COLLECTIVE TRUST

COLLECTIVE TRUST

Why Schools Can't Improve Without It

Patrick B. Forsyth
Curt M. Adams
Wayne K. Hoy

Foreword by
Barbara Schneider

Teachers College
Columbia University
New York and London

Published by Teachers College Press, 1234 Amsterdam Avenue, New York, NY 10027

The authors would like to acknowledge the use of previously copyrighted material: Appendix 1.1, copyright © 1983 by Hoy & Kupersmith; Appendix 1.2, copyright © 2009 by Hoy; Appendix 3.1, copyright © 2003 by Hoy & Tschannen-Moran; Appendixes 3.2, 3.3, and 3.4 copyright © 2004 by Forsyth & Adams; Appendix 3.5, copyright © 2009 by Adams & Forsyth.

Library of Congress Cataloging-in-Publication Data

Forsyth, Patrick B., author.
    Collective trust : why schools can't improve without it / Patrick B. Forsyth, Curt M. Adams, Wayne K. Hoy ; Foreword by Barbara Schneider.
        p. cm
    Includes bibliographical references and index.
    ISBN 978-0-8077-5167-1 (pbk. : alk. paper)   1. Educational change—United States—Longitudinal studies.   2. Trust—United States—Longitudinal studies.   I. Adams, Curt M., author.   II. Hoy, Wayne K., 1938–, author.   III. Title.
    LA217.2.F66 2011
    371.2'07—dc22

                                                                                    2010045086

ISBN 978-0-8077-5167-1 (paper)

Printed on acid-free paper

Manufactured in the United States of America

18   17   16   15   14   13   12   11   8   7   6   5   4   3   2   1

To my father, Robert Louis Forsyth, who in his 88th year continues to inspire with his wit, vitality, humor, and generosity.

—PBF

To my wife, Vicky, for ten amazing years and many more to enjoy.

—CMA

To our granddaughter, Amaya Bella Hoy, and the future.

—WKH

Contents

Foreword

The past decade will certainly be referred to as the era in which major efforts were directed at school reform. Every sitting president over the last 10 years has made education a national priority by either advocating and passing legislation or allocating enormous resources to improve the nation's schools. Most of these initiatives focus on: organizational change such as charter schools; enhancing teacher effectiveness through new certification standards, tenure provisions, and merit pay; and school accountability measures that require frequent testing and school and teacher penalties for poor student performance. What has received less attention is the quality of relationships that can foster successful leadership, teamwork, and shared values regarding the importance of the academic and personal welfare of the students in the school. Strong social ties formed on mutual expectations and obligations of responsibility can promote positive norms that lead to relational *trust* in a school community. Trust emerges as the lubricant for strengthening relationships among teachers, students, administrators, and parents.

In the early 1990s Anthony Bryk and I, along with two then graduate students, Julie Kochanek and Sharon Greenberg, embarked on a 10-year journey that sought to understand what conditions in schools facilitated school reform. Using extensive case data from 12 elementary schools and city-wide surveys from Chicago teachers, we formed a theory of relational trust. Through a series of analyses drawing on the disciplinary fields of sociology, political science, and organizational behavior and management we were able to show how reciprocal exchanges among participants in a school community cumulate in a socially defined organizational property that we termed *relational trust*.

In our book, *Trust in Schools: A Core Resource for Improvement*, we discuss how social relationships in schools are particularly fragile as they stem from vulnerabilities of power and authority that school leaders have with regard to their staff, teachers with their students and parents, and parents with teachers. Trust can overcome these vulnerabilities by strengthening the relational ties among all the members of the school community when grounded in mutual respect, competence, integrity, and shared values that promote the academic and social welfare of the students. The presence or absence of relational trust has important consequences for both the functioning of the school and its capacity to engage in fundamental change. We showed how relational trust can enhance the effectiveness of school leaders and personnel and pave the way for school reform.

Our ideas of relational trust were appearing at the same time that several other researchers were also working on similar ideas. Some of these scholars had entered the field earlier and had begun developing their own constructs and measures regarding the concept of trust. What is especially interesting about this work is that whether one is defining trust as a relational or collective property of school organizations, researchers agree that social relationships in communities are what make trust a key element in promoting school effectiveness.

Collective Trust: Why Schools Can't Improve Without It, by Patrick Forsyth, Curt Adams, and Wayne Hoy, the newest book on the importance of trust in school, is an excellent complement to our work on relational trust. Tracing their own studies over the past 30 years, this volume describes how they and others have conceptualized, measured, and analyzed the properties of collective trust. Their conceptual understandings of collective trust and results, which bear a strong affinity to our work, suggest that there is a growing cumulating knowledge base on the importance of social relationships for school improvement.

Organized into nine chapters, the volume is intended to provide: a framework and set of measures for studying collective trust; empirical evidence from several studies on the utility of trust for facilitating change; and tools for school personnel to use for evaluating the presence and strength of trust in their schools. What is especially unique about this book is that it is written by three generations of researchers who have selected this topic as the cornerstone of their work. This intergenerational quest for understanding and documenting the value of collective trust has built an integrated and cohesive argument for why policymakers and practitioners need to pay closer attention to trust in schools.

The evidence, measures, and interpretations of why and how collective trust operates in schools is important as administrators and others seek ways to form productive school communities that have as their central goal the academic and social welfare of the students. Our research and that of these authors continues to show that reform programs are unlikely to succeed unless there are strong relationships in the organization that embrace similar values. But it is not just values; trust requires articulated expectations of responsibility and commands high levels of performance from not only teachers but also administrators, students, and parents.

—Barbara Schneider, Michigan State University

Preface

Collective Trust is the culmination of nearly 3 decades of research, beginning at Rutgers University and continuing at Ohio State University, Oklahoma State University, and the University of Oklahoma. The objectives of this volume are threefold:

- To provide educational researchers and other scholars with a sound theoretical framework and a set of reliable and valid measures to study collective trust
- To bring together the considerable cumulative empirical evidence about trust in schools and begin to integrate and make sense of it
- To provide practitioners with a set of tools to evaluate the trust culture of their schools with an aim toward school improvement

The book is unusual in two ways. First, we examine what has been a continuous agenda of scientific inquiry by the same researchers for decades; it is difficult to find such concerted effort and continuity in educational research. Second, the book's authorship is a collaboration of three generations of researchers—from Wayne Hoy to his student, Patrick Forsyth, to his student, Curt Adams; we all continue in our quest to understand trust and improve schools through sound theory and research.

This book is written for anyone who is intrigued by the general topic of organizational trust as well as for those educators who sense the pivotal importance of trust in schools. The theory and research reported not only is of interest to researchers and educational leaders; it also is useful for organizational scholars, sociologists, and other behavioral and social scientists. Although clearly not written in the style of an "airport" minute-manager, the analyses give a readable, persuasive, and useful understanding of the role trust plays in school success. Educational leaders will find it informative and practical.

Collective Trust is suitable as a text or auxiliary text for courses on leadership, school culture, community relations, and research. It is an ideal text for courses on educational research and design, clearly tracing, as it does, the 25-year history of a significant and ongoing research agenda focused on school trust and involving the development of an important and useful body of knowledge. The chronology of theoretical development, along with accumulating empirical findings, demonstrate the integrative and self-corrective features of social science.

ORGANIZATION OF THIS BOOK

We begin our analysis of trust in schools by first describing in Part I the foundations of collective trust (Chapters 1–3), beginning with the early studies and moving to the current theoretical model for the formation of collective trust and its measurement. In Part II we summarize the research findings on trust in schools (Chapters 4–8) by examining the conditions that enhance collective trust, the consequences of trust, the close relationship between a culture of trust and school effectiveness, the relationship between leadership and collective trust, and the role of trust in the formation of social capital and academic optimism. Finally, in Part III we conclude with implications of what we know about trust (Chapters 9–10) for educational policy and practice.

Practitioners interested in using this book for school improvement can safely skip Chapter 3, which deals with the development of scales to measure collective trust, and Chapter 8, which examines the role of collective trust in two related theoretical systems. On the other hand, do not neglect Chapters 2, 6, and 9; these chapters are particularly useful for understanding the dynamics of collective trust and for improving schools.

Throughout the book we have provided concrete examples for the more abstract explanations in this volume. In addition, we call to your attention the following helpful features:

> *Figures and tables* in each chapter summarize and demonstrate the key relations that we are explicating.
> A *summary* is provided at the conclusion of each chapter that highlights the major concepts, ideas, and propositions.
> *Appendixes* are found at the end of the text that provide the actual measures that were used in our research.

We encourage all researchers and practitioners to use any of the instruments in this book. There is no fee. Simply reproduce them and use them in your research and organizational development. We invite you to join us in our quest to understand and improve schools.

ACKNOWLEDGMENTS

We have many to thank for their contributions to this work as it has evolved over the years. Colleagues from three generations have contributed ideas, suggestions, and corrections: Anita Woolfolk Hoy, Laura Barnes, William Kupersmith, Roger Goddard, Roxanne Mitchell, C. John Tarter, Michael DiPaola, Megan Tschannen-Moran, Page Smith, and Jeffrey Geist. Students at our respective universities have been subjected to various parts of this volume and have contributed with their insights and critique. The errors, of course, are ours alone. We gratefully acknowledge the support of Oklahoma State University and The Ohio State University, which provided PBF and WKH with sabbaticals to begin organizing and writing this book. We thank our families, spouses and children (Elena, Connor, Patrick, Vicky, Brody, Noah, Anita, Wayne K., Maritess, Kelly, and Liz)—all of whom contributed in ways they don't know and some they do—for giving us their blessing to take this on. We are deeply indebted to our graduate assistant Katherine Curry (University of Oklahoma), whose careful attention to detail and assistance with technical editing has been invaluable. We also express sincere appreciation to our editors at Teachers College Press, especially Brian Ellerbeck, who were willing to take a chance on a different kind of book.

This volume represents a true collaboration with the three authors contributing equally, while offering unique skills and gifts to the process.

PBF
CMA
WKH
January 1, 2010

Foundations of Collective Trust

Part I consists of three chapters. The first chapter describes early research exploring school trust. While demonstrating that trust is important for understanding schools, early studies also underscored the need for controlling confounding variables, which often produced erroneous conclusions.

Chapter 2 situates research on schools in the broader context of sociological and organizational theory. We emphasize the nature of and need for collective trust by contrasting it with interpersonal trust within organizations. Finally, and perhaps most important, we derive a theory of collective trust to explain its dynamics in organizations and to guide future research.

Chapter 3 details the evolution of the measurement of collective trust in schools. We present strong evidence for the reliability and validity of our measures as we discuss the psychometric properties of faculty trust in principals, colleagues, and clients (parents and students); parent trust in the school and in the principal; and student trust in teachers and in the principal.

CHAPTER 1

Early Studies in School Trust

Key to evaluating a claim about the importance of relational trust for school improvement is the ability to reliably measure differences in this organizational property across school communities and over time.

—Anthony Bryk and Barbara Schneider,
Trust in Schools: A Core Resource for Improvement

Trust is the keystone of successful interpersonal relations, leadership, teamwork, and effective organizations. This book is about collective trust—the trust that groups have in individuals and in other groups. We have been engaged in the empirical study of collective trust for nearly 3 decades, and the current inquiry is a summary of what we have learned about trust in schools during that time. Our research on trust started in the 1980s at Rutgers University and then, after a brief break, continued first at The Ohio State University and then at Oklahoma State University (Forsyth, 2008) and the University of Oklahoma. In early 2000 we were joined in the systematic study of trust in schools by researchers at the University of Chicago (Bryk & Schneider, 2002; Kochanek, 2005).

FACULTY TRUST: A DEFINITION AND ITS REFERENTS

Although trust has been recognized as an important aspect of organizational life for decades (Golembiewski & McConkie, 1975; Likert, 1967), early analyses of trust were general and global. The empirical study of organizational trust is of more recent vintage. The beginnings of the systematic study of trust in schools date back to the early 1980s when Hoy and his colleagues (Hoy & Henderson, 1983; Hoy & Kupersmith, 1985) began a set of school investigations on organizational trust in which they conceptualized trust and developed both constitutive and operational definitions.

Definition of Trust

The initial definition of trust, based on the work of Rotter (1967) and Golembiewski and McConkie (1975), was as follows:

> Trust is a generalized expectancy held by the work group that the word, promise, and written or oral statement of another individual, group, or organization can be relied upon (Hoy & Kupersmith, 1985, p. 2).

Notice that trust is defined at the collective level; it is the trust of the work group. Moreover, trust can be viewed in relation to any number of reference groups such as the principal or the school organization. Using the general definition above, Hoy and Kupersmith (1985) added the notions that trust involves confidence in others and the belief that others are acting in the best interest of the relevant party. Thus faculty trust is a collective form of trust in which the faculty has an expectancy that the word, promise, and actions of another group or individual can be relied on and that the trusted party will act in the best interests of the faculty.

Referents of Trust

The faculty can trust a variety of referent groups, including the principal, colleagues, and the organization itself. Consider the following:

1. Faculty trust in the principal—the faculty has confidence that the principal will keep his or her word and act in the best interests of the teachers.
2. Faculty trust in colleagues—the faculty believes teachers can depend on each other in difficult situations and rely on the integrity of their colleagues.
3. Faculty trust in the school organization—the faculty can rely on the school district to act in its best interest and be fair to teachers.

Each of these three varieties of trust suggests an expectancy that the trusted party is reliable and can be counted on to act in the best interests of the faculty. Each is also a collective property; the party doing the trusting is the faculty as a whole; hence, trust is a collective variable.

Measuring Faculty Trust

Hoy and Kupersmith (1985) developed three scales to measure each of these varieties of trust. Teachers at each school described overall trust in their school. The items were worded to capture the trust of the faculty as a whole rather than the trust of the individual; that is, the reference is to "teachers in this school." Scores of all the teachers are averaged to tap the extent to which the faculty trusts the principal, colleagues, or the organization. Reliabilities for all the scales were consistently in the .90 to .97 range. The three scales are found in Appendix 1.1.

Not surprisingly, as predicted, the three scales are moderately correlated with each other; when the faculty trusts the principal, the faculty is likely to trust colleagues as well as the school organization. Hoy and Kupersmith (1985) also provide predictive and construct validity evidence for the three scales.

The three faculty trust scales described above provided the measurement tools to explore and test relationships between faculty trust and a number of school properties. Hoy and his colleagues examined the relationships between trust and principal leadership, school climate, and school effectiveness. We now turn to those studies to see what they tell us about the power of trust.

PRINCIPAL AUTHENTICITY

In some schools, principals are open, transparent, and inclusive, whereas in other schools they obfuscate and leave teachers in the dark about decisions and why and how they are made. In the latter schools, behavior is often forced and shallow: individuals appear as actors on a stage who have memorized their lines and perform their parts with neither enthusiasm nor commitment. Most individuals believe they know authentic behavior when they experience it; they can describe people who tell it like it is as well as others who are phonies. Yet there is not an abundance of research on authenticity in general and leadership authenticity in particular because it is such a slippery concept. It is one thing to talk about genuine and real behavior, but it is quite another to articulate a clear and concise definition of authenticity.

Elements of Authentic Behavior

Hoy and Henderson (1983) conceptualized and measured the extent to which the behavior of a principal is perceived by teachers as authentic. They identify three basic aspects of leader authenticity:

- Accountability
- Nonmanipulation of others
- Saliency of self over role

Let's examine each of these basic elements of leader authenticity. Accountability is behavior for which the leader accepts responsibility, including admitting mistakes and errors. The leader accepts responsibility for not only his or her behavior, but also for mistakes of subordinates; there is no "scapegoating" or "passing the buck." Authentic leaders do not manipulate people; they treat them with respect and as individuals rather than as inanimate objects that are pawns in a game. Finally, authentic leaders break through the barriers of role stereotyping and behave in ways that are appropriate to their personal and situational needs. Such leaders are not bound to rigid role expectations; in fact, they demonstrate a saliency of self over role demands.

One problem in attempting to measure authenticity is the distinction between perceived authenticity in a given situation and actual authenticity as judged by some external objective standard. Hoy and Henderson (1983) avoided this dilemma by opting for a measure of authenticity based on the perceptions of teachers. They argued that it is the teachers' perceptions that drive their behaviors, and they developed a reliable and valid measure of teachers' perceptions of leader authenticity (Hoy & Henderson, 1983), which is the measure of authenticity used in subsequent research we will discuss.

Leader Authenticity and Faculty Trust

Hoy and Kupersmith (1984) also proposed that principal authenticity is a key element in the development of faculty trust. They argued that a leader's openness and candor generate a belief that the principal is not out to harm them and that they can rely on the principal. The argument for linking leader authenticity and faculty trust is based on the assumption that principals who are willing to admit their own mistakes, who do not manipulate teachers, and who are real in the sense that they do not hide behind their formal authority (i.e., are authentic) create an atmosphere amenable to faculty confidence, intimacy, and trust. The authenticity-trust relationship is not unidirectional, however. Although leader authenticity produces faculty trust, it is also likely the case that faculty trust enables leaders to be open, transparent, and authentic. The predicted relationship is reciprocal with each variable reinforcing the other.

The Authenticity–Faculty Trust Hypothesis

A test of this theory was supported in a study of 45 elementary schools in New Jersey (Hoy & Kupersmith, 1984) and in a study of 87 middle schools (Hoffman, Sabo, Bliss, & Hoy, 1994); the authenticity of the principal's behavior was strongly related to faculty trust in the principal. Moreover, the greater the leader authenticity of the principal, the stronger the faculty trust in the organization and in colleagues, but these latter two relationships, although statistically significant, were not as strong as the direct link between principal authenticity and faculty trust in the principal. It appears principals have power to earn the trust of teachers by behaving authentically, but their power to get colleagues to trust each other is more circumscribed.

The later study of trust in middle schools (Hoy, Hoffman, Sabo, & Bliss, 1996) also extended our knowledge about the authenticity-trust relation by examining teacher authenticity and faculty trust. Not surprisingly, authentic behavior by teachers was strongly related to faculty trust in colleagues and to faculty trust in principal. In brief, authenticity and trust may be two sides of the same coin.

SCHOOL CLIMATE

Personality is to the individual what climate is to the organization. Just as individuals have personalities, so too do organizations; the "personalities" of schools are called their *organizational climates*. There are a variety of ways to conceptualize school climate, but two common perspectives examine climate in terms of either the openness or health of the interactions among participants. The Organizational Climate Description Questionnaire (OCDQ) measures the openness of school climate, whereas the Organizational Health Inventory (OHI) assesses the health of school climate (Hoy & Miskel, 2008; Hoy, Tarter, & Kottkamp, 1991). We now turn to the research on school climate and faculty trust for both of these perspectives.

Openness of School Climate

Although many people had made the case for the importance of trust in organizations, there were few studies that examined trust in schools prior to 1980. Some had argued that trust was necessary for establishing effective interpersonal relations (Hughes, 1947), for improving communication (Zand, 1972), for establishing emergent leadership (Gibb, 1969), for building teamwork (Paul, 1982), and for initiating successful organizational change (Ouchi, 1981). However, not withstanding its popularity as a concept for commentary and admonition, there was remarkably little empirical research on trust in schools.

After the development of the Hoy-Kupersmith measures of trust in schools, a series of climate studies was undertaken at Rutgers University. In one such study, Tarter, Bliss, and Hoy (1989b) argued that openness in the relationships between teachers and the principal as well as openness in relationships among teachers were both closely related to the degree of trust in the school. In other words, open school climates and an atmosphere of trust go together.

Authentic relations characterize open principal behavior with teachers. The principal creates a work environment that is supportive and helpful, encourages teacher initiative to solve problems, and frees teachers from administrative busywork so that they can focus on the teaching-learning task. In marked contrast, closed behavior is close, controlling, and nonsupportive.

The Openness–Faculty Trust Hypothesis

Not surprisingly, the empirical data also supported a climate of openness-trust relationship in a study of high schools in New Jersey (Tarter & Hoy, 1988). Openness in the climate of a school and trust in interpersonal relationships complemented each other. The relationship between climate and trust, however, was more clearly specified in this research. Openness in the leadership of the principal was the major predictor of faculty trust in the principal, whereas openness in interpersonal relationships was the major predictor of faculty trust in colleagues. Although openness and trust are positively associated, they are different, albeit related, concepts. There was another interesting finding in this study. Faculty trust in colleagues was independent of principal behavior; that is, teachers could trust colleagues even if they were skeptical of their principals.

Two other studies, one of elementary schools (Hoy et al., 1991) and one of middle schools (Hoffman et al., 1994), also confirmed the openness-trust relationship. Regardless of the level of the school (elementary or secondary), it appeared that open school climate facilitates faculty trust and strong faculty trust reinforces a climate of openness.

Health of School Climate

Just as the openness of a school's climate is inextricably bound to trust in schools, so too is the organizational health of a school. *Organizational health* refers to the extent to which there is integrity in the educational program (institutional integrity), efficient administration (principal influence), and a strong academic emphasis. The leadership of the principal is committed to high standards of performance (initiating structure), while simultaneously attending to the personal and professional needs of teachers (consideration). Healthy schools are committed to teaching and learning; they set high, but achievable, academic goals and mobilize their resources to attain those ends (resource support). Teachers in healthy schools like their principal, their colleagues, and their students and have high morale, which is expressed in enthusiasm and pride in their school. In sum, institutional integrity, initiating structure, consideration, principal influence, resource support, academic emphasis, and morale form a collective set of variables that determine the health of interactions in schools.

The Health–Faculty Trust Hypothesis

It should not be surprising that the relationship between organizational health and faculty trust in schools is also positive and significant. Regardless of school level (Hoy & Sabo, 1998; Tarter & Hoy, 1988), the healthier the climate of the school, the greater the degree of faculty trust. Similar to the openness-trust relationship, the health-trust relationship is nuanced. Although overall school health is positively related both to faculty trust in the principal and to trust in colleagues, the considerate and consistent leadership of the principal is more critical to generating faculty trust in principal, whereas the enthusiasm and friendliness of teachers are more strongly related to trust among colleagues. In brief, an integrative theme of trust runs though the interactions of faculty and administrators in healthy schools. Healthy school climates promote faculty trust, but faculty trust also reinforces healthy school interactions; school health and faculty trust are mutually dependent.

The early research on trust in schools focused on its relationships with authenticity and school climate, but it also made an attempt to link trust in schools to the effectiveness of schools. We turn to the trust-effectiveness relationship next.

SCHOOL EFFECTIVENESS

Effectiveness is the acid test of the functioning of any organization. What makes an organization effective? There are several problems with the question. The most basic is, What is organizational effectiveness, and how do we measure it? There are no easy answers here.

Elements of School Effectiveness

The criteria for organizational effectiveness are numerous and ambiguous at best; in fact, after a thorough review of literature on organizational effectiveness, Cameron (1984) concluded that no list of criteria had been formulated that was either necessary or sufficient for evaluating the construct of organizational effectiveness. Not much has changed in the interim to overturn his verdict. At one point he and his colleague (Cameron & Whetton, 1996) tried to make the case that quality was a more appropriate concept for educational organizations than effectiveness, but the quality perspective has not replaced the quest for effective organizations.

Hoy, Tarter, and Wiskowskie (1992), however, did try to link faculty trust and school effectiveness. They used a Parsonian perspective to guide their formulation (Parsons, 1961). They posited that effective schools meet the Parsonian imperatives of

1. Accommodating to their environments
2. Setting and attaining goals
3. Maintaining solidarity within the system
4. Preserving a unique value system

Fortunately, Mott (1972) had earlier developed a model of organizational effectiveness for his study of hospitals that closely paralleled the Parsonian approach; he used quantity and quality of product, efficacy, adaptability, and flexibility to measure effectiveness. He argued that these attributes define the ability of an organization to mobilize its centers of power for action, to achieve its goals, to fulfill worker needs, and to adapt. Mott's research provided strong evidence that his measure of effectiveness was valid and highly reliable in assessing the effectiveness of hospitals.

Faculty Trust–School Effectiveness Hypothesis

Miskel and his colleagues (Miskel, Fevurly, & Stewart, 1979; Miskel, McDonald, & Bloom, 1983) adapted the Mott measure and used it successfully to study the effectiveness of schools, and Hoy and his colleagues (Hoy et al., 1992) followed suit as they examined the relationship between faculty trust and school effectiveness in elementary schools. They used the adapted Mott scale as an *index of perceived organizational effectiveness*. Hoy and Ferguson (1985) had already demonstrated that the index correlated with many other measures of school effectiveness, including student achievement, thus providing validity for the use of the scale in schools. (See Appendix 1.2 for the index.)

Hoy, Tarter, and Wiskoskie (1992) studied 44 elementary schools in New Jersey. Although their basic research question focused on the relation of a "culture of trust" and school effectiveness, they were also interested in school climate properties that influenced trust. In particular, they used *supportive leadership* and *collegial teacher behavior*, both subtests of the Organizational Climate Descriptive Questionnaire. Supportive leadership is principal behavior that demonstrates an authentic concern for teachers,

openness to ideas, and respect for the professional competence of teachers; it is an index of principal openness and professionalism. Collegiality is
teacher behavior that supports open and professional interactions among
teachers; it is an index of teacher openness and professionalism. Both these
climate variables were hypothesized to be related to school trust as well as
to school effectiveness. Moreover, a culture of trust was expected to predict
school effectiveness.

First, the initial correlation analyses supported the predicted relationships. For the most part, climate properties were significantly related
to faculty trust as well as to school effectiveness, and faculty trust in
colleagues—but not faculty trust in the principal—was related to school
effectiveness. Next, several theoretical models were developed and tested
using path analysis, which is a more sophisticated statistical approach that
enables researchers to explain networks of relationships among such variables as climate, trust, and effectiveness in schools.

A Test of a Theoretical Model of School Effectiveness

The final path analysis provided a much cleaner and clearer picture of the
network of relations. The bivariate relationships between supportive leadership and effectiveness and between supportive leadership and faculty trust in
colleagues were spurious. The path analyses revealed that supportive leadership led to collegiality among teachers and to faculty trust in the principal,
but neither was directly related to effectiveness. Collegiality of teachers and
teacher trust in the principal affected faculty trust in colleagues, which in
turn produced school effectiveness. Only faculty trust in colleagues was directly related to effectiveness in this study.

The same study was replicated a few years later with middle schools
(Tarter, Sabo, & Hoy, 1995). The results were slightly different. Here the
best model to explain school effectiveness showed that both forms of faculty
trust were directly related to school effectiveness, but that supportive principal leadership influenced faculty trust in the principal, whereas collegial
teacher behavior influenced the faculty trust in colleagues. See Figure 1.1
for a comparison of the models. It is clear that faculty trust is important in
influencing school effectiveness for both elementary and secondary schools,
albeit in slightly different paths.

Although this research on effectiveness and trust was a good beginning,
there were several limitations. First, the measure of effectiveness was a subjective one based on the assessment of organizational participants. Second,
the study was limited to a rather small set of elementary and middle schools
in New Jersey. Finally, the trust variable was limited to faculty trust in only
two referent groups—teachers and principals.

Figure 1.1. Comparison of Path Models of school effectiveness for elementary and middle schools.

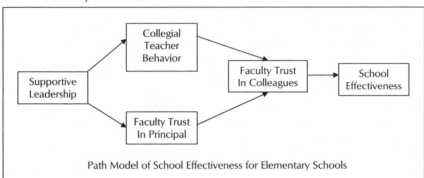

Path Model of School Effectiveness for Elementary Schools

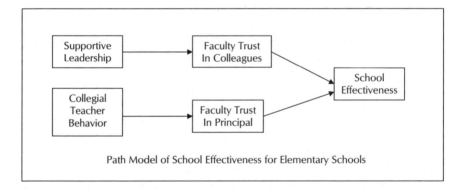

Path Model of School Effectiveness for Elementary Schools

Faculty Trust and Academic Achievement

A few years later, Hoy and Sabo (1998) explored the relation between faculty trust and school achievement in a large study of New Jersey middle schools. They argued that although there were many school outcomes that might be used to measure school effectiveness, student achievement was one outcome that virtually everyone agreed was an index of effective schooling. Moreover, achievement outcomes had the added benefit of being quite objective because they relied on actual student performance (standardized test scores) rather than teacher assessments. Thus they used statewide student achievement scores in math, reading, and writing as well as the more subjective Mott index as indicators of school effectiveness.

Once again, faculty trust in the principal and faculty trust in colleagues were positively related to all these effectiveness measures. The correlations between the trust measures and student achievement measures were in the weak to moderate range (.27–.40), whereas the correlations between the two trust measures and the more subjective measure of effectiveness were positive and stronger (.56–.72). School climate openness and school health were also significantly and positively related to student achievement and overall school effectiveness.

A study of a large sample of New Jersey high schools (Hoy et al., 1991) produced similar results for these secondary schools; however, a disconcerting piece of evidence also surfaced. In earlier analyses of the relationships between faculty trust and achievement, the researchers had neglected the socioeconomic status (SES) of the schools. Coleman's landmark study of schools (Coleman et al., 1966) documented the strong association between SES and academic achievement in schools. The Coleman report concluded that most of the variance in school achievement was a function of family background differences rather that school factors.

What happens when SES is added to the mix of variables explaining student achievement and school effectiveness? The results are disastrous. Suddenly, none of the faculty trust variables—trust in the organization, trust in the principal, or trust in colleagues—makes a significant difference in achievement. SES overwhelms the trust variables, climate variables, and most other school variables, for that matter. So what appeared to be a pivotal role for trust in explaining student achievement and school effectiveness disappears.

This is not to say that trust, openness, authenticity, and health are not important positive features of the school, because clearly they are. They make a difference on the affective aspects of school life. For example, they nurture teacher satisfaction and morale; they make schools more interesting and comfortable places in which to work and to learn. But it may be that their influence on the cognitive development of students had been overemphasized. At least the systematic empirical evidence in the early 1990s led to the conclusion that SES was a dominant force in the academic success of students. Clearly the strong impact of SES, a variable not very amenable to quick change, put a damper on the Rutgers faculty trust and climate studies. Empirical data has a way of doing that—of unraveling our best theories and explanations.

It was not until the late 1990s and the new millennium before research began to refocus attention on trust in schools (Hoy & Tschannen-Moran, 1999, 2003; Tschannen-Moran & Hoy, 2000). A new series of studies on school trust began at Ohio State University as Hoy and his colleagues reconceptualized trust and added new aspects of trust that were more directly related to student achievement in schools. What, if anything, was missed in the early studies on school trust? In the subsequent chapters, we will examine more recent studies of trust that have emerged at The Ohio State University, the University of Chicago, Oklahoma State University, and the University of Oklahoma, which make a strong case for the importance of trust in schools, albeit a different kind of trust.

SUMMARY

The results of the early studies of trust conducted at Rutgers University painted a picture of the importance of trust in the life of a school. Faculty trust was inextricably related to such concepts as authenticity, openness, leadership, morale, and healthy interpersonal dynamics among students, teachers, and administrators. Many of these relationships are reciprocal, that is, they are mutually dependent. They enhance each other simultaneously.

As we tried to explain how these concepts were related to effectiveness and student achievement, we discovered that bivariate analyses of these variables were often misleading and spurious. More sophisticated multivariate statistical analyses are necessary if we are to get a more complete understanding of the dynamics of effective school organizations and student achievement. Moreover, controls are important in research design and statistics. In all studies of effectiveness and achievement, SES must be controlled because it is so strongly related to achievement and so intransigent; we must find school variables that promote school success and high achievement in spite of low SES.

The Rutgers studies were a modest beginning but an important first step in the study of faculty trust and school climate (see Figure 1.2 for a summary of research findings). In the end, the Rutgers studies of school trust raised as many questions as they answered, but they did provide the impetus for an important line of inquiry that flourishes today at a number of universities.

Figure 1.2. Summary of Rutgers University studies on faculty trust.

Definition: *Faculty trust* is the collective expectancy of the faculty that the word, promise, and actions of another group or individual can be relied upon and that the trusted party will act in the best interest of the faculty.

Referents of faculty trust: The principal, colleagues, and the organization.

Empirical Findings:

1. Principal authenticity and faculty trust are positively related (Hoy & Kupersmith, 1985; Hoy, Hoffman, Sabo, & Bliss, 1996).
2. Faculty trust in the principal, in colleagues, and in the organization are positively correlated with each other (Hoy & Kupersmith, 1985; Hoy et al., 1996).
3. Open school climate is positively related to faculty trust in the principal and in colleagues (Hoy, Tarter, & Kottkamp, 1991; Hoffman, Sabo, Bliss, & Hoy, 1994).
4. The health of school climate is positively related to faculty trust in the principal and in colleagues (Hoy et al., 1991; Hoy & Sabo, 1998).
5. Both the openness and health of the school climate are positively related to school effectiveness (Hoy et al., 1991; Hoy & Sabo, 1998).
6. In elementary schools, supportive principal leadership is positively related to both collegial teacher behavior and trust in the principal; both of which are related to faculty trust in the principal, which is directly related to school effectiveness (Hoy, Tarter, & Witkoskie, 1992). But in middle schools, the relationships are slightly different; supportive leadership is directly related to faculty trust in the principal, but collegial teacher behavior influences faculty trust in colleagues. Both types of trust are directly related to school effectiveness (Tarter, Sabo, & Hoy, 1995).
7. Faculty trust in colleagues and faculty trust in the principal were both positively correlated with student achievement; however, the socioeconomic status (SES) of students overwhelms both trust variables. In other words, when SES is controlled, the effects of these two aspects of trust on school achievement disappear (Hoy et al., 1991; Hoy & Sabo, 1998).

CHAPTER 2

Conceptual Foundations and the Formation of Collective Trust

Most of us notice a given form of trust most easily after its sudden demise. . . . We inhabit a climate of trust as we inhabit an atmosphere and notice it as we notice air, only when it becomes scarce or polluted.

—Annette Baier, *Moral Prejudices*

We set for ourselves the task of developing a distinctive conceptual framework and definition of collective trust to use in our analysis of schools. In Chapter 1 we reviewed early efforts to define and measure trust in schools, but increasingly, throughout the past 20 years, social scientists from a variety of disciplines turned to the study of trust. Is there now a converging body of literature in which scholars of different disciplines agree about the essential nature of trust? Surprisingly, the answer is, Yes; we exploit that convergent literature to improve and refine our earlier definition of trust and identification of the common elements of trust. Based on our review, we first propose a more comprehensive definition of trust and then formulate and explicate a general model of collective trust.

COMMON FEATURES OF TRUST

Psychologists usually frame their conceptions of trust at a micro level in terms of individuals who trust and are trusted and emphasize the internal cognitions that lead to such trust (Deutsch, 1962; Rotter, 1967). By contrast, sociologists conceive of trust as a macro- or meso-level property of social relationships among people, groups, and institutions (Coleman, 1990; Granovetter, 1985; Zucker, 1986). Nonetheless, there are basic conceptual similarities in the perceptions of trust regardless of discipline or level (Rousseau, Sitkin, Burt, & Camerer, 1998). Most scholars (Deutsch, 1962;

Fukuyama, 1996; Kramer & Tyler, 1996; Mishra, 1996; Tschannen-Moran & Hoy, 1998; Zucker, 1986) agree that trust has the following attributes:

- Multiple levels (e.g., individual, group, and organization)
- Different referent roles (e.g., in schools: teachers, principals, colleagues, students)
- Multiple facets (benevolence, reliability, competency, honesty, and openness)
- Interdependence
- Confident expectations
- Risk
- Vulnerability

Vulnerability, Risk, and Interdependence

At the most basic level, *vulnerability* is a common thread that runs through most expositions of trust regardless of discipline. Those who trust make themselves vulnerable to others in the belief that those they trust will act in ways that are not harmful or detrimental to them; trusting individuals have a positive expectation in the actions of those whom they trust. Vulnerability and confident expectations of outcomes are crucial aspects of trust.

Risk is another primary element in psychological, sociological, and economic analyses of trust (Coleman, 1990; Rotter, 1967; Rousseau et al., 1998; Williamson, 1993). Of course, being vulnerable often leads to risk and risk-taking behavior. Without some vulnerability there is little risk, at least when risk is defined as "perceived probable loss" (Chiles & McMacking, 1996). Both risk and vulnerability create an opportunity for trust; that is, sometimes trust is a choice. At other times, however, choice is more limited; circumstances and events constrain trust. In egalitarian situations, for example, trust is a choice, but in hierarchical relations, trust may be the only reasonable course of action. But in either case, when the expected, positive behavior occurs, trust is strengthened. Uncertainty regarding the intentions of one party to act in the best interests of another is the source of risk (Lewis & Weigart, 1985), and risk creates trust opportunities.

Finally, there can be no trust without *interdependence*; that is, the interests of one party cannot be achieved without reliance upon another (Rousseau et al., 1998). If there is no interdependence, there is no need for trust. Trust relations are rooted in interdependence among people, groups, and organizations. Interdependence, like risk, is a matter of degree, but the more interdependence in social relations, the more essential trust becomes.

In sum, trust can occur and be analyzed at various levels and with different role referents. Three common elements are the basis of most trust definitions. Trust is seen as a condition in which people or groups find themselves *vulnerable* to others under conditions of *risk* and *interdependence*. In such situations, trust requires that one party has confidence that another party will act in positive fashion and in its best interests. Vulnerability, risk, and interdependence are necessary conditions for trust; thus, variations in these aspects over the course of a relationship may alter the level and form that trust takes (Rosseau et al., 1998).

Under conditions of vulnerability, risk, and interdependence, trust can be thought of as the extent to which a trustor (one who trusts) perceives a trustee (the trust referent) as trustworthy. From the literature has emerged a set of sources of trustworthiness or facets of trust (categories of perceived behaviors of trustees) that enable trustors to make judgments about a trustee's trustworthiness. For example, if a potential trustor perceives a potential trustee acting benevolently, the trustor is more likely to judge the trustee as trustworthy and eventually bestow his or her trust.

Facets of Trust

There are at least five sources or facets of trust that can be gleaned from the interdisciplinary literature; benevolence, reliability, competence, honesty, and openness are common elements that are found in most discussions of trust (Hoy & Tschannen-Moran, 1999; Tschannen-Moran & Hoy, 2000). We describe each of these in greater detail.

BENEVOLENCE. The most common condition of trust is a sense of benevolence—the confidence that the trusted person or group will protect one's interests. We depend on the goodwill of others to act in our best interests. In ongoing interactions, future behavior or deeds may not be specified because of a mutual attitude of goodwill. Trust is the assurance that another party will not exploit one's vulnerability even when the opportunity is available (Cummings & Bromily, 1996). Put simply, trust involves the "accepted vulnerability to another's possible but not expected ill will" (Baier, 1986, p. 236). In situations of interdependence, faith and confidence in the benevolence or altruism of others are critical to trust.

RELIABILITY. Reliability is the extent to which one can rely upon another for action and goodwill. At its most fundamental level, reliability has to do with predictability; however, predictability alone is insufficient. What is required is the combination of reliability with benevolence; that is, when something is required from another person or group, the individual can be relied upon to supply it (Butler & Cantrell, 1984; Mishra, 1996; Rotter, 1967). Reliability implies a sense of confidence that one's needs will be met in positive ways. One need neither invest energy worrying about whether the person will come through nor make alternative plans. Most interactions unfold over time, and there is a lag between when a commitment is made and when it is fulfilled. The degree to which a person believes that outcomes will be forthcoming and positive reflects the extent of trust.

COMPETENCE. There are times when good intentions are not enough. When a person is dependent on another and some level of skill is involved in fulfilling an expectation, a person who means well but does not have the competence is not trusted (Baier, 1986; Butler & Cantrell, 1984; Mishra, 1996). For example, the patient of a young surgeon may feel that this doctor wishes very much to heal her, but if the doctor is inexperienced, the patient is unlikely to trust the physician. Many organizational tasks rely on competence. For example, when the success of a project depends on team participation, trust will depend on confidence that deadlines will be met and that the work will be of sufficient quality to meet project goals.

HONESTY. Honesty speaks to character, integrity, and authenticity. Rotter (1967) defined trust as "the expectancy that the word, promise, verbal or written statement of another individual or group can be relied upon" (p. 651). Truthful statements conform to "what really happened" from that person's perspective and when one's word about future actions is kept. Accepting responsibility for one's actions, not distorting the truth, and not shifting blame to another exemplifies authenticity (Tschannen-Moran & Hoy, 1998), and integrity is the positive correspondence between a person's statements and deeds. Most scholars and researchers see honesty as a pivotal feature of trust (Baier, 1986; Butler & Cantrell, 1984; Cummings & Bromily, 1996); in fact, honesty is assumed when we think of trust.

OPENNESS. Openness is the extent to which relevant information is shared; actions and plans are transparent. Openness makes individuals vulnerable because it signals a kind of reciprocal trust—a confidence that information revealed will not be exploited and that recipients can feel the same confidence in return. People who are guarded in the information they share provoke suspicion; others wonder what is being hidden and why. Just as openness promotes trust, withholding and secrecy breed distrust and suspicion. Individuals who are unwilling to extend trust through openness end up isolated (Kramer, Brewer, & Hanna, 1996). Openness and transparency produce trust.

In sum, trust is a state in which individuals and groups are willing to make themselves vulnerable to others and take risks with confidence that others will respond to their actions in positive ways, that is, with benevolence, reliability, competence, honesty, and openness.

THE SOCIOLOGY OF COLLECTIVE TRUST

In the remainder of this chapter, we call attention to the fact that trust can exist at a variety of levels: between individuals, among group members, and between groups (Webber, 2002). We want to make the case that in many organizations trust between groups plays a particularly germane role in effective operation and goal achievement. In a later chapter we will argue that collective trust is most important in organizations composed of highly interdependent groups whose common task is complex and uncertain.

Trust is necessitated by risk and the presence of at least two entities, a trustor and a trustee. Without risk, there is neither a need for, nor the possibility, of trust (Currall & Judge, 1995; Das & Teng, 1998; Deutsch, 1962; Kee & Knox, 1970; Mayer, Davis, & Schoorman, 1995). Humans can, of course, trust inanimate things like bridges, but our focus in this book is on people trusting people and groups, especially within the context of formal organizations, and more specifically, within schools.

Distinguishing Between Interpersonal Trust and Collective Trust

To understand what we mean by collective trust, it is important to first describe interpersonal trust so that we can properly distinguish the two. Interpersonal trust refers to the trust that a single individual has for another in a situation that carries risk. Legal or socially enforceable contracts can reduce risk and the need for trust in one-on-one social exchanges, but most human exchanges carry some level of risk requiring some level of trust.

As we mentioned earlier, trustors may calculate the level of risk based on the existence of a contract; social norms; control mechanisms; and especially, the behavioral history, reputation, or credentials of the trustee. However, to the extent that risk exists, entering into an exchange often requires trust. Thus, interpersonal trust emerges in situations having some risk and where the trustor cognitively evaluates conditions based on personal experience and then makes a calculated leap of faith that the trustee will act according to expectation.

The formation of interpersonal trust is often accompanied by the formation of positive affect such as "liking." Together, the history of the trustee's trustworthiness, along with personal regard, can create an almost thoughtless trusting relationship such as is often found in small rural communities. There, people know each other's history, can anticipate each other's behavior, and have positive emotional expectations—all conditions short-circuiting the need for extensive calculation of trustworthiness. The small town is often a low-risk environment. In higher-risk situations, where the behavior of the trustee is less certain because of the absence of a personal relationship and known behavioral history, the inclination and decision to trust is usually preceded by careful calculation.

The distinction between interpersonal trust and forms of social trust is often overlooked, partly because, in both cases, trust formation processes consist of psychological or cognitive activity. Even in the case of simple interpersonal trust, the cognitive process starts with the observation of another's behavior and has meaning only insofar as it affects the subsequent dispositions and behaviors of the trustor toward the trustee.

Scholars continue to define trust as a psychological state (Jones & George, 1998; Rousseau et al., 1998). Yet some of these same scholars also urge that trust be studied at various analytical levels (Rousseau et al., 1998). Lewis and Weigert (1985) are quite explicit about this, suggesting, "From a sociological perspective, trust must be conceived as a property of collective units, ongoing dyads, groups, and collectivities, not of isolated individuals" (p. 968). In their landmark study of school trust, Bryk and Schneider (2002, 2003), explore a kind of social trust (relational trust) based on social interactions, mutual dependencies, and power asymmetry among school members. School level trust is seen as emerging from individual discernments and interpersonal exchanges within role sets (e.g., principal-teachers). For Bryk and Schneider, relational trust is a joining together of individual discernments.

Obviously, interpersonal trust can be examined wherever you have two or more people. We can study interpersonal trust between family members, members of a club, and individuals who make up a public school. And clearly, knowledge about interpersonal trust has importance for learning about human behavior. Interpersonal trust, however, is not the focus of this book. Instead, our focus is on what we have called "collective trust," an organizational and sociological perspective rather than a psychological one (Rousseau et al., 1998).

The earliest trust studies conducted in schools (see Chapter 1) recognized that the trust of interest was the trust various groups have for other groups and role incumbents. That is, in the very first empirical studies of school trust, Hoy and Kupersmith (1984) focused their inquiry and measurement on faculty trust in colleagues, the principal, and the school district. Faculty trust scores were aggregated to calculate a school-level variable used to predict various outcomes. However, in this and other early school trust studies, there was little discussion of how these school level variables came to be organizational properties or how they differed from interpersonal trust among school individuals.

In answer to the question, Why is it important to distinguish between interpersonal and collective trust? We make the following assertions: First, collective trust makes a distinct and significant contribution to understanding organizational phenomena over and above explanations facilitated by interpersonal trust. Second, when studying social organizations, collective trust, like other normative and cultural conditions, should be an important predictor of organizational outcomes. Last, the ways we can conceptualize and operationalize collective trust, using such constructs as homogeneity, saturation, density, and reciprocity, provide unique insight into the social workings of organizations.

Collective trust, we argue, is distinct and complementary to interpersonal trust. It is formed and exists as a social property (Lewis & Weigert, 1985). It is a social phenomenon rooted in multiple social exchanges among members of a group. It has an existence separate from dyadic relationships and experiences. Its referent is another group or individual. We can, for example, speak of the collective trust that the faculty group of a school has for the parent group. Formally, we define collective trust as a stable group property rooted in the shared perceptions and affect about the trustworthiness of another group or individual that emerges over time out of multiple social exchanges within the group. These socially constructed shared trust beliefs define the group's willingness to be vulnerable to another group or individual.

Forms of Collective Trust

Before we explain the formation of collective trust in schools, we need to define the forms of collective trust that appear in the literature. Collective trust in school organizations exists in multiple school groups and between different relational dyads. As identified in Table 2.1, the specific form of trust depends on the trustor, that is, the group judging the trustworthiness of another; and the trustee, the group or individual who is the object of the trust. Trustor groups include the primary members of schools: teachers, students, parents, and the principal. Trustees consist of these same school members along with the school as a collective entity. Based on the two dimensional table, several forms of trust are possible in schools, but only eight forms have been operationalized and appear in the educational literature. These forms are defined by trustor group (e.g., faculty, parent, and student) and the referent or object of its trust. Some forms, represented by "X" in Table 2.1, are either not possible or have yet to be studied.

FACULTY TRUST. The bulk of trust research in schools investigates the nature and function of faculty trust. Faculty trust studies specify the teaching faculty as the trustor group with trustees consisting of clients and teaching colleagues (school groups), principals (individuals), and schools (organizations). Clients refer both to parents and students.

There are four forms of faculty trust found in Table 2.1: faculty trust in the principal, faculty trust in colleagues, faculty trust in clients, and faculty trust in schools. When referring to a specific form of faculty trust, for example, faculty trust in colleagues, we identify the faculty as the trustor group and the specific trustee. When referring to all four forms of faculty trust we use faculty trust as an abbreviated identifier of the four different forms.

PARENT TRUST. The Oklahoma studies extended the trust literature to include parent perceptions of school authorities. Previous to the Oklahoma research, Hoy and colleagues, as well as Bryk and Schneider, treated parents as the referent of faculty trust. The primary forms of parent trust specify parents as trustors and principals (individuals), teachers (groups), and schools (organizations) as trustees. These trustor-trustee patterns lead to three forms of parent trust: parent trust in the principal, parent trust in teachers, and parent trust in schools. It is possible to also measure parent trust in students and parent trust in other parents, but these latter two forms of trust have not been operationalized or studied.

Similar to faculty trust, the trustor and trustee are specified when defining a specific form of parent trust. For example, parent trust in principal, parent trust in schools, and parent trust in teachers. The more general parent trust descriptor is used when referring to all forms of parent trust.

STUDENT TRUST. The Oklahoma studies also extended forms of trust to include the student role group. Two forms of student trust were

Table 2.1. The forms of collective trust

Trustors	Trustees (Referents)			
	Principal	Colleagues (Teachers)	Clients (Students/Parents)	School
Faculty	G to I	G to G	G to G	G to O
Parents	G to I	X	X	G to O
Students	G to I	G to G	X	X
Principal	X	X	X	X
Key:	G = Group	I = Individual	O = Organization	X = Empty

Note: Our definition of collective trust requires that the trustor be a group. The trustee may be an individual, group, or organization. The trustor will always be listed first and the referent or trustee second.

operationalized: student trust in the principal and student trust in teachers. Student trust measures student perceptions of other school groups or the principal. Previous to these measures, student trust was specified as teacher perceptions of students, clearly not a valid indication of student affect. Student trust is the general descriptor used when referring to both forms of student trust. Even though student trust in classmates or student trust in parents have not been operationalized, these forms of student trust are theoretically possible.

COLLECTIVE TRUST MODEL

In this section, we present a brief synopsis of our model of collective trust, followed by a more extensive discussion, which links elements of the model to organizational and trust theory and research. The model is portrayed graphically in Figure 2.1.

The core of the model is the social construction of shared trust beliefs within interdependent groups of an organization. The model depicts three contextual elements that condition the formation of collective trust:

1. *External context* includes all environmental influences and experiences that have shaped and continue to shape the values, attitudes, and expectations of individual group members.
2. *Internal context* focuses on the influences and conditions (e.g., structure and culture) within an organization that affect the values, attitudes, and expectations of individuals and groups within the organization.
3. *Task context* is the set of constraints inherent in the group's particular task or specialty (e.g., clarity and complexity of the task, ease of measurement of outcomes, and interdependence with other groups and individuals) that establish the levels of trust necessary for group and organizational effectiveness.

Collective trust is a social construction, which emerges during repeated exchanges among group members. This process parallels the formation of personal trust but occurs at the group level. Unlike personal trust, which is an individual cognitive construction, collective trust is socially constructed out of talk and nonverbal interactions among group members. During social exchanges, group members, both consciously and unconsciously, share their perceptions about previously observed behaviors of other groups (e.g., parents or students) and their members as well as their personal interpretations and feelings about those behaviors.

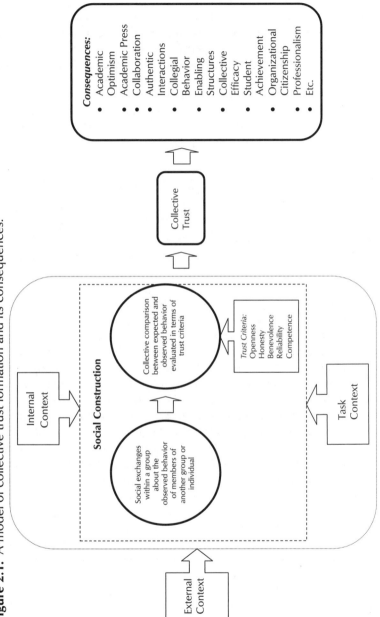

Figure 2.1. A model of collective trust formation and its consequences.

Evaluations are made by comparing observed with expected behavior, and the comparisons accumulate as evidence of trustworthiness using the criteria of openness, honesty, benevolence, reliability, and competence. Out of multiple exchanges over time, a group consensus emerges producing socially constructed, shared, collective trust beliefs about another group or individual, which have important consequences (e.g., academic optimism, student achievement, and collective efficacy). Once formed, collective trust acts as other group norms whose embrace by new group members is a condition of their integration and full membership. The elements of this collective trust model are defined and summarized in Figure 2.2. We now turn to an explication and elaboration of the model.

Collective Trust Formation

Collective trust is a relevant construct for analyzing most social organizations. To be clear, the focus of collective trust is groups within larger social entities. We will primarily use the term *group* to designate these units; however, sometimes other terms like *subgroup, role group,* and *collectivity* may seem to better fit the context.

Collective trust is an especially useful construct for studying organizations composed of interdependent groups, often organized by role or organizational function. Having reviewed existing empirical research on school trust, we found schools to be such organizations, and thus, we use schools as our extended analytical case. Our discussion relies remotely on the exchange theories of George Homans (1950, 1974) and Peter Blau (1964), which have recently been met with renewed interest, and the sociology of groups as explored by Mills (1967) and Cartwright and Zander (1953).

The extent of a group's interdependence on another group or individual has importance for this discussion because high levels of dependence correspond with risk, thereby establishing the need for high levels of collective trust. Organizations like public schools are made up of role groups that are highly interdependent (Bryk & Schneider, 2002), which contributes to their complexity and unpredictability. For example, the parents of a school are vulnerable to the teachers on whom they depend for their children's development, but teacher behavior is difficult to predict.

Yet, at the same time, children spend most of their day outside school under the legal guardianship of adults, usually parents or other relatives. High parent performance expectations for children, commitment to education, monitoring attendance, and homework support are critical to school/ learning success. Thus, teachers also depend on parents because parent support is necessary for learning and child development, and the power of teachers to provide this support is limited. Interdependence amounts to

Figure 2.2. Collective trust formation.

Many organizations (for example, most service organizations) are composed of role or functional groups, which are dependent on other groups or individuals for their own success and that of the organization. Distinct from interpersonal trust and trust among group members, collective trust is a group belief that emerges through the social construction of shared perceptions about the trustworthiness of another group or individual. The elements and process described below constitute a model explaining the formation of collective trust.

1. *Context:* Three contextual elements condition the formation of collective trust.
    A. *External context* consists of the sum of environmental forces that have shaped and continue to shape the values, attitudes and expectations of individual group members.
    B. *Internal context* consists of the sum of forces within the organization that shape the values, attitudes, and expectations of individuals and groups within the organization. These include existing group beliefs about the trustworthiness of other individuals and groups whose cooperation is necessary, inside and outside the organization.
    C. *Task context:* Dependent groups are also affected by the nature of their particular task or specialty, its clarity, complexity, and measurability of success.
2. *Social exchange:* Repeated social exchanges among group members are influenced by, and often have as their content, previous individual observations, interpretations, and feelings about the trustworthiness of another group.
3. *Social construction:* These social exchanges catalyze a process of social construction that parallels the formation of interpersonal trust, but that occurs at the group level. This social process includes the sharing within the group of individual expectations for appropriate behavior by members of another group (expressed in terms of openness, honesty, benevolence, reliability, and competence) and comparisons to observed behavior of members of another group, resulting in an emergent consensus about the trustworthiness of another group.
4. *Collective trust:* The group's consensus about the trustworthiness of another group becomes a shared belief.
5. *Consequences:* The socially constructed shared belief constrains behavior of the group and has significant consequences for the group, other groups or individuals it cooperates with, and the organization as a whole.

reciprocal risk between groups, resulting in the dynamic character of collective trust and its requirement for constant nurturing.

As repeated cycles of social exchange demonstrate the probability of another group's trustworthy behavior, trust is enhanced (Rousseau et al., 1998); however, a break or interruption in the cycle of reciprocated trustworthy behavior can initiate the dissolution of trust (Serva, Fuller, & Mayer, 2005). High levels of interdependence between groups require high levels of reciprocated trust.

Context of Trust Formation

Here we discuss the three distinct types of context that affect the formation of collective trust in organizations.

EXTERNAL CONTEXT. Common experiences and contextual effects will be shared by many or all members of a group; however, some experiences affect only a few. Schein (2004) calls attention to the idiosyncratic "assumptions, expectations, and patterns of coping" from the external context that each member brings to the collectivity (p. 67). From the perspective of collective trust formation, external context and its effects, embedded as individual attitudes, characteristics, and so on can be said to condition a group's capacity and disposition to trust. This capacity and disposition to trust can be described collectively as we seek to compare groups and their likelihood to trust. For example, groups will differ greatly with respect to the kinds and degree of diversity found within them. There is extensive evidence that diverse values, worldviews, and background experiences negatively condition the emergence of trust, social integration, and communication (Earle & Cvetkovich, 1995; Northcraft, Polzer, Neal, & Kramer, 1995; Smith et al., 1994; Triandis, Hall, & Ewen, 1965; Wiersema & Bantel, 1992). Comparing groups with respect to value divergence or convergence should predict the likelihood of emerging collective trust.

INTERNAL CONTEXT. In the model of collective trust, we identify a second set of influences called *internal context*, which refers to organizational conditions immediately surrounding groups. Among the potential avenues through which organizational conditions may affect a group and its capacity to trust another group or individual, we list an organization's structure, leadership, employee evaluation system, clarity of goals, history, and facilities.

How should internal context be conceptualized as conditioning a group's capacity and disposition to trust other social entities? Studying families, Anderson (1971) has proposed four propositions that serve as a starting place. Keep in mind, however, that they were deduced from studies of intra-group, not collective trust, formation. These propositions are adapted here to fit the group context. The first proposition derives more clearly from the external context as described earlier. The latter three propositions, however, help us organize possible effects of internal context:

- As group homogeneity increases, so too does trust
- As organizationally necessitated social exchange within a group increases, so too does trust
- As size and complexity of the host organization increases, trust decreases
- As social change and volatility within the organization increases, trust decreases

In sum, we can begin examining the internal context in which a group operates by noting required communication levels, organizational size, and organizational stability.

TASK CONTEXT. The model of collective trust formation analytically distinguishes task complexity as a significant element separate from internal and external context. The nature of an organization's task, whether complex or simple, affects the social construction of collective trust. As Thompson (1967) explained in his comparison of organizations differing in task complexity, manufacturing technology is simple and straightforward. It involves taking in standard raw material; enacting an invariable and simple, linear, standard process; and finally emitting a standard product. By contrast, complex technologies take in nonstandard raw material, enact nonstandard processes, and produce a nonstandard product. Schools, for example, take in children whose motivation, prior knowledge, and skill are variable. The process of enacting learning is necessarily variable, adapted to individual and group learning needs. The product is variable as well. The relative complexity of an organization's technology has important consequences for collective trust formation, as we demonstrate in Chapter 7.

Social Construction

The social construction of collective trust is a multilevel process. Figure 2.1 portrays the theoretical elements of its formation: context (already discussed), social construction, social exchange, collective trust, and consequences. Again, keep in mind that we are not concerned with the formation of interpersonal trust within a group, but rather the formation of collective trust of one group for another group or individual.

To understand the process of social construction of collective trust, it is instructive to consider what happens when an outsider attempts to become a member of an existing group within a larger organization. In this situation, the social construction of the group's trust for another is already in place. For example, a new teacher is exposed to the faculty's shared beliefs about parent trustworthiness as they interact with their new colleagues. The level of collective trust for the parent group has become a shared belief, a cultural assumption in Schein's (2004) terms. To a greater or lesser extent, a newcomer's successful integration into the group will depend on accepting its shared normative system, including its beliefs about another group's trustworthiness. (For an extended discussion of a newcomer's socialization into a group, see Mills, 1967.)

Group beliefs and attitudes are typically made known by the group's elites who often articulate the group's identity to newcomers as they are socialized. The intensity of these norms and beliefs soon becomes apparent to newcomers through repeated social exchanges and socialization. Newcomers encountering existing social constructions have a need to conform to the "common wisdom" to gain and sustain their personal status within the group (Pfeffer, 1982). They are first drawn into the "common view" for reasons related to acceptance and presentation of self in a favorable light (Mulkay, 1971).

The point is that if collective trust exists in a group, it is a social phenomenon, not simply an aggregation of trust experiences and beliefs of individual group members. Collective trust is very much like culture, said to consist of "shared cognitive representations in the minds of individuals" (Romney, Boyd, Moore, Batchelder, & Brazill, 1996, p. 4699). Although related, collective trust is distinct from the beliefs of individual group members and thus is more stable and not as dependent on an individual's idiosyncratic experiences as is interpersonal trust.

We take up the question of how the existing collective trust beliefs were socially constructed in the first place. Chester Barnard (1938) talked long ago about the fact that when individuals become part of a cooperative group, they are unavoidably drawn into social exchanges they would otherwise not have been a part of. These exchanges have both emotional and cognitive consequences. Homans (1950) has called the changes in attitudes of group members resulting from their membership "the primary focus of social psychology" (p. 109). The more group members interact, the more alike they become (Homans, 1974; Young & Parker, 1999). Social exchanges tend to produce people who both think alike and have common feelings; they also develop shared norms and perceptions, such as beliefs about the trustworthiness of another group or individual.

Clearly, the members of a group do have personal experiences and evidence about the trustworthiness of another group's members upon which they base their personal decision to trust or not to trust other individuals. Cognitively, these individuals have made judgments about the trustworthiness of individuals in another group, and they have probably shaped personal feelings about them as well (Lewis & Weigert, 1985). Beyond the realm of personal trust for others, however, it

> is often important to the members of a group that they achieve a consensus concerning the relations between their group and its social surroundings—which groups can be considered as allies, which as enemies, how the group compares with others. (Cartwright & Zander, 1953, p. 143)

A group's process for deciding if another group or individual is trustworthy and likely to cooperate is indeed important in organizational life, particularly when groups are interdependent. During social exchanges that occur naturally and necessarily among members of a group, stories, experiences, and opinions about the observed behaviors of another group's members will be expressed. Reported behavior will be compared to the behavioral expectations held by the group. Believing that the other group will act in a trustworthy manner, the group judges observed behavior against criteria of trustworthiness. A kind of balance is achieved in the grist of multiple exchanges (Homans, 1974) that shapes the norm—in this case, collective trust beliefs. Once a shared belief has formed, deviate views are sanctioned (Napier & Gershenfeld, 1999).

The criteria used in shaping a group's trust for another are identical to the criteria used by individuals to assess trustworthiness during the formation of interpersonal trust. They include the consideration of evidence that the referent group acts openly, honestly, benevolently, reliably, and competently. For example, collective trust of faculty in parents emerges through the multiple social exchanges that teachers have with each other. Teachers share their first- and secondhand evidence about parental behavior. These exchanges take place in the shadow of existing, shared perceptions and norms governing "how teachers talk about parents in this school," "how teachers feel about parents in this school," and so on. Over time, as parent behavior is discussed and evaluated against the expectations teachers have for parent behavior and against criteria of trustworthiness, teachers socially construct a common set of beliefs about the trustworthiness of parents.

Collective Trust

The emergent level of collective faculty trust is not the product of a single story or the experiences of a single teacher, but rather is negotiated as various bits of information, interpretations, and feelings are recounted over time during the day-to-day social exchanges among teachers. The result is a property of the teacher group, a social phenomenon we call *collective trust*. Thus, while interpersonal trust is shaped cognitively by individuals and filtered only through their own experiences, collective trust "evens out" individual perceptions, while being influenced and constrained by the existing norms, feelings, beliefs, and social pressures of the group. As Lewis and Weigert (1985) point out, "The cognitive content of trust is a collective cognitive reality that transcends the realm of individual psychology" (p. 970).

Consequences

School trust research during the past 20 years has shown that collective trust has far-reaching consequences for schools and their effectiveness. For example, the collective faculty trust is related to such outcomes as academic optimism, professionalism, and school achievement. Figure 2.1 captures the dynamics and key features that we believe explain the social construction of collective trust that we have just described.

SUMMARY

In this chapter, we begin to build the case for a theory of collective trust. First, we reviewed the multidisciplinary trust literature and discovered a consistent, but evolving, conceptualization of trust as a state in which individuals and groups are willing to make themselves vulnerable to others and take risks with confidence that others will respond to their actions in positive ways, that is, with benevolence, predictability, competence, honesty, and openness.

Next, we defined collective trust and introduced the construct as a stable group property rooted in the shared perceptions and affect about the trustworthiness of a group or individual that emerge over time out of multiple social exchanges within the group. The socially constructed shared trust beliefs define the group's willingness to be vulnerable to another group or individual.

Finally, we proposed and explicated a theoretical model for the development of collective trust in all organizations, which is based on group theory and social exchange theory.

CHAPTER 3

Measuring Collective Trust in Schools

There appears to be widespread agreement on the importance of
trust in human conduct, but unfortunately there also appears to be an
equally widespread lack of agreement on a suitable definition of the
construct.

—LaRue Hosmer, *Trust*

Although trust has long been the subject of philosophers and politicians,
the systematic investigation of trust by social scientists and educational researchers is of more recent vintage. In the late 1950s, the impetus for the
empirical study of trust came from the escalating suspicion of the Cold War
and the hope that social science research might provide answers to the dan-
gerous and costly arms race (Deutsch, 1958).

In the late 1960s, in response to a generation of young people who had
become disenchanted with authority and alienated from the establishment,
the study of trust shifted to individual personality traits (Rotter, 1967). By
the 1990s, with shifts in technology and society, the study of trust had become popular and important in sociology (Coleman, 1990), in economics
(Fukuyama, 1995), and in organizational science (Kramer & Tyler, 1996;
Shaw, 1997).

In Chapter 1 we described the beginnings of our study of collective
trust in schools, which were based on the work of Rotter (1967) and Golembiewski and McConkie (1975). In this chapter we will briefly review our
early definition of trust and its measure, and then move to the more recent elaborations of definitions and refined measures of collective trust in
schools, which have guided our research for the past two decades.

EARLY DEFINITION AND MEASURE OF COLLECTIVE TRUST

Initially, we defined trust as a "generalized expectancy held by the work
group that the word, promise, and written or oral statement of another

individual, group, or organization can be relied upon" (Hoy & Kupersmith, 1985, p. 2). The work group in our research was the faculty as a whole; thus, the first collective definition of trust was based on the faculty's descriptions of trust relationships in their schools.

Recall that we used three referents of collective trust: the *principal*, *colleagues*, and the *school*. In a pilot study and then a series of factor analyses, Hoy and Kupersmith (1985) identified seven items for each referent of trust. Each of the three collective trust scales had high reliabilities of .93 for faculty trust in the principal, .93 for faculty trust in colleagues, and .82 for the school organization. The questionnaire for this, our first collective measure of trust, is found in the Appendix 1.1.

DEVELOPMENT OF A REFINED MEASURE OF COLLECTIVE TRUST

At Ohio State in the late 1990s we decided to take another look at the trust literature because studies of the concept were burgeoning in the social sciences and seemed useful to the analysis of relationships in schools. We undertook a comprehensive review of the literature on trust (Tschannen-Moran & Hoy, 2000), which indentified a host of different definitions. With one exception (Frost, Stimpson, & Maughan, 1978), however, all were multifaceted.

Most definitions of trust were based on a general and common belief that trust meant relying on individuals or groups to act in ways that were in the best interest of the concerned party. Although the literature on trust is diverse, it has some common threads running through it regardless of whether the focus is on the individual, organization, or society itself. We were most interested in organizational and collective trust.

Trust relationships are based on interdependence; the interests of one party cannot be achieved without reliance on another group or individual (Rousseau et al., 1998). If there is no interdependence, there is no need for trust. Interdependence in a relationship typically creates vulnerability, which is a common feature of trust (Baier, 1986; Bigley & Pearce, 1998; Coleman, 1990; Mayer et al., 1995; Mishra, 1996). Trust involves taking risks and making oneself vulnerable to another party or group with confidence that the other will act in ways that are not detrimental to the trusting party.

Facets of Trust

We gleaned five facets of trust from our extensive literature review (Tschannen-Moran & Hoy, 1998, 2000). In the previous chapter we developed each of these facet of trust; hence, here will only briefly review each facet.

- *Benevolence* is the "accepted vulnerability to another's possible but not expected ill will" (Baier, 1986, p. 236).
- *Reliability* combines a sense of predictability with benevolence. In a situation of interdependence, when something is required from another person or group, the individual or group can be relied upon to supply it (Butler & Cantrell, 1984; Mishra, 1996; Rotter, 1967).
- *Competence* is the ability to perform as expected and according to standards appropriate to the task at hand. For example, in schools, students are dependent on the competence of their teachers
- *Honesty* is the person's character, integrity, and authenticity. Statements are truthful when they conform to "what really happened" from that person's perspective.
- *Openness* is the extent to which relevant information is shared; it is a process by which individuals make themselves vulnerable to others.

A Refined Definition of Collective Trust

The second wave of trust studies at The Ohio State University evolved from our comprehensive review of the trust literature (Tschannen-Moran & Hoy, 2000) and was guided by the following multifaceted definition:

> *Trust* is a faculty's willingness to be vulnerable to another party based on the confidence that the latter party is benevolent, reliable, competent, honest, and open.

Remember that in our analyses faculty trust is a collective property—the extent to which the faculty as a group is willing to risk vulnerability. Moreover, faculty trust has multiple referents; initially, we focused on four:

- Faculty trust in students
- Faculty trust in colleagues
- Faculty trust in the principal
- Faculty trust in parents

DEVELOPING MEASURES OF FACULTY TRUST: THE TRUST SCALES

Using the conceptual formulation of trust just developed, a team of researchers wrote items for a measure of faculty trust. For each trust referent (student, colleagues, principal, parent), items were crafted to include all five facets of trust. Although there were no existing measures for trust that fit the proposed conceptual framework, items from the Hoy and Kupersmith (1985) scales provided a starting point. An analysis of their items, however, revealed that none of them tapped either competency or openness; hence, new items were added to the existing ones to measure the missing facets of trust. In addition, sets of items were written for faculty trust in students and in parents, making sure that each facet of trust was represented for each referent group.

Format of Trust Scales

The format of the Trust Scales is a 6-point Likert response set ranging from strongly disagree (1) to strongly agree (6). Teachers are asked to indicate the extent to which they agreed with the items. Sample items from each of the four levels of trust being measured include:

- Teachers in this school trust their students.
- The principal is in this school is competent in doing his or her job.
- Teachers in this school are reliable.
- Teachers can count on parents in this school to support them.

An Overview of the Development Plan

Items were developed to measure each proposed facet of trust in the following steps:

1. The researchers created a pool of items.
2. A panel of experts reacted to the items.
3. A preliminary version was field tested with teachers.
4. A pilot study as done with a small group of schools to test the factor structure, reliability, and validity of the instrument.
5. Two large-scale studies were conducted to assess psychometric properties of the measures.

Pool of Items

We created a pool of items to measure all the facets and referents of faculty trust. Specifically, willingness to risk vulnerability and five facets of trust—benevolence, reliability, competency, honesty, and openness—were considered as the items were written. Four referents of faculty trust—student, teacher, principal, and parent—guided the creation of the four separate sets of trust items.

Panel of Experts

To evaluate the content validity of the items, the Trust Scale was submitted to a panel of experts, all professors at The Ohio State University from the College of Education and the Fisher Business School. Panel members were asked to judge which facet of trust each item measured. There was strong agreement among the judges. In those few cases where the panelists disagreed, the items were eliminated or retained and the question of the appropriate category was left to an empirical test using factor analysis. There was consensus in the panel that the items measured all the facets of trust for each referent group.

Field Test

A field test with public school teachers was conducted to evaluate the clarity of instructions, appropriateness of the response set, and face validity of the items. Six experienced teachers were asked to examine and respond to the items and give some feedback. Again there was general agreement that the items were clear and reasonable and had face validity. In a few instances, specific comments led to minor modification of an item.

Pilot Study

After the panel review and field test, 48 items remained and were used in a pilot study to explore the factor structure, reliability, and validity of the measure.

SAMPLE. A sample of 50 teachers from 50 different schools in five states was selected to test the psychometric properties of the Trust Scales. Half of the schools selected were schools with reputations of relatively high conflict and the other half had relatively low conflict among the faculty.

INSTRUMENTS. In addition to the 48 trust items, teachers were asked to respond to a self-estrangement scale (Forsyth & Hoy, 1978), a sense of powerlessness scale (Zielinski & Hoy, 1983), a teacher sense of efficacy scale (Bandura, n.d.), and one item measuring the perception of conflict in the school. These additional measures were used to check the predictive validity of the trust scales. It was predicted that each aspect of trust would be positively related to sense of teacher efficacy and negatively related to self-estrangement, sense of powerlessness, and degree of conflict.

DATA COLLECTION. Data were collected from 50 different schools through two procedures. Researchers identified about a third of the schools as coming from either low-trust or high-trust schools, and teachers were asked to respond to our questionnaire. The other two thirds were sent the questionnaire by mail. Ninety-one percent of those contacted agreed to participate and returned usable questionnaires.

FACTOR ANALYSIS RESULTS. The items were submitted to a principal axis factor analysis to test whether they loaded strongly and as expected. Although we anticipated four factors, only three strong factors emerged. The three-factor solution was supported by a scree test and made conceptual sense. Surprisingly, the items for trust in students and trust in parents loaded together on a single factor. Teachers did not distinguish between trusting students and trusting parents. Thus, the two sets of items combined into a single factor, which was called "Trust in Clients." The clients in this case are students and parents; both are recipients of the services offered by schools. The other two factors, as predicted, were Trust in the Principal and Trust in Colleagues. On the whole, factor loadings were strong and loaded together with other items from the same subtest.

Decisions of whether to retain, eliminate, or modify each of the items were based on theoretical (conceptual fit) and empirical (factor loadings) grounds. When an item loaded at .40 or above on more than one factor, it typically was removed. In a few cases, however, such items were retained because either the conceptual fit was strong or the item could be modified to enhance the conceptual fit. For example, the item, "Teachers in this school trust their students," loaded strongly on Trust in Clients at .75 but also loaded on Trust in Colleagues at .43. This item was retained because of its strong conceptual fit with trust in clients. Any item that failed the empirical test of loading .40 or higher on at least one factor was eliminated. Likewise, regardless of the factor loading, any item that loaded on the wrong factor conceptually was eliminated. Finally, redundant items were eliminated when another item measured the same property of trust and had an even stronger loading. The final product was a 35-item questionnaire.

CONTENT ANALYSIS. Each level of trust was examined to make sure that all facets of trust (benevolence, reliability, competence, honesty, and openness) were represented in each scale, and indeed that was the case. The factor structure also supported the construct validity of the trust measures; items generally loaded correctly for each referent of trust.

ONE DIMENSION WITH FIVE FACETS. All five facets of trust covaried to form a single, coherent pattern of trust for principals, colleagues, and clients. In other words, the five facets of trust came together to provide a unidimensional measure of trust for each referent group.

VALIDITY AND RELIABILITY. The pilot study produced a 35-item survey that reliably measured three kinds of collective faculty trust: Trust in the Principal (alpha = .95), Trust in Colleagues (alpha = .94), and Trust in Clients (alpha = .92).

We examined the validity of the measures and their ability to distinguish trust from other related constructs. Predictive validity of the measures of trust was strong. As expected, self-estrangement, powerlessness, and conflict were all negatively related to dimensions of trust, whereas teacher sense of efficacy was positively related to the subscales of trust. The results of the correlational analyses are summarized in Table 3.1.

Further Testing of the Trust Scales

Having developed a measure of trust in field and pilot studies, the next step was to evaluate the Trust Scale in other samples of schools.

AN ELEMENTARY SAMPLE. The population for this phase of the study was the elementary schools within one large urban midwestern school district. Ninety percent of the schools contacted agreed to participate, resulting in a sample of 50 elementary schools.

The factor structure for the Trust Scale was very similar to that found in the pilot study and demonstrated a stable factor structure. Kerlinger (1973) argues that factor analysis is perhaps the most powerful method of construct validation, and the findings of this study support the construct validity of faculty trust. The proposed faces or facets of trust—benevolence, reliability, competence, honesty, and openness—vary together and belong to an overall conception of trust that is coherent. Moreover, the facets of trust are present for each referent of trust.

In addition, reliabilities for the three subscales were even higher than those found in the pilot study. Using Cronbach's alpha coefficient, the reliabilities were .98, .98, and .97 for faculty trust in the principal, colleagues, and clients

Table 3.1. Validity evidence: Correlations between trust and criterion variables

Subscale	1	2	3	4	5	6	7
1. Faculty Trust in Principal	(.95)	.54**	.40**	−.47**	−.22	−.28**	.46**
2. Faculty Trust in Colleagues		(.94)	.62**	−.32**	−.31**	−.76**	.30*
3. Faculty Trust in Clients			(.92)	−.51**	−.31*	−.56**	.47**
4. Powerlessness				(.83)	.42**	.38**	−.55**
5. Self-Estrangement					(.88)	.36**	−.61**
6. School Conflict						—	−.28*
7. Teacher Efficacy							(.87)

Note: Alpha coefficients of reliability are on the diagonal.

*p < .05, **p < .01

respectively. In brief, the factor structure of the trust measures was stable, and the reliability and validity of each of the three measures were strong.

A SECONDARY SAMPLE. To this point, our analysis of trust focused on elementary schools. Would the same structure of trust emerge in secondary schools? Would faculty trust in students and parents combine into a unitary measure of trust, or would it separate into two aspects of trust? Would the trust scales used at the elementary level work as well at the secondary level? We addressed these questions by studying a sample of 97 high schools in Ohio.

Regardless of level, elementary or secondary, faculty trust in students and in parents combined to form one unitary construct of faculty trust in clients. Once again, a three-factor solution was best and explained about 70% of the variance. The factor analytic results of the two samples were remarkably similar. The factor structure was consistent and stable; all items loaded as predicted and defined three dimensions of trust: faculty trust in the principal, in colleagues, and in clients (students and parents). Alpha coefficients of reliabilities for the three scales were also high—faculty trust in principal (.98), faculty trust in colleagues (.93), and faculty trust in clients (.93).

OMNIBUS TRUST SCALE (T-SCALE)

At this point in the instrument development, there were two slightly different versions of the trust scale—one for elementary schools and one for secondary schools. To simplify, we decided to develop one shorter scale that could be used for either elementary or secondary schools. The goal was to create an omnibus scale, such that each subscale

1. Measured the three referents of faculty trust
2. Contained all five facets of trust
3. Had high reliability
4. Was parsimonious
5. Correlated strongly with the original elementary and secondary subscales

To accomplish these aims, we compared the factor loadings for each item for the elementary and secondary samples (see Table 3.2). The factor loadings were quite high for most of the items; in fact, there were only two items that had low loadings, which we dropped. Next, we eliminated some items that were redundant measures for each facet, making sure that all facets of trust were measured for each subscale.

The result was an Omnibus Trust Scale of 26 items that measured the three aspects of faculty trust: faculty trust in colleagues, in the principal, and in clients. When the alpha coefficients of reliability were recalculated for the

Table 3.2. Items and factor loadings for the Omnibus Trust Scale (T-Scale)

Subscales and Items	Facet	Factor Loadings	
		Elementary	Secondary
Faculty Trust in Principal			
1. The teachers in this school have faith in the integrity of the principal.	(O)	.92	.92
2. The principal in this school typically acts in the best interests of the teachers.	(R)	.94	.94
3. The principal doesn't tell teachers what is really going on.*	(O)	−.89	−.84
4. Teachers in this school trust the principal.	(V)	.88	.97
5. The principal of this school does not show concern for teachers.*	(B)	−.91	−.84
6. The teachers in this school are suspicious of most of the principal's actions.*	(V)	−.86	−.91
7. Teachers in this school can rely on the principal.	(R)	.94	.97
8. The principal in this school is competent in doing his or her job.	(C)	.92	.91
Faculty Trust in Colleagues			
1. Teachers in this school typically look out for each other.	(B)	.91	.83
2. Teachers in this school trust each other.	(V)	.91	.74
3. Even in difficult situations, teachers in this school can depend on each other	(R)	.93	.79
4. Teachers in this school have faith in the integrity of their colleagues.	(H)	.92	.73
5. Teachers in this school are suspicious of each other.*	(V)	−.89	−.66
6. Teachers in this school do their jobs well.	(C)	.71	.43
7. When teachers in this school tell you something you can believe it.	(H)	.84	.63
8. Teachers in this school are open with each other.	(O)	.91	.74
Faculty Trust in Clients (Students and Parents)			
1. Teachers in this school trust their students.	(V)	.79	.72
2. Students in this school can be counted on to do their work.	(R)	.90	.83
3. Students in this school care about each other.	(B)	.89	.80
4. Students here are secretive.*	(O)	−.75	−.30
5. Teachers here believe that students are competent learners.	(C)	.75	.81
6. Teachers can count on parental support.	(R)	.91	.82
7. Teachers in this school believe what parents tell them.	(H)	.84	.72
8. Teachers think that most of the parents do a good job.	(C)	.90	.90
9. Parents in this school are reliable in their commitments.	(R)	.91	.81
10. Teachers in this school trust the parents.	(V)	.89	.89

H = Honesty; B = Benevolence; C = Competence; O = Openness; V = Risk of Vulnerability; R = Reliability; * = Reverse the scoring.

See Appendices for the Omnibus Trust Scale (T-Scale).

shorter scale, they remained high (above .90) for both samples. Moreover, the omnibus subscales correlated highly with the longer subscale versions for both samples; neither was lower than .96. The Omnibus T-Scale is found in Appendix 3.1 and also on line at www.waynekhoy.com. Researchers and school practitioners are invited to use the scale for research purposes and administrators for professional and organizational development. Just download the scale, copy it, and use it.

PARENT TRUST IN SCHOOLS SCALE (PTS-SCALE)

Thus far we have described the development of our three measures of faculty trust in the principal, in colleagues, and in clients (students and parents). We now turn to our collective measures of parent trust in the school and in the principal. This phase of the study of collective trust was done at Oklahoma State University and the University of Oklahoma (Forsyth, Adams, & Barnes, 2002).

The same definition and conceptual framework was used in this series of studies as has been used in research on faculty trust at The Ohio State University. That is, all five facets of trust were an integral part of each measure; in fact, factor analysis confirmed that the facets of trust were all part of a single measure for each of these referents of trust.

Item Development

The Oklahoma researchers constructed 27 Likert-type items to capture perceptions of parents regarding the benevolence, reliability, competence, honesty, and openness of the school. Items were written from a parental perspective to parallel items contained in previously validated trust scales, namely the Organizational Trust Inventory of Cummings and Bromiley (1996) and Omnibus T-Scale of Hoy and Tschannen-Moran's (1999, 2003). The construct relevance of the items was evaluated by a panel of 11 graduate doctoral students in a seminar on the study of trust.

Field Test

The parents of children in three school districts completed the 27-item parent trust of school scale. Items had an 8-point response set ranging from "strongly disagree" to "strongly agree." Of the 10 participating schools, two were lower elementary (K–3), two were upper elementary (4–6), three were middle (7–8), and three were high schools. Two of the school districts sent surveys home with students, and they were returned to the child's teacher. One district distributed surveys during parent-teacher conferences.

All surveys were returned to the researchers within 2 weeks after distribution. Participating parents remained anonymous, and over 71% (429/600) returned the surveys, 5% of which were discarded as unusable because they were incomplete. The number of useable surveys remained adequate for the factor analysis procedures. The parents and schools were representative of urban, suburban, and rural communities in Oklahoma.

Factor Analysis

The data from the 429 parents were subjected to a series of principal axis factor analyses, all of which supported a single factor solution containing all five of the facets of trust. The goal of the successive factor analyses was to develop a parsimonious measure of trust with good psychometric properties. The 27-item scale was reduced to a 20-item scale and then to a 10-item short form without sacrificing either validity or reliability. For details of this factor analytic study, see Forsyth et al. (2002). The items for final factor analysis are found in Table 3.3. The alpha coefficient of reliability for the scale was .95 with all the items loading strongly on this unidimensional factor. The complete Parent Trust in School Scale is found in Appendix 3.2.

PARENT TRUST IN PRINCIPAL SCALE (PTP-SCALE)

The Parent Trust in Principal Scale was developed using the same procedures and parent sample as that for the Parent Trust in School Scale with a different referent, the principal. First, the items were developed using our conceptual

Table 3.3. Items and factor loadings for the Parent Trust in School Scale (PTS-Scale)

Parent Trust in School	Facet	Factor Loading
1. This school always does what it is supposed to.	(R)	.70
2. This school keeps me well informed.	(O)	.79
3. I really trust this school.	(H)	.88
4. Kids at this school are well cared for.	(B)	.84
5. This school is always honest with me.	(H)	.83
6. This school does a terrific job	(C)	.85
7. This school has high standards for all kids.	(C)	.83
8. The school is always ready to help.	(B)	.89
9. I never worry about my child when he/she is there.	(R)	.69
10. At this school, I know I'll be listened to.	(O)	.89

H = Honesty; B = Benevolence; C = Competence; O = Openness; R = Reliability.

See Appendix 3.2 for the PTS Scale.

framework for trust, and then a 27-item version of the scale was factor analyzed to reduce the number of items to 20. Next, the 20-item scale was refined
to a 15-item short form with sound psychometric properties. The alpha coefficient of reliability was .95, all facets of trust were represented in the scale,
and the final factor analysis confirmed a strong, single factor.

The items for final factor analysis are found in Table 3.4. All the items
loaded strongly on one unidimensional factor. The complete final version of
the Parent Trust in Principal Scale is found in Appendix 3.3.

STUDENT TRUST IN FACULTY SCALE (STF-SCALE)

Another perspective on collective trust that has received scant attention is
student trust. The Oklahoma researchers also developed a measure of student trust using the same conceptual framework.

Item Development

Similar to faculty trust and parent trust, student trust is a condition that
surfaces through interactions perceived as open, honest, reliable, competent,

Table 3.4. Items and factor loadings for the Parent Trust in Principal Scale
(PTP-Scale)

Parent Trust in Principal	Facet	Factor Loading
The principal of this school		
1. Is good at his/her job.	(R)	.79
2. Can be counted on to do his/her job.	(R)	.85
3. Is well intentioned.	(B)	.77
4. Is always honest.	(H)	.84
5. Invites criticism and praise from parents.	(O)	.76
6. Is very reliable.	(R)	.89
7. Has high standards for all kids.	(C)	.86
8. Is always ready to help.	(B)	.84
9. Treats everyone with respect.	(B)	.86
10. Keeps an open door.	(O)	.83
11. Owns up to his/her mistakes.	(H)	.80
12. Knows how to make learning happen.	(C)	.92
13. Is always there when you need him/her.	(R)	.85
14. Is trustworthy.	(H)	.89
15. Likes to talk to parents.	(O)	.76

H = Honesty; B = Benevolence; C = Competence; O = Openness; R = Reliability.
See Appendix 3.3 for the PTP Scale.

and benevolent; therefore, items were generated to measure each of these facets of student trust. The items were written such that the response set was a 4-point scale, ranging from strongly disagree (1) to strongly agree (4). A 4-point scale is more appropriate for attitudinal questions distributed to young students than a 6- or 8-point scale (Royeen, 1985). Multiple items for each facet of trust were drafted and included in a 13-item questionnaire.

Sample of Students

Data were collected from a sample of seventh, eighth, and ninth graders from three schools within one school district. The demographic characteristics of this sample included Caucasian students (25%), African Americans (32%), Hispanics (30%), and Native Americans (12%). Forty-seven percent of the students qualified for the federal lunch program.

Exploratory Factor Analysis

The initial factor analysis indicated one strong factor, which explained most of the variance. The Student Trust in Faculty Scale, like the Parent Trust Scale, was unidimensional. In other words, the facets of openness, honesty, benevolence, competence, and reliability converged into a single factor, and loadings for all the items were high, ranging of .62 to .85 (see Table 3.5).

Reliability and Validity

Reliability, as measured by Cronbach's alpha, was .90, suggesting strong internal consistency among the items. The structure of the factor analysis supported the construct validity, as did concurrent and predictive validity procedures. As predicted, academic efficacy and student identification with school were both significantly correlated with student trust in teachers. In addition, a test of a hierarchical growth model of language arts achievement (Adams & Forsyth, 2009b) supported the validity; trust was the crucial variable in the analysis as theoretically anticipated. The Student Trust in Faculty Scale is found in Appendix 3.4.

STUDENT TRUST IN PRINCIPAL SCALE (STP-SCALE)

Our final measure of collective trust is another one that has received almost no attention. The Oklahoma researchers also developed a measure of student trust in the principal using the same trust formulation as other measures.

Table 3.5. Items and factor loadings for the Student Trust in Faculty Scale (STF-Scale)

Student Trust in Teachers	Facet	Factor Loading
1. Teachers are always ready to help.	(B)	.79
2. Teachers at this school have high expectations for all students.	(C)	.69
3. Teachers at this school are easy to talk to.	(O)	.80
4. Students are well cared for at this school.	(B)	.82
5. Teachers at this school always do what they are supposed to.	(R)	.76
6. Teachers at this school really listen to students.	(O)	.85
7. Teachers at this school are always honest with me.	(H)	.77
8. Teachers at this school do a terrific job.	(C)	.84
9. Students can believe what teachers tell them.	(H)	.69
10. Teachers at this school do not care about students.*	(B)	−.62
11. Teachers at this school are good at teaching.	(C)	.82
12. Students learn a lot from teachers in this school.	(C)	.79
13. Students at this school can depend on teachers for help.	(R)	.84

H = Honesty; B = Benevolence; C = Competence; O = Openness; R = Reliability.

*Reverse the scoring.

See Appendix 3.4 for the Student Trust in Faculty Scale (STF Scale).

Item Development

The Oklahoma researchers (Barnes, Adams, & Forsyth, 2002) generated 20 trust items using a 4-point scale, ranging from always (1) to never (4). A simplified response set was used on recommendation of child development experts, and items were reviewed by reading specialists to confirm that items and instructions did not exceed a fourth-grade reading level. Four items were written for each of the five facets of trust, this time with the principal as referent.

Sample of Students

A stratified random sample was drawn from all 836 public schools in one quadrant of a midwestern state. These schools were located in 101 districts, 91 of which gave the researchers permission to collect data. Ultimately 79 schools were included, consisting of 22 elementary schools, 30 middle schools, and 27 high schools. The sample was nearly identical to the state's entire population in ethnic group proportion and socioeconomic status (SES). Data were collected from students in 5th, 7th, and 11th grades. Instruments were delivered to or mailed to all subjects and returns were by prepaid U.S. postage. Up to four follow-up mailings were done, and random replacement was used for respondents whose surveys were returned as undeliverable. The response rate was 56%, 1,836 out of 3,239 instruments returned.

Factor Analysis Results

A series of principal axis factor analyses were performed resulting in one, strong unidimensional factor explaining 65 % of the variance. All the facets of openness, honesty, benevolence, competence, and reliability converged into a single factor with loadings for all the items high, ranging of .69 to .84 (see Table 3.6). Ultimately the scale items were reduced from 20 to 12 without loss of theoretical coverage of the facets or internal consistency.

Reliability and Validity

Cronbach's alpha of .95 provided strong evidence of internal consistency among the items. The structure of the factor analysis demonstrated construct validity; items measured the construct as predicted. Predictive validity

Table 3.6. Items and factor loadings for the Student Trust in Principal Scale (STP-Scale)

Student Trust in Principal	Facet	Factor Loading
The principal in my school		
1. Is nice.	(B)	.77
2. Likes students.	(B)	.79
3. Is fair.	(O)	.80
4. Is helpful.	(C)	.83
5. Does what he/she says he/she will do.	(R)	.69
6. Is there for students.	(R)	.80
7. Tells the truth to students.	(H)	.80
8. Makes time to talk.	(O)	.69
9. Is smart.	(C)	.79
10. Can be trusted.	(H)	.82
11. Does the job well.	(C)	.84
12. Treats students with respect.	(B)	.81

H = Honesty; B = Benevolence; C = Competence; O = Openness; R = Reliability.

See appendices for the Student Trust in Principal Scale (STP-Scale).

was also supported; high school students had significantly lower trust in the principal than students in elementary or middle schools (Adams, 2003). The Student Trust in Principal Scale is found in Appendix 3.5.

SUMMARY

Trust was conceptualized with multiple facets; the willingness to risk or be vulnerable is inherent in all trust relations, as are the facets of benevolence, reliability, competence, honesty, and openness. Thus our constitutive definition of collective trust was *a group's willingness to be vulnerable to another party based on the confidence that the latter party is benevolent, reliable, competent, honest, and open.*

This conceptual perspective of trust proved useful and powerful. All the conditions of trust were found empirically; in fact, factor analytic techniques demonstrated that all facets of trust were found in each variant of collective trust. In all, we developed seven valid and reliable scales of collective trust:

1. Faculty trust in principal
2. Faculty trust in colleagues
3. Faculty trust in clients (students and parents)
4. Parent trust in school
5. Parent trust in principal
6. Student trust in faculty
7. Student trust in principal

In schools, faculty trust tends to be pervasive. When teachers trust their principal, for example, they are also more likely to trust each other and their clients. Conversely, distrust also tends to breed distrust. Broken trust is likely to ripple through the system.

The analyses of collective trust in schools indicated that they were related to other school variables in predictable ways. For example, teachers' sense of powerlessness and estrangement were negatively related to all the variants of faculty trust and positively related to teacher sense of efficacy. Also, not unexpectedly, the greater the degree of faculty trust in a school, the less the degree of conflict. All the aspects of trust measured by our trust scales were related to other school variables as predicted. For instance, student trust in schools was positively related to academic efficacy as well as students' propensity to identify strongly with their school. Also as anticipated, high school students had significantly lower trust in the principal than did elementary or middle school students.

Another intriguing finding of the study was that for both elementary and secondary samples, faculty trust in students and parents converged. The relationship was so strong that the trust for the two groups was indistinguishable. Faculty trust for the two referents merged to form a single factor, which we called faculty trust in clients (students and parents). When teachers trust the students, they also trust their parents, and vice versa, at every grade level.

In sum, a multifaceted definition of trust was developed based the extant literature. That definition was operationalized and confirmed and led to the development of a set of collective trust scales for schools. Each scale proved to be reliable and valid and provided the basis for our comprehensive study of collective trust in schools. The first half of this chapter draws heavily from the work of Hoy and Tschannen-Moran, 2003.

PART II

Research on Collective Trust

In Part II we turn to the research evidence. Chapter 4 examines what school researchers have discovered concerning the antecedents of collective trust. Knowledge about such antecedents paves the way for causal exploration and theoretical modeling and provides guidance to those who want to improve the culture of trust in schools.

Chapters 5 and 6 together scrutinize the influence of collective trust. Chapter 5 presents a chronology of consequences of collective trust, cataloguing the research by dependent variables. Chapter 6 continues the analysis, but focuses on the particular consequences of trust for school effectiveness. We develop and present an original model of student achievement to guide research and practice.

Chapter 7 integrates the organizational literature with the school trust literature to examine power in organizations. In particular, we consider collective trust as an important feature of school leadership and organizational structure that promotes cooperation in schools. The sources of school leadership are modeled to show how structure, persuasion, and trust supplement each other.

Chapter 8 situates collective trust in two theoretical systems: social capital and academic optimism, both of which are pivotal in promoting social action in schools.

CHAPTER 4

Antecedents of Collective Trust: School Evidence

Authentic trust emerges when people have grown to have a deep and abiding trust in one another. Each relies on the other in a full and complete way, resting in interdependence and vulnerability without anxiety.

—Megan Tschannen-Moran, *Trust Matters*

In this chapter, we discuss the empirical evidence on the antecents of collective trust. Although identifying predictors of trust is important, of greater significance is the explanation of how and why individual and organizational factors influence the formation of collective trust. We accomplish the latter by developing a set of propositions for establishing and sustaining collective trust.

Our theoretical model identifies external and internal contextual factors that are said to affect the social construction of trust. External context is defined by the partly shared and partly idiosyncratic social-historical environment that exists beyond the organizational boundaries of schools, yet it shapes the attitudes and beliefs of those in schools. Internal context is made up of within-school structural and normative conditions that constrain or incite individual and group behavior. As we demonstrate in this chapter, the dynamic relationship between external and internal forces within social networks shapes collective trust. We explore the literature with two questions in mind: What external factors and internal conditions build and sustain collective trust in school groups? How does the interaction of these conditions shape collective trust?

EXTERNAL ANTECEDENTS

Although collective trust exists within the various role groups that make up schools, its formation within groups is nonetheless influenced by the environment outside the school. Individuals view schooling through what Schneider and Reichers (1983) call cognitive schemata, the values and beliefs that frame how individuals perceive the world. Diverse views of teaching and learning can prevent school members from reaching agreement on role-specific expectations necessary for trust formation. Collective judgments are difficult to obtain without a shared set of expectations and obligations against which to gage the trustworthiness of an individual or a group (Bryk & Schneider, 2002). Absent a shared understanding of a group's responsibility, individual orientations, not collective beliefs, become the dominant criteria for judging the trustworthiness of other groups or individuals (Young & Parker, 1999).

We use an example to illustrate the importance of shared expectations in collective trust formation. It is generally expected that teachers will communicate evidence of student performance to parents. If such communication does not occur or is infrequent, collective parent trust of teachers is likely to suffer. Teachers in this case are violating norms defined by the school culture. On the other hand, if teachers consistently communicate information about student performance to parents, but observe no noticeable parental intervention, faculty trust in students and parents is likely to suffer.

What happens if communicating student performance to parents is an expectation of some parents, but is not a shared expectation of the collective parent group? How might this affect collective trust? We argue that group norms are more deterministic of collective trust than are individual beliefs. If a specific norm has not been established, that is, the collective expectation does not exist within the group, then in our example, communicating performance would not produce or violate collective trust. Subjective perceptions of individual parents and teachers who expect performance to be communicated might diminish, but the collective trust of the group would not suffer until the parents as a group define this practice as an expectation and obligation of teachers.

The example illustrates how collective trust depends on congruence between group expectations (i.e., social norms) and actual behavior. A pattern of behavior inconsistent with socially accepted role expectations is likely to diminish collective trust. If, as in our example, a norm requiring teachers to report student performance to parents has not been institutionalized, parents are less likely to base judgments of teacher trustworthiness on this behavior. Social norms, once established, are the behavioral standard used to judge the actions of others, more so than formal policies (Blau, 1955). So, how does such a norm come to exist in schools? Norms are partly determined by the external school environment's effect on individual and group behavior, a relationship we explore in more detail by examining research evidence.

Research Findings on External Conditions

The relationship between external social conditions and collective trust has rarely been studied. To our knowledge, external factors, such as federal and state policies, business involvement, and mass media, have not been scrutinized for their relation to collective trust formation in schools. Trust studies that do take into account external conditions primarily focus on the differential effect of minority and economic compositions of schools. Studies by Smith, Hoy, and Sweetland (2001) and Hoy, Smith, and Sweetland (2002) found that faculty trust in colleagues and principals were not strongly affected by the economic and minority composition of schools. In these studies, subjective teacher perceptions of the school climate were stronger predictors of collective trust than objective measures of school demographics.

In contrast, a study by Goddard and Tschannen-Moran (2001) found socioeconomic status of students to be a significant predictor of faculty trust in clients, but minority status to be only marginally associated. Goddard, Salloum, and Berebitsky (2006) found both socioeconomic and minority status had a significant direct effect on faculty trust in clients. Moreover, the findings of Bryk and Schneider (2002) on interpersonal trust indicate that ethnic composition of the school community did matter in teacher trust formation, but the economic status of the school community did not. For collective parent trust, Adams, Forsyth, and Mitchell (2009) found that socioeconomic status of students, as a lone predictor variable, accounted for significant variance in parent trust, but when considered in combination with normative conditions such as student identification with school, its influence weakened.

Interpretation of the Evidence

To understand the effects of external context on collective trust within schools, it is necessary to first distinguish the different configurations of trustors and trustees. All but one of the previous studies treated the faculty group as the trustor and teaching colleagues and clients (students and parents) as the referent (Bryk & Schneider, 2002; Goddard, Salloum, & Berebitsky, 2006; Goddard & Tschannen-Moran, 2001; Hoy et al., 2002; Smith et al., 2001). Adams et al. (2009) specified the parent group as the trustor and schools as the referent. Economic status and minority composition were only significant predictors of collective trust when parents and students were either the trustor or referent. Faculty trust in colleagues and faculty trust in the principal were not as sensitive to the demographic context of schools.

It is not surprising that social composition (i.e., economic and minority status) would have the strongest relationship with faculty trust in clients and parent trust in schools. Trust is largely a response to a perception of the intentions of others (Bryk & Schneider, 2002; Hoy & Tschannen-Moran, 1999), and social differences coupled with power asymmetry between teachers and parents often create suspicion rather than trust. Schools can mitigate suspicion through positive social interactions between parents and teachers, but they cannot wipe clean the slate of past experiences that influence parent dispositions toward school or teacher dispositions toward parents. If interactions are based on incongruent expectations and orientations, collective trust is less likely to emerge.

The social nature (Lewis & Wiegert, 1985; Rousseau et al., 1998) of collective trust is visible in the cumulative evidence of studies that specify economic and ethnic factors as predictive conditions. If collective trust were only a psychological state, as Jones and George (1998) argue, we would expect the negative effects of poverty and minority status to hold across school populations. The evidence does not support such an absolute relationship. When statistically significant, the effects of ethnicity and economic status on collective trust were lessened by normative school conditions (such as school climate) associated with cohesive relational networks (Adams & Forsyth, 2007b, Adams et al., 2009; Goddard, Salloum, & Berebitsky, 2006; Goddard & Tschannen-Moran, 2001).

Collective trust can and does exist in high-poverty, high–ethnic minority schools. Bryk and Schneider (2002) found this to be true within an elementary school they studied in Chicago where educators and parents were successful at coalescing values and beliefs around a common educational vision. They note that the cooperative work environment became a mechanism by which trust emerged and was sustained. The success of some high-poverty, high-minority schools in promoting trust raises an important question about its formation process. If the effect of external conditions on collective trust is not universal across schools, why does it hinder trust formation in some school environments but not others?

As the evidence suggests, poverty or ethnic status of families does not necessarily lower trust. Although social and economic conditions can erect hidden barriers that make it difficult for the type of relational networks associated with collective trust to emerge, trust building in high-poverty and high-minority schools is enhanced when school processes connect and unify school group members. Group cohesion is needed before expectations and responsibilities can be collectively defined and accepted. The external context of schools can present challenges to developing cohesive relationships, but as long as internal conditions support cooperative and interdependent transactions among school members, collective trust can exist.

INTERNAL ANTECEDENTS

Internal school context is defined by the organizational conditions immediately surrounding teaching and learning. These conditions consist of contextual factors like school size, management structures like accountability plans, and normative features like shared decision making. It is the internal context that gives life to a school's culture or personality. School leaders are responsible for shaping organizational culture; they execute this responsibility through direct transactions with teachers, students, parents, and community members (Northouse, 2001) and by aligning structural components with organizational goals (Mintzberg, 1989). It is not surprising to find compelling evidence that leadership matters for collective trust (Bryk & Schneider, 2002; Kochanek, 2005; Tschannen-Moran, 2004).

As important as effective leadership is for a healthy school culture and the overall performance of a school, the formation of collective trust does not exclusively fall on the shoulders of strong leaders. Teachers, parents, students, and principals share responsibility for the existence of internal conditions associated with collective trust. To distinguish among the internal antecedents, we classify predictive conditions as behavioral, cognitive, and affective mechanisms.

Research Findings on Behavioral Mechanisms

Power is a useful lens to view the behaviors supportive of collective trust. For school leaders, power can be dichotomized as positional or personal (Northouse, 2001), depending on how authority is exercised. Authority is a control mechanism for behavior, and as Hoy and Miskel (2008) note, "[It] is a basic feature of life in schools because it provides the basis for legitimate control of administrators, teachers, and students" (p. 221). Hoy and Miskel further argue that effective school leaders rely less on formal and more on informal authority to build loyalty and establish consensus. The use of power by principals, both in how they interact directly with teachers and how they use structures to shape interactions among school members, has direct and indirect consequences on collective trust (Hoffman, Sabo, Bliss, & Hoy, 1994; Hoy et al., 1992; Tarter et al., 1989b; Tarter et al., 1995; Tschannen-Moran & Hoy, 1998; Smith et al., 2001).

Principals who are viewed by teachers as authentic—that is, they accept responsibility, are nonmanipulative, and rely on personal authority—are more likely to be perceived as trustworthy (Hoy & Kupersmith, 1984). Similarly, principal-teacher interactions viewed by teachers as supportive (Hoffman et al., 1994; Hoy et al., 1992; Tarter, Bliss, & Hoy, 1989a; Tarter et al., 1995), open (Tarter et al., 1989b), collegial (Tschannen-Moran &

Hoy, 1998), and considerate (Smith et al., 2001) strengthen faculty trust in the principal. Conversely, principals who attempt to control teacher behavior by formal power alone are likely to see their trust wither. Tarter and colleagues (1995) found that directive leadership, an observable feature of formal power, diminished the perceived trustworthiness of principals.

As Kochanek (2005) suggests, there are circumstances in schools that require principals to use formal power, such as removing an ineffective teacher, but these situations do not necessarily undermine trust. A teacher pressured to leave a school certainly would not perceive the principal as supportive; however, one disgruntled teacher does not define collective trust. Rather, normative conditions that reflect a pattern of behavior that is consistent with role expectations and responsibilities define collective trust. Removing ineffective teachers speaks to the competence of the principal, and teachers generally would see this action as supportive of the school's mission. In sum, the research substantiates the role of supportive principal behavior as a means by which leaders can build and sustain trust.

In addition to principal-teacher relationships, school leaders build a foundation for constructive social interactions among teachers through their use of structural and normative mechanisms as a means of promoting cooperation and shared inquiry around instructional issues. Principals who use structures and processes to leverage human and social capital as a tool for school improvement are more likely to build and sustain faculty trust. To illustrate, Louis (2007) found that administrators in high-trust schools created cultures that encouraged risk taking, shared inquiry, and instructional innovation as means to improve instruction and achievement. Cosner (2009) discovered that principals generated collegial trust by reengineering formal structures to allow for more teacher interaction, to create more space for teacher collaboration, and to make professional development more site specific. Informal processes, such as book clubs and evening socials, were used in combination with changes to formal structures to successfully build collegial trust.

In conclusion, supportive, open, authentic, and collegial teacher-principal interactions can lead to faculty trust in colleagues and principals (Hoffman et al., 1994; Hoy et al., 1992; Tarter et al., 1989b; Tarter et al., 1995; Tschannen-Moran & Hoy, 1998). How principals use organizational structures and cultures also matters for faculty trust (Geist & Hoy, 2004; Smith et al., 2001; Tschannen-Moran, 2001; Tschannen-Moran & Hoy, 1998). Behaviors and structures that support healthy communication within schools are not limited to faculty trust in colleagues and principals. Faculty trust in clients and parent trust in schools also benefit from collaborative, professional, engaged, and academically oriented interactions among teachers, parents, and students (Adams et al., 2009; Hoffman et al., 1994; Tarter et al., 1989b; Tschannen-Moran, 2001).

Research Findings on Cognitive Mechanisms

Cognitive mechanisms represent shared beliefs among group members toward the human and social capacity of the school (Hoy, Tarter, & Woolfolk Hoy, 2006b). Behavioral and cognitive mechanisms differ in that measures of behavior capture perceptions of one party's pattern of action (i.e., to be collaborative, to be supportive, to be open, to be engaged, etc.), whereas cognitive conditions are group or organizational level beliefs about the performance capability of the school. For instance, a shared belief in the collective capability of teachers derives from discernments of the faculty's agency vis-à-vis the context of the teaching task, not just the behavior of a few effective teachers within the school (Goddard, Hoy, & Woolfolk Hoy, 2000, 2004). The primary cognitive conditions predictive of collective trust relate to beliefs about school structures, organizational processes, and collective efficacy.

Public schools depend on bureaucratic features to coordinate teaching and learning, but such structures are not necessarily coercive or hindering; in fact, they can enable the work of teachers (Adler & Borys, 1996). Structures enhance the performance of schools if they enable cooperation, shared inquiry, open communication, and shared decision making (Hoy & Sweetland, 2001). Not surprisingly, when teachers perceive structures as enabling, their collective trust in the principal and colleagues increases (Geist & Hoy, 2004; Hoy & Sweetland, 2001). In contrast, perceived hindering structures attenuate faculty trust. Teacher perceptions of enabling structures also account for much of the development of parent trust in schools (Adams & Forsyth, 2007a, 2007b).

Collective trust is shaped as much by informal work processes as by formal structures. Whereas formal structures are the rational mechanisms that regulate teaching and learning, informal processes are shaped by the actual behavior and social interactions of school members that collectively help to define the personality of the school (Tarter et al., 1989b). Mindfulness is an important organizational trait of schools. Mindful schools detect problems early, search below the surface to better understand phenomena, maintain close attention to teaching and learning, respond quickly and appropriately to problems, and defer to knowledge and expertise over formal power (Hoy, Gage, & Tarter, 2006). Collective trust profits from schools that operate mindfully.

Case studies of high- and low-trust schools corroborate the importance of mindful school processes for collective trust. Louis (2007) found that the degree of teacher influence and control over the instructional design was the primary difference between low- and high-trust schools. Teachers in high-trust schools reported feeling valued for their professional knowledge and involved in the design of the instructional program. Conversely, teachers in low-trust schools felt voiceless and uninvolved in the development of the instructional design. Mindless behaviors and processes can paralyze schools. Bryk and Schneider (2002) observed how conflicts over power, control, and legitimacy across school groups (i.e., teachers, the principal, and the school leadership council) in one Chicago elementary school dominated social interactions to the point where the knowledge and expertise held by each group was discounted. The result was salient distrust within the school.

Teacher beliefs concerning structures and processes used to coordinate teaching and learning matter for collective trust, but so too do beliefs in the instructional capability of the faculty as reflected in collective efficacy. Collective efficacy is a powerful determinant of faculty trust in clients and faculty trust in colleagues. In fact, Tschannen-Moran and Goddard (2001) found that collective efficacy explained more school-level variability in faculty trust in clients than other school-level predictors. Given the social nature of trust, we are not surprised that cognitive conditions, most especially those related to perceptions of enabling structure, a state of organizational mindfulness, and beliefs about instructional efficacy, are antecedents of collective trust.

Research Findings on Affective Mechanisms

Affective conditions establish an emotional bond between individuals and the school. Organizational theorists (Argyris, 1964; Herzberg, 1966; McGregor, 1960) have for some time touted the performance benefits associated with aligning work processes with individual needs, but the effects of this alignment are not limited to performance; trust benefits as well. Lewicki and Bunker (1996) claim that an emotional identification with a group or an organization is the foundation for trust. Likewise, Lewis and Weigert (1985) view feelings as a primary source of trust. Feelings can include such emotions as enthusiasm, distress, frustration, or excitement (Jones & George, 1998). Trust is extremely sensitive to feelings and emotions; negative feelings would make an individual or group apprehensive about risking vulnerability whereas positive ones elicit confidence in the trustee.

Organizational identification and commitment are two affective mechanisms linked to better job performance, (Vandenberghe, Bentein, & Stinglhamber, 2004), increased motivation (Lee, 1971), and reduced absenteeism (Riketta, 2005). Identification and commitment have consequences for school groups as well. For example, students who identify with school and feel a sense of belonging to their school will naturally trust their teachers more. A similar effect exists for teachers and parents who identify with and are committed to the school; trust is stronger with an emotional attachment

(Adams et al., 2009; Tarter et al., 1995). Consistent with these findings, Tschannen-Moran and Hoy (1998) found feelings of professionalism among teachers to be strongly related to faculty trust in colleagues, but only marginally associated with faculty trust in the principal. Smith and colleagues (2001) found teacher morale to be predictive of faculty trust in colleagues but not faculty trust in the principal or clients.

Turning to parents and students, Adams and colleagues (2009) discovered that student identification with school was strongly related to parent trust in school; the more students felt connected to the school, the more their parents trusted the school. Trust between proximate role groups is another powerful affective mechanism. Adams and Forsyth (2009b) found that strong parent trust in the school had the reciprocal consequence of stronger faculty trust in parents and students. In high-poverty elementary schools, Adams (2010) found that student trust was largely dependent on teachers' trusting students. Strong emotional attachments at the group level can give life to collective trust.

EMPIRICAL MODEL AND PROPOSITIONS

Empirical evidence provides support for our belief that collective trust sources include the external and internal contexts of schools. Poverty level and minority composition are two external conditions found in the literature to influence faculty trust in clients and parent trust in schools but not faculty trust in colleagues or faculty trust in the principal. Supportive leaders, enabling structures, and school identification are examples of internal conditions that build and sustain collective trust. Our objective in this section is to move from a general theory of collective trust (presented in Chapter 2) to empirically derived propositions on its formation.

Our theoretical model in Chapter 2 articulates a general explanation of collective trust, whereas evidence synthesized in this chapter presents a more nuanced understanding of the interaction between internal and external sources of trust. Our model depicted in Figure 4.1 shows internal school conditions mediating the external context effects. That is, the degree to which poverty and minority composition shape collective trust depends on the degree to which these social conditions influence behavioral, cognitive, and affective mechanisms in schools. Social elements within the internal and external context can reinforce shared values, or they can isolate school groups, thereby diminishing collective trust. School leaders have marginal control at best over the external context, but they are responsible for structures used to coordinate teaching as well as the organizational culture; indeed, structure and culture have the greatest potential to shape collective trust.

Figure 4.1. Generalized model of external and internal context interaction

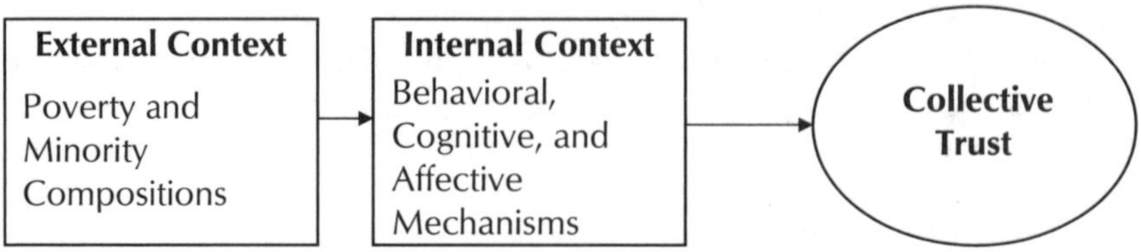

Our propositions address the question, What types of school structure and culture build collective trust? There are, of course, no absolutes that apply to every school, nor is there a single factor that outweighs other antecedent conditions. However, the evidence reviewed in this chapter, and synthesized in our propositions, can help us understand why patterns of collective trust exist in some schools but not in others.

Behavioral Propositions

There is evidence that supportive, collegial, and transformational principal behaviors are strongly related to faculty trust in the principal, while collegial, professional, and collaborative teacher behaviors are related to faculty trust in teaching colleagues. Trust-provoking behaviors for all school members relate to open, professional, and respectful interactions centered on helping students learn. Specifically, for principal-teacher and teacher-teacher interactions, behaviors consistent with the prevailing technical knowledge and effective practice as defined by the field elicit trust. We advance the following propositions related to behavioral mechanisms:

1. Leadership that enables teachers to use their technical knowledge and expertise enhances faculty trust in the principal.
2. Leadership that is based on continuous feedback, open communication, collaborative problem solving, and deference to expertise promotes faculty trust in the principal and faculty trust in colleagues.
3. Teacher collaboration around effective instructional strategies and student needs is positively related to faculty trust in colleagues.
4. External context that blocks collaboration within the school hinders collective trust.
5. Supportive, cooperative, and relational oriented behaviors of school members facilitate collective trust.

Cognitive Propositions

Cognitive mechanisms are defined by the shared beliefs within school groups that underlie both individual and collective action. Collective trust is shaped by how school members perceive formal structures regulating teaching and learning, beliefs about the instructional efficacy of the faculty, and perceptions about the mindfulness of the school organization. Faculty trust in the principal, faculty trust in colleagues, and parent trust in schools are three trust forms dependent on bureaucratic structures being responsive to the complex nature of teaching and learning. Formal structures that support effective instruction and cooperative interactions are powerful sources of collective trust. Other cognitive mechanisms linked to collective trust, such as collective efficacy, are enhanced by enabling school environments. We advance the following propositions related to cognitive mechanisms.

1. School structures perceived to enable cooperation and promote collective action promote collective trust.
2. Collective teacher efficacy is positively associated with faculty trust in clients, faculty trust in colleagues, and student trust in teachers.
3. Perceived influence on instructional and school decisions facilitates collective trust within school groups.
4. External effects on the formation of collective trust are mediated by perceptions of school structure, collective efficacy, and decisional influence.

Affective Propositions

Affective mechanisms provide the psycho/social bonds that make other trust mechanisms possible. Healthy affective conditions produce supportive structures and behaviors. Positive morale and a shared sense of belonging are affective conditions associated with faculty and parent trust. A shared feeling of fulfillment and satisfaction with the teaching task is linked to faculty trust in colleagues. Schools where students share a strong sense of belonging and value for education also tend to have higher parent trust. Finally, collective trust within one role group for another has a powerful reciprocal effect. When parent trust in school is strong, so too is faculty trust in clients. Likewise, when teachers trust students, students are more likely to trust teachers. We advance the following propositions related to affective mechanisms.

1. A shared sense of belonging among group members supports collective trust among all school members.

2. Positive morale and attitudes among group members are positively related to collective trust.
3. A group's collective trust in one school group is positively related to collective trust in other school groups.
4. External context effects on the formation of collective trust are mediated by affective conditions.

Convergent Postulate

Behavioral, cognitive, and affective mechanisms are more interrelated than they are independent. To illustrate, directive leadership behaviors are likely to create hindering structures and hindering structures are likely to breed alienation. Conversely, supportive leadership leads to enabling structures and enabling structures promote self-actualization. The optimal social environment for collective trust is one where the internal, external, and task contexts function synergistically. This leads us to our convergent postulate: the level of collective trust within a school is proportional to the degree of convergence among value orientations, behaviors, structures, and norms.

IMPLICATIONS FOR SCHOOLS

Building collective trust in schools starts with leadership. All three major analyses of school trust are written primarily for educational leaders (Bryk & Schneider, 2002; Kochanec, 2005; Tschannen-Moran, 2004). Each book provides vignettes of missteps, as well as effective practices, made by school leaders as they worked to engage a school community in continuous improvement. The evidence reviewed for this chapter supports the vital role of school leaders in collective trust formation; however, the research also suggests that school leaders are an insufficient source of collective trust.

Although we often judge school performance on the basis of school leadership (Schmidt, 2008), many factors affect teaching and learning besides principals. Given the social nature of collective trust, it is important that our implications for schools address not only leadership, but also how the external environment and relevant school groups share in the responsibility for building and sustaining a culture of collective trust.

The Role of School Leaders

School leaders are directly responsible for nurturing organizational structures so that each school group accepts responsibility for student learning. Social cohesion and shared responsibility result from interactions that are both personal and professional in nature. In contrast, relationships based on power lessen collective trust (French & Raven, 1968). A primary task of the principal is to minimize conflict and to facilitate cooperative interactions around a common vision. Successful leaders are able to mitigate conflict in schools by removing barriers that hinder interactions, marginalize parents, usurp the expertise and autonomy of teachers, and prevent the emergence of a shared vision.

Kochanek (2005) argues that principals need to reduce vulnerabilities through successful low-risk interactions before building trust, but her conjecture ignores the relationship between vulnerability and trust. Without vulnerability there is no need to trust (Hoy & Tschannen-Moran, 1999; Lewis & Weigert, 1985; Nooteboom, 2002; Rousseau et al., 1998). It is not the role of school leaders to reduce vulnerabilities but instead to make it possible for school agents to take risks. Principals do this by being supportive, open, collegial, authentic, and considerate as well as by cultivating boundary spanning cooperation that encourages collective, not unilateral, problem solving (Geist & Hoy, 2004; Hoffman et al., 1994; Hoy et al., 1992; Smith et al., 2001; Tarter et al., 1989a; Tarter et al., 1995; Tschannen-Moran, 2001; Tschannen-Moran & Hoy, 1998).

The Role of the External Environment

The role of the external environment in collective trust is to support social action at the school level. To be supportive, external policies, in particular, must balance the need to regulate against the need for local autonomy. A good balance provides the support and resources by which school communities can unite members around common goals and unique instructional issues (Schmidt, 2008). A poorly fitting context can produce a set of pressures, structures, or constraints that limit the agency of a school community to define its pressing needs and to develop appropriate improvement plans targeted at these needs (Schmidt, 2008). School improvement and reform emerges from within schools, not the external environment.

The Role of Teachers

In many ways, teachers are the leverage point for collective trust. Teacher behaviors shape parent trust in schools and student trust in teachers; teacher beliefs about formal structures are associated with their trust in the principal and parent trust in schools; and teacher instructional agency affects colleague trust. School leaders control structures, and to a lesser extent norms, but teachers make the difference for collective trust. Their actions determine the extent to which teaching and learning will be open and collaborative or closed and isolated. There are more opportunities for collaborating with colleagues and parents, sharing best practices, discussing student needs, analyzing student data, and reflecting on practice when teachers allow classrooms to become a type of scholarly commons where ideas and information are exchanged (Hatch, 2006).

The Role of Parents

Parents have as much responsibility for their child's learning as do teachers; both parents and teachers have an important role to play. The parental role is indeed different from the teacher's, but just as critical for student performance. We think that parental responsibility is a more critical determinant of trust than parent involvement. When parents are reliable and committed to their child's developmental needs, supportive of the learning process, and honest in their interactions with school authorities, collective trust between parents and teachers is likely to be stronger. Responsibility exists when parents control factors that affect the learning and development of their child. Broad indicators of parental responsibility would include being aware of a child's behavior and performance in school, communicating with teachers, reinforcing school expectations at home, and providing a healthy home learning environment (Hatch, 2006; Hoover-Dempsey & Sandler, 1997). There are social and economic factors that make it challenging for some parents to address these responsibilities; however, they do not absolve parents of their obligations.

In summary, the preceding role descriptions should be used as a loose framework to guide the formation and sustenance of collective trust. The danger in decontextualizing the role of each school group lies in the gross simplification of the actual process of trust formation. Micro political factors, such as power, control, and conflict (Angus, 2008), as well as cultural characteristics that shape value orientations, will affect the degree to which groups can collectively act in ways that promote trust. Our role descriptions were derived from a general understanding of collective trust and its formation. Interventions specific to individual schools will depend as much on the context of the school as our suggested guidelines.

SUMMARY

The cumulative evidence on collective trust formation is useful for researchers who seek to test propositions on its development and for practitioners who strive to use collective trust as a resource for school improvement. Two findings from our analysis are particularly noteworthy. First, as our theoretical model postulates, external and internal context interact in the social construction process. It was encouraging to find that internal conditions mediate the effects of external conditions. In essence, collective trust can be built by school communities, almost regardless of the external environment.

The second noteworthy finding addresses the necessary balance between behavioral, cognitive, and affective mechanisms for building or enabling collective trust. That is, trustworthy behaviors are inseparable from thoughts and feelings. The likelihood of an individual or group trusting another depends on the observed behaviors of others. Feelings and beliefs, whether shared by a school group or held by an individual, are the source of trustworthy behaviors. The shared feelings and beliefs that have consequences for collective trust reflect the structures used to coordinate teaching and learning, the behavior of other school groups, and the behavior of members within one's own school group.

We agree with other scholars on the important role of principals in collective trust formation, but we also recognize that principals, as effective as some are, cannot build unilaterally a culture of collective trust. Collective trust emerges from social interactions within and among groups. School leaders can configure structures to support interactions among school members, but the degree of cooperation is still dependent on school member willingness to interact cooperatively.

CHAPTER 5

Consequences of Collective Trust: School Evidence

Trust . . . has important consequences for the functioning of a school
and its capacity to engage in fundamental change.
—Anthony Bryk and Barbara Schneider, *Trust in Schools*

The amount of empirical research accumulated over 25 years on the consequences of various facets of school trust is significant. Our summary of empirical research on the consequences of collective school trust has excluded
from consideration studies that exclusively explore school effectiveness or
academic performance as a consequence of trust; we present these findings
in Chapter 6.

Three empirical-research clusters on school trust have emerged. These
clusters can be differentiated by their primary host university, key researchers, and conceptual-measurement approaches.

The first cluster has Wayne K. Hoy as the common denominator along
with an exclusive focus on faculty trust. It is divided into two phases; the
first began in 1985 at Rutgers University and included W. K. Kupersmith,
James Bliss, C. John Tarter, Dennis Sabo, L. Witkowski, and K. Barnes,
among other scholars. The second phase emerged with the turn of the millennium at The Ohio State University when Hoy and a new set of colleagues
and students reconceptualized faculty trust and recalibrated its measures.
Key colleagues in this phase included Megan Tschannen-Moran, Roger D.
Goddard, Anita Woolfolk-Hoy, C. John Tarter, and Page A. Smith.

A second cluster is associated with the work of Anthony Bryk and
Barbara Schneider at the University of Chicago, together with their colleagues Sharon Greenberg and Julie Kochanek. This work is distinguished
by seminal theoretical development, the conceptualization of relational trust
in schools, and an extensive empirical project based on teacher trust under
conditions of change following the Chicago School Reform Act of 1988.
First reported in 1995, their work culminated in the publication in 2002 of

Trust in Schools: A Core Resource for Improvement, a volume in the prestigious Rose Series in Sociology (Bryk & Schneider, 2002).

A third cluster is associated with Patrick B. Forsyth, Curt M. Adams, Laura L. B. Barnes, Roxanne Mitchell, and colleagues at Oklahoma State University and the University of Oklahoma. The unique contribution of this cluster is its development and subsequent research on collective parent and student trust. That is, whereas the first two clusters exclusively focused on the trust beliefs of teachers, this work explored parent and student trust beliefs in an effort to capture authentically the reciprocal nature of collective trust.

Paralleling the organization by research clusters, this chapter's focus on trustor groups begins with collective faculty trust, then moves to parent trust, and concludes with a brief discussion of student trust. As previously mentioned, the earliest empirical work done by Hoy and colleagues in the early 1980s consisted exclusively of faculty trust. Just as it makes up the earliest series of trust studies in schools, faculty trust continues to be the most frequently studied form of trust. Thus, in order, we take up the consequences of faculty trust and parent trust. Only a few student trust findings have been reported. Both primary trustor groups included here have been studied with multiple trustees, as for example, faculty trust in parents, colleagues, principal, and school.

THE RUTGERS STUDIES

As described in Chapter 1, Hoy and Kupersmith (1985) introduced the conceptual work done in schools that launched nearly all empirical examination of school trust. Recall that three measures were developed, one for faculty trust in the principal, one for faculty trust in colleagues, and another for faculty trust in the school organization. This Rutgers phase includes regular publications through 1998 (Hoy & Kupersmith, 1985; Hoy, Sabo, & Barnes, 1996; Hoy, Tarter, & Wiskowskie, 1992; Tarter, Bliss, & Hoy, 1989b; Tarter, Sabo, & Hoy, 1995; and Tschannen-Moran & Hoy, 1998).

From the start, Hoy and his colleagues balanced a psychological understanding of trust formation and function with an appreciation for trust as an important social or organizational phenomenon. Most of the findings from the Rutgers phase summarized in Chapter 1 treated faculty trust as a dependent variable; that is, they explored antecedents of faculty trust. One general finding from those studies was that all the forms of faculty trust were moderately related to each other. Faculty trust in the principal was related to faculty trust in colleagues and faculty trust in school. In sum, the early studies proposed and tested a definition of collective trust, examined the relations among the forms of trust, focused on predictors of faculty trust, and started to explore the role of trust in school effectiveness.

THE OHIO STATE STUDIES

An event that took place at the Stanford University Graduate School of Business in May 1994 signaled a change in the intensity of interest in trust research among general organizational researchers as well as those who study trust in schools. The Stanford symposium papers were published in 1996 as *Trust in Organizations: Frontiers of Theory and Research* (Kramer & Tyler, 1996). These papers are cited in virtually all subsequent trust research, in the studies reviewed here (where trust is an antecedent influence), and in other school studies that examine the consequences of trust formation.

Two studies, "Five Faces of Trust: An Empirical Confirmation in Urban Elementary Schools" (Hoy & Tschannen-Moran, 1999) and "A Multidisciplinary Analysis of the Nature, Meaning, and Measurement of Trust" (Tschannen-Moran & Hoy, 2000) established the current and enduring paradigm for the empirical examination of trust in schools. These publications also mark the beginning of the second phase of Hoy and colleagues' trust research on faculty trust. Most of the research done in this phase explored some aspect of academic performance or school effectiveness as a consequence of collective trust. As already mentioned, we will examine the effectiveness studies in Chapter 6.

There are at least three studies in the cluster that focus on nonachievement outcomes, and these are discussed here in chronological order. The first is an investigation into the extent to which collective faculty trust explains decisional influence (Tschannen-Moran, 2001). Stated in simple terms, all the variants of faculty trust predicted decisional influence. Thus, when the faculty trusts the principal, teachers see themselves as influencing management decisions. When faculty trust colleagues, they see teacher committees influencing instructional decisions and parents influencing policy decisions. When the faculty trusts clients (students and parents), teachers see themselves as influencing management decisions as well as instructional decisions. Faculty trust in clients is also related to parent influence over policy decisions.

In another study, Tschannen-Moran (2003) examined the relationships between faculty trust in the principal, transformational leadership, and organizational citizenship. Transformational leadership includes individualized influence, inspiration motivation, intellectual stimulation, and individualized consideration (Bass, 1985, 1998). There has been some empirical research on transformational leadership in schools, mostly by Leithwood and colleagues (Hipp, 1997; Hipp & Bredeson, 1995; Leithwood & Jantzi,

2000; Leithwood & Steinbach, 1993). Here, Tschannen-Moran explored both transformational leadership and a theoretically related concept, organizational citizenship, defined as employee behavior that goes beyond formal job responsibilities (Bateman & Organ, 1983; Organ, 1988, 1997).

This leadership study replicates the research by Podsakoff, MacKenzie, Moorman, and Fetter (1990), which found that transformational leadership's relationship to organizational citizenship was mediated by employee trust of the leader. Tschannen-Moran (2003) found, unexpectedly, that although the relationship between transformational leadership and faculty trust in principal was strong, there was no relationship between transformational leadership and organizational citizenship. Apparently, the relationship between transformational leadership and organizational citizenship is more complex than either Podsakoff or Tschannen-Moran anticipated. One finding, however, stands out: Faculty trust in the principal is more strongly related to organizational citizenship than transformational leadership.

Finally, the Ohio State cluster includes a study probing the consequences of faculty trust on levels of bullying and teacher protection of students against bullying in elementary schools in Texas (Smith & Birney, 2005). The general hypothesis predicted that faculty trust prevents bullying and enhances the teacher willingness to protect students. The results support the hypothesis. Faculty trust in clients was related to lower levels of student bullying. Similarly, faculty trust in colleagues was also strongly related to teachers protecting their students from bullies. Faculty trust in the principal, however, was related to neither bullying nor protection.

THE UNIVERSITY OF CHICAGO STUDIES

In another series of school trust studies, Anthony Bryk and Barbara Schneider (2002) of the University of Chicago examined relational trust. They did not set out to study trust, but instead, sought to explain differences in school improvement and capacity to improve the Chicago Public Schools over a 10-year period. This work serendipitously pointed to trust as a critical social phenomenon. Their derivation of the "relational trust" construct answered perplexing questions about why some schools appeared to embrace change and others remained ineffectual. Bryk and Schneider rejected earlier trust conceptualizations common in psychology and economics based on either shared belief systems or contracts as inappropriate for application to the study of public schools. Instead, Bryk and Schneider (2002, 2003) proposed a trust perspective anchored in the role relationships of the school community that require reciprocal trust (teacher-principal, teacher-student, teacher-parent, and parent-principal).

In Bryk and Schneider's version of relational trust theory (see Chapter 2), the focus is on trust among teachers, parents, students, and administrators. For them, relational trust describes the extent to which there is synchrony with respect to each groups' understanding of its and other groups' expectations and obligations. For example, when teachers have views about their own and the principal's responsibilities that are consistent with those of the principal, we can speak of synchrony.

For relational trust to grow and be reinforced, however, both teachers and principal must repeatedly discern the behavior of the other as consistent with mutually held expectations. What emerges is relational trust, which they assert is an organizational property of schools because

> its constitutive elements are socially defined in the reciprocal exchanges among participants in the school community, and its presence (or absence) has important consequences for the functioning of the school. (Bryk & Schneider, 2002, p. 22)

Thus, trust perceptions of individual members of school role groups, revealed in social exchanges, and reinforced over time, produce interpersonal and intrapersonal trust.

Although their theoretical approach comes close to the theory of collective trust we advanced in Chapter 2, their theory of relational trust does not rely on the group process elements that we see as integral to understanding trust formation in schools. Bryk and Schneider's measures are similar to those used by Hoy and his colleagues at The Ohio State University. Both approaches are aligned with Mishra (1996). Bryk and Schneider, however, collapsed trust scores for each school (teacher trust of principal, parents, and fellow teachers) into a composite that enabled them to examine the effects of school trust on math and reading performance. Their general finding was that teacher trust

> is highly predictive of school productivity trends [i.e., improving math and reading performance]. Schools reporting strong positive trust levels in 1994 were three times more likely to be categorized eventually as improving in reading and mathematics than those with very weak trust reports. (Bryk & Schneider, 2002, p. 111)

Bryk and Schneider argue that trust does not directly affect academic performance, but fosters organizational conditions, which in turn promote activities that do directly affect learning. Four specific organizational conditions they identified and measured were

1. Orientation to innovation (teacher "can do" attitude and internalized responsibility

2. Outreach to parents
3. Professional community (collaborative work practices, personal commitment to improve teaching and school operations)
4. High expectations and high academic standards.

They found that these four conditions were more likely to improve if a school was characterized by high relational trust at the start of the study. Schools whose relational trust increased between 1994 and 1997 were also more likely to see positive changes in organizational conditions ultimately related to school effectiveness.

The Bryk and Schneider reports, especially their book *Trust in Schools* (2002), are a first longitudinal, contextualized study of trust's importance in a social enterprise like public schooling. Using both case study and survey methods, these scientists discovered the salience of trust when they were not looking for it, and then embraced it to develop a specialized trust theory related to schools as organizations.

THE OKLAHOMA STATE AND UNIVERSITY OF OKLAHOMA STUDIES

In 2001, Patrick Forsyth gathered colleague Laura Barnes and seven graduate students at Oklahoma State University–Tulsa to begin a multiyear study of school trust. From the outset, this team sought to examine student, faculty, and parent trust. The Oklahoma series of studies is derived from this original project using a new set of measures developed by the team. With a conscious intention to make its work compatible with the Ohio State studies, the Hoy measures of faculty trust were used. Forsyth and his colleagues developed and tested parallel measures for parent trust in school, parent trust in principal and student trust in principal. The Oklahoma research both replicates earlier studies (school effectiveness, parent decisional influence) and introduces previously unexamined trust effects (e.g., parent involvement and student identification with school).

Forsyth, Barnes, and Adams (2006) used a canonical correlation approach to study the combined effects of parent trust (external trust) and faculty trust (internal trust) on a set of school outcomes. They explored a set of outcomes that included collective teacher efficacy, enabling school structure, and academic performance.

The researchers examined the relationships between the predictors (parent and teacher trust along with SES) and collective teacher efficacy, enabling school structure and academic performance. The study produced four distinct, polar patterns of collective trust and consequences. The first pattern, called *classic ineffective*, describes schools where there is low parent trust, low faculty trust, and low SES, resulting in low collective teacher efficacy beliefs, hindering school structures, and low academic performance. The second pattern, *classic effective*, describes schools with converse conditions, that is, schools with high parent trust, high faculty trust, and high SES, resulting in high collective teacher efficacy beliefs, enabling school structures, and high academic performance.

The researchers found a third pattern, *bunker*, that describes schools where high faculty trust and low SES predict enabling school structures and low academic performance. This seems to be the situation where the school professionals have despaired of succeeding with students and parents but make the school work internally for themselves. Finally, a fourth, called *internal dysfunctional*, is where low faculty trust and high SES predict hindering structures and high academic performance. Here high academic performance seems to flow from external social and economic advantage, despite the school's failure as an institution. These latter two patterns are not hypothetical; they exist.

This study points to the intriguing existence of nonprominent patterns of variable relationships that can be missed by researchers and policy makers alike. The findings reveal that parent trust adds explanatory power over and above faculty trust for the predominant effectiveness patterns; however, parent trust plays no significant role in bunker and internal dysfunctional patterns of school effectiveness. Clearly, parent trust appears to be critical to effective structural school patterns.

How parent trust affects parent school involvement and influence was the subject of a study using a sample evenly distributed across elementary, middle, and high schools (Barnes, Mitchell, Forsyth, & Adams, 2005). The data demonstrated that parent trust in school directly predicts parent involvement and parent perceptions of their influence on school decisions; but the latter perceptions did not affect parent involvement in school. Interestingly, parent trust in principal did not predict either parent involvement or parent influence.

Mitchell and Forsyth (2004) investigated the relationship between student and parent trust of the principal and student identification with school. A first study explored the simple relationship between parent and student trust and student identification, taking into consideration SES and school level. Student identification was conceptualized and measured as having two components: (1) feelings of belongingness and (2) valuing school and school related outcomes (Voelkl, 1997). Trust of the principal (student and parent) declined by school level, elementary trust of the principal being highest. SES was not significantly related to other variables in the study. Examining the effects of school level and parent trust in the principal on student identification, only school level proved to be a significant factor. Student trust in the principal and school level were both related to student identification.

A second study explored the direct effects of SES, school level, external trust (combination of parent trust in school, parent trust in the principal, and student trust in the principal), and internal trust (combination of faculty trust in the principal, faculty trust in clients, and faculty trust in colleagues) on academic performance. The mediation effect of student identification was also explored (Mitchell & Forsyth, 2005). Academic performance was directly predicted by SES, external trust, and internal trust. Student identification was directly predicted by school level and external trust, but not internal trust or SES. In turn, student identification directly predicted academic performance. The research suggests that enhancing parent and student trust may have potential for overcoming the negative effects of poverty on school effectiveness.

MAKING SENSE OF COLLECTIVE TRUST'S CONSEQUENCES

In this chapter, we have reviewed empirical findings related to school trust, an array of collective trust's consequences emerging over more than 25 years from three distinct research series. In the process we identified 47 propositional findings that point to consequences of collective trust, including propositions about trust and academic achievement, which are examined in Chapter 6. These propositions have been portrayed as simple relationships in Figure 5.1. This collection of findings brings us to the threshold of a new task. Homans (1967) has noted that at some point in time an economy of thought may be achieved and "no longer does it [science] face just one damn finding after another. It has acquired an organization, a structure" (p. 32). The ultimate purpose of scientific research is to produce explanations of phenomena (theory), and these explanations consist of propositions linked together to form coherent and useful theory. In the remaining section of this chapter, we set out to develop a parsimonious and coherent explanatory framework of collective trust consequences. We think of it as a tentative first effort to draw together disparate findings, making sense of and ultimately making useful the extensive body of trust research in schools.

Although we contribute here to the trend of parsing trust in its many forms (interpersonal, collective, and multiple possible combinations of trustors and referents), there is some evidence that trust may be a generalized disposition. Thus, the multiple forms of trust may well be interrelated. Clearly, evidence exists in the school literature that various forms of faculty trust are strongly correlated as indicated earlier in Chapter 1 (Hoy & Kupersmith, 1985).

Figure 5.1. Empirical consequences of trust findings stated as propositions

Hoy Cluster, Rutgers Phase

1. Teacher Trust in Principal is positively related to Teacher Trust in School Organization.
2. Teacher Trust in Principal is positively related to Teacher Trust in Colleagues.
3. Teacher Trust in Principal is positively related to Principal Authenticity.
4. Teacher Trust in Principal is positively related to School Climate (Health).
5. Teacher Trust in Colleagues is positively related to Teacher Trust in School Organization.
6. Teacher Trust in Colleagues is positively related to Principal Authenticity.
7. Teacher Trust in Colleagues is positively related to School Effectiveness.
8. Teacher Trust in Organization is positively related to Principal Authenticity.

Hoy Cluster, Ohio State Phase

9. Teacher Trust in Principal is unrelated to math/English achievement.
10. Teacher Trust in Principal is positively related to teacher influence on management decisions, teacher committee influence on instructional decisions, and parent influence on school policy.
11. Teacher Trust in Principal is positively related to Principal Transformational Leadership.
12. Teacher Trust in Principal is unrelated to Organizational Citizenship.
13. Teacher Trust in Principal is unrelated to Bullying or Teacher Protection in Students.
14. Teacher Trust in Colleagues is positively related to math/English achievement.
15. Teacher Trust in Colleagues is positively related to teacher committee influence on instructional decisions and parent influence on school policy.
16. Teacher Trust in Colleagues is positively related to Teacher Protection in Students from Bullying.
17. Teacher Trust in Clients is positively related to math/English achievement.
18. Teacher Trust in Clients is positively related to teacher influence on management decisions, teacher committee influence on instructional decisions, and parent influence on school policy.
19. Teacher Trust in Clients is positively related to Teacher Protection in Students from Bullying.

20. Teacher Trust in Clients is negatively related to Bullying.
21. Principal Trust in Students is positively related to math/English achievement.
22. Principal Trust in Teachers is unrelated to math/English achievement.
23. Academic Optimism (including Teacher Trust in Clients) is positively related to student achievement (even controlling for school size and SES).

University in Chicago Cluster

24. Relational Trust (combined Teacher Trust in Principal, Colleagues, and Parents) is positively related to Teacher "can do" orientation to innovation and internalized responsibility.
25. Relational Trust is positively related to Parent Outreach.
26. Relational Trust is positively related to "Professional" Community.
27. Relational Trust is positively related to high Academic Standards and Expectations.
28. Relational Trust is positively related to School Improvement (math and reading).

Oklahoma State Cluster

29. Teacher Trust in Principal is positively related to Enabling School Structures.
30. Teacher Trust in Principal is positively related to Collective Teacher Efficacy.
32. Teacher Trust in Colleagues is positively related to Enabling School Structures.
33. Teacher Trust in Colleagues is positively related to Collective Teacher Efficacy.
34. Teacher Trust in Colleagues is positively related to Academic Performance.
35. Parent Trust in School is positively related to Enabling School Structures.
36. Parent Trust in School is positively related to Collective Teacher Efficacy.
37. Parent Trust in School is positively related to Academic Performance.
38. Parent Trust in School is positively related to Parent Involvement and School Activities
39. Parent Trust in School is positively related to Parent Influence on School Policy.
40. Parent Trust in Principal is unrelated to Parent Involvement or Influence.
41. Student Trust in Principal is positively related to Student Identification.
42. Student Trust in Principal is negatively related to School Level (grade).

Figure 5.1. (Continued)

43. Parent Trust in Principal is negatively related to School Level (grade).
44. External Trust (Parent Trust in School, Parent Trust in Principal, Student Trust in Principal) is positively related to Academic Performance.
45. Internal Trust (Teacher Trust in Principal, Teacher Trust in Colleagues, Teacher Trust in Clients) is positively related to Academic Performance.
46. External Trust (Parent Trust in School, Parent Trust in Principal, and Student Trust in Principal) is positively related to Student Identification.
47. Internal Trust (Teacher Trust in Principal, Teacher Trust in Colleagues, and Teacher Trust in Clients) is positively related to Student Identification.

Other Findings
1. Teacher trust varies by trust target (i.e., principal, colleagues, organization).
2. Teacher Trust in Client is more important than SES in predicting academic achievement.
3. Multidimensional trust (i.e., wherein the trust perceptions in multiple school role groups are measured) predicts important school outcomes more powerfully than the trust perceptions in a single-role group.

None of the school research reviewed here is experimental and very little of it is longitudinal. How then can we model causal direction when examining studies of collective trust and other variables? The term *reciprocal causality* is sometimes used to describe the relationship between trust and its consequences (Golembiewski & McConkie, 1975). The claim, for example, that trust enables cooperation is not diminished by the assertion that cooperation also promotes trust (see Cook & Cooper, 2003, p. 235). Trust has consequences that can be measured, but in some cases, reciprocal causality makes it difficult to establish bold claims and assign proportions of cause and effect between trust and other variables with which trust forms a normative system. Thus, we prefer to use the less strident term *consequences* when we see conditions that appear to emerge in the presence of collective trust.

If we sort the findings reported above with respect to their nontrust correlates or dependent variables, they fall into four general categories: (1) the relationships among the various role-based collective trusts, (2) climate/affect consequences, (3) structure consequences, and (4) behavioral consequences. Figure 5.2 depicts these consequences and our effort to draw theoretical linkages among them. The model portrays collective trust as having consequences for both climate/culture features of groups and organizations, as well as structural features. Structure and climate, in turn, have consequences for behaviors and group or organizational outcomes. Collective trust also has direct consequences for behavior and group/organizational outcomes. Notice that all the relationships are portrayed in the model with double-headed arrows, acknowledging the likelihood of reciprocal causality.

Generally, careful examination of available empirical findings supports the conclusion that collective trust, like interpersonal trust, most frequently functions as a lubricant for social and individual action. That is, trust tends to indirectly facilitate social enterprise. This explanation is consistent with Dirks and Ferrin's (2001) findings that trust generally has direct effects on perceptions and attitudes while having indirect, inconsistent, and weaker effects on work behavior and other outcomes. Their work also supports the notion that trust can have simultaneous direct and moderating effects. The school trust studies reveal trust's indirect consequences on cooperation and other behaviors and outcomes through the group's climate and affective dispositions, and through the group's formal and informal structures.

Consequences for Climate and Affect

There is evidence from all three research series that collective trust has positive and significant consequences for a variety of school climate and affect features. The oldest and most prolific series (Hoy and colleagues) provides ample evidence that faculty trust, with its various referents (principal, colleagues, organization, and clients), shapes the climate and affective environment of the school. Faculty trust appears to have positive consequences for principals, providing an environment in which they are perceived by teachers as practicing transactional leadership and acting authentically. Faculty

Figure 5.2. Consequences of collective trust.

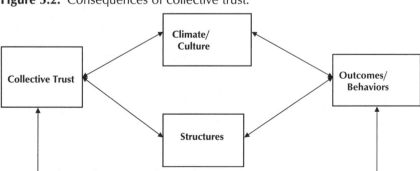

trust in the principal has been shown to be especially important for a wide array of teacher attitudes, perceptions, and beliefs, including school climate and collective teacher efficacy. Bryk and Schneider (2002) add to this list of consequences of collective faculty trust "increased professional community," a teacher "can do" orientation, high academic standards, and teacher internalized responsibility.

Parent trust (Forsyth, Adams, and colleagues), as might be expected, has climate and affect consequences through its direct influence on collective teacher efficacy and on student identification with school. Thus, parent trust boosts the climate and affective dispositions of two other groups, teachers and students. It should be pointed out that student identification with school is positively affected by teacher, faculty, and student trust in the principal.

In short, the collective trust norms inherent in the various role groups of the school community are part of a network that shapes the organizational climate and affective dispositions found in schools. High levels of collective trust, in its many forms, are found in school climates characterized as positive, energetic, and optimistic. Finally, consistent with both organizational and school research, we can predict that trust has positive consequences for behaviors, including cooperation and other important school outcomes through its effects on climate.

Consequences for Structure

There are a number of school trust studies relating various facets of trust to structural elements of the school. A cautionary note should, however, be emphasized: All the structural variables in these studies were measured as perceptions of either teachers or parents. Both faculty trust in the principal and faculty trust in colleagues are related to teacher perceptions that bureaucratic structures in the school (formalization and centralization) enable rather than hinder teacher work. Formalization has mostly to do with rules and procedures. Centralization is associated with hierarchy and relative concentration of decision making at the top of the organization. When teachers trust each other and the principal, they are also more likely to view the school's structures as enabling. Parent trust in school also has the effect of increasing teacher perceptions of existing school structures as enabling, rather than hindering, their work.

Faculty trust is also related to teacher perceptions that the faculty has influence on management and instructional decisions, as well as the perception that parents have influence on school policy.

Parent trust in school appears to have consequences for school structure as well. As mentioned, parent trust in school is associated with teacher views that school structure is enabling. Parent trust is also associated with parent perceptions of their own influence on school policy.

Thus, both faculty trust and parent trust have very significant consequences for how both groups view the organizational structures of the school. Although there is little evidence about actual structural differences between high-trust versus low-trust schools, it may be that perceptions about structure are more important than actual differences. Just as with climate, perceptions about group and organizational structures, conditioned by trust, have consequences for behaviors, cooperation, and other important school outcomes.

Consequences for Behavior and Outcomes

Most of the school research on the direct outcomes of collective trust are concerned with academic performance. Chapter 6 deals with this subject exclusively. As for other behaviors and outcomes, the findings are mixed. Faculty trust in the principal does not affect teacher behavior to prevent student bullying; however, faculty trust in colleagues and clients do. Bryk and Schneider's (2002) combined indicator of faculty trust is associated with teacher behaviors of outreach to parents and instructional innovation. Finally, parent trust in school is associated with parents' involvement with their children's education, both at home and at school.

The number of studies focused on outcomes directly the result of trust, other than academic performance, is limited. Additionally, there is no apparent explanation for why some behaviors and outcomes may be directly affected by collective trust and others are not.

SUMMARY

What can we say we know about collective trust and its consequences? Of the three forms of collective trust that have been studied in schools (faculty trust, parent trust, and student trust), all have been associated with important school consequences. Collective trust has both direct and indirect consequences. Variables that appear to mediate between collective trust in schools and other outcomes are structure, culture, and climate. These mediating variables, in turn, have consequences for group or organizational goals and interests. For example, enabling structures and positive climates have beneficial consequences for goal achievement, cooperative behaviors, and other desirable outcomes.

We began the sense-making section by noting Homans's (1967) charge that accumulated empirical findings can finally be transformed into tentative explanations of phenomena. Our conceptual framework becomes a first interpretation of findings, a theoretical holding pattern for generating future hypotheses, and a place to bring contradictory and confirmatory findings that will further specify the relationships between collective trust and its consequences. Perhaps more important, these initial efforts to simplify the complexity of collective trust and its consequences for schools can offer practitioners conceptual capital for reflection and experimentation.

CHAPTER 6

Collective Trust and School Effectiveness

Good schools are intrinsically social enterprises that depend heavily
on the cooperative endeavors among various participants who
comprise the school community.
—Anthony Bryk and Barbara Schneider, *Trust in Schools:*
A Core Resource for Reform

The focus of this chapter is on the relationship between collective trust in
schools and school effectiveness. The early Rutgers research on trust (see
Chapter 1) foreshadows development of this body of research on effectiveness. There are both theoretical and practical issues surrounding the linking
of trust and effectiveness. Although most researchers agree that organizational effectiveness is the critical test of any organization, there is no generally accepted set of criteria for evaluating organizational effectiveness. Some
studies of effectiveness focus on the quality of inputs, others assess the efficiency of the internal operations, and still others insist that outcome per-
formances are the key to determining the effectiveness of the organization.

SCHOOL EFFECTIVENESS

School effectiveness is an umbrella term for an approach to evaluating
schools. Some researchers consider schools effective if they are successful at
attracting resources; for example, district per pupil expenditure is viewed as
an index of effectiveness. Others assess the effectiveness of schools in terms
of how well the internal operations function; for example, they examine the
level of conflict or satisfaction. Finally, others claim that organizations must
be evaluated in terms of the quality of their products or the value added to
their output.

In education, academic achievement is currently in vogue as state and federal agencies require multiple assessments of student performance. The *No Child Left Behind* (NCLB) legislation of 2001 mandated that student performance improve over the years until students graduate. Virtually everyone agrees that student growth and achievement are critical factors of school effectiveness.

Currently, for good or ill, school effectiveness is typically measured in terms of student achievement on multiple sets of standardized tests. We view student performance as a crucial aspect of school effectiveness but see it as only one important criterion. Thus, our analysis of the trust-effectiveness link will center on academic achievement of students, but it will also include other, more subjective measures of school effectiveness.

Objective Measures

In this chapter, objective indicators of school effectiveness are the percentage of students who pass a graduation test, aggregated scores from standardized tests reported by states for schools, or standardized test scores from the Metropolitan Achievement Test or the Iowa Basic Skills Tests. We typically use reading and mathematic scores and occasionally social studies, writing, and language scores. Admittedly, these are not perfect indicators of academic performance, but they are reliable measures of student achievement, and they have been used by states to measure academic progress. Standardized tests have the virtue of being objective measures at the individual level that are routinely administered by schools and are rough indicators of the success of schools when aggregated. However, aggregation of data has its share of problems. For example, students are nested within classes, and such hierarchical arrangements produce problems of the appropriate unit of analysis as well as issues of under- and overestimation of observed relationships among the variables (Bryk & Raudenbush, 1992).

Subjective Measures

The subjective index of school effectiveness that we use in this chapter is based on the theoretical work of Talcott Parsons (1960) and the empirical development of Paul Mott (1972) and Cecil Miskel and his colleagues (Miskel, Fevurly, & Stewart, 1979; Miskel, McDonald, & Bloom, 1983). As we noted in Chapter 1, Parsons (1961) presents the conceptual underpinnings of a multidimensional definition of effectiveness in his presentation and development of the four functional imperatives. If organizations are to survive and be effective, they must accommodate their environments, achieve their goals, maintain solidarity among their parts, and create and maintain a successful motivational system.

Mott (1972) developed an operational system to measure general organizational effectiveness, which is remarkably consistent with Parsons's formulation. Mott argued that "effective organizations are those that produce more and higher quality outputs and adapt more effectively to environmental and internal problems than do other, similar organizations" (p. 124). In particular, he measured the quantity and quality of the product, the efficiency of production, and the flexibility and adaptability of the organization in hospitals by asking employees to respond to a series of questions tapping each of these criteria. Although Mott's index is a subjective measure based on perceptions of employees, he carefully demonstrated its validity as a measure of effectiveness in hospitals by demonstrating its high correlation with a number of more traditional and objective measures of hospital effectiveness.

Likewise, Hoy and Ferguson (1985), with some minor adaptations, confirmed the index's validity as an overall measure of school effectiveness. They showed that the school index of effectiveness (see Appendix 1.2) was significantly related to all four of Parsons's imperative functions of effective schools, including measures of student performance. Thus, in a few of the studies reported in this chapter, we will use the subjective index of effectiveness (as we did in Chapter 1), whereas in most studies we use objective measures of student achievement as indicators of school effectiveness.

EARLY RESEARCH: THE RUTGERS UNIVERSITY STUDIES

The original definition of faculty trust was developed, refined, and measured at Rutgers University. This early research focused primarily on the nature of the collective trust of the faculty, including three referents of trust—faculty trust in the principal, in colleagues, and in the organization. In addition, the research explored relationships between aspects of faculty trust and principal behavior (e.g., authenticity), school climate, school health, and the influence of trust and climate properties on school effectiveness.

Collective Trust and School Effectiveness

Throughout this chapter, we refer to *faculty trust* as a shorthand way to speak of the collective trust of the faculty. We begin by briefly reviewing the results of the earlier Rutgers studies that explored the collective trust–school effectiveness relation.

Recall that in two separate Rutgers studies, collective trust was related to school effectiveness as measured by the subjective measure of effectiveness in Appendix 1.2. In both elementary (Hoy et al., 1992) and middle schools (Tarter et al., 1995), there was a positive path between school climate properties, faculty trust, and school achievement, albeit slightly different paths for elementary and middle schools (refer to Figure 1.1).

Collective Trust and School Quality

At Rutgers, the relationship between collective trust and positive school outcomes was also examined. The concept of quality was studied using multivariate techniques to assess the positive performance of schools. Quality is a construct that some substitute for overall effectiveness (Cameron, 1984; Cameron & Whetton, 1996). It is a broad term that encompasses many positive properties of an organization's output.

In the case of schools, the index of quality dealt not only with outcomes but also with the means to achieve those ends. Using a large, diverse sample of middle schools, Hoy and Sabo (1998) factor analyzed a set of indicators that they postulated were measures of school quality. The indicators included collective trust in principals and in colleagues; SES; authenticity; openness; perceived effectiveness; healthy interpersonal dynamics; and mathematics, reading, and writing achievement. Not surprisingly, all these indicators loaded strongly on the same factor—school quality. The factor loadings on this school quality index for faculty trust in the principal and in colleagues were both very strong. Clearly, collective trust in schools is an important aspect of good schools.

Collective Trust and Student Achievement

Early attempts at Rutgers to link collective trust with student achievement measured by statewide proficiency tests in reading, writing, and mathematics were unsuccessful (Hoy et al., 1991). When socioeconomic status (SES) of the school or the district was added to regression equations predicting academic achievement, only SES was significantly associated with student achievement. The wealth of school families (SES) in study after study was the key to explaining variance in student achievement, a stubborn and discomforting fact because socioeconomic status does not lend itself to easy change. At this stage, collective trust seemed unimportant in explaining student achievement. These early studies on collective trust were unable to refute Coleman's landmark study (Coleman et al., 1966), which documented the strong relation between SES and academic achievement and concluded that family background factors were much more important than school factors in accounting for student achievement.

THE OHIO STATE STUDIES: THE MISSING LINK

There was a brief hiatus in the study of collective trust in schools as Wayne Hoy moved from Rutgers University to The Ohio State University, but in a few years, he and his students again had begun to pursue, refine, and expand the study of school trust.

A new aspect of trust was introduced in this phase of the research, *faculty trust* in students and parents. Initially, trust in students and trust in parents were conceptualized as separate components of faculty trust, but that turned out not to be the case. In every factor analysis performed on these two referents of trust (Hoy & Tschannen-Moran, 2003; Smith et al., 2001; Tschannen-Moran & Hoy, 1998), only one factor emerged.

Apparently faculty trust in students and parents represents only one dimension of trust in schools; when the faculty trusts parents, it also trusts the students and vice versa. This discovery of the unidimensionality of collective trust in students and parents (sometimes called faculty trust in clients) was a serendipitous finding at the time; however, more recently Bryk and Schneider (2002) also encountered the same phenomenon in their longitudinal study of the Chicago Public Schools. They explained that, especially in elementary schools, teacher-student trust operates primarily through teacher-parent trust.

The surprise was that collective trust of students and parents, unlike its other referents, was positively related to student achievement, even after controlling for socioeconomic and other demographic characteristics. The researchers were unable to find any large, empirical, quantitative study in which *collective trust* in either colleagues or the principal was directly related to student achievement when SES was controlled.

In fact, it seems likely that the reason the earlier research could not link collective trust with student achievement, controlling for SES, was that the wrong referent of the collective trust was studied. Faculty trust in students and parents is the key to fostering student achievement; faculty trust neither in colleagues nor in the principal is linked to student achievement. In brief, trust relations with parents and students are the critical referents when it comes to explaining student achievement.

Collective Trust in Clients and Student Achievement

We now turn to a series of studies that examined the relation between collective trust in clients (parents and students) and school achievement.

THE EVIDENCE. Goddard, Tschannen-Moran, and Hoy (2001) performed the first study to connect collective faculty trust in clients with student achievement. Using hierarchical linear modeling, they demonstrated that collective trust in students and parents was directly related to student achievement in a sample of urban elementary schools. The study was a major breakthrough because, as we have seen, it is extremely difficult to find school-level variables that affect student achievement when controlling for SES. SES typically overwhelms all other variables in explaining student achievement and therein lies the rub. The SES of the family is difficult to change even in the long run and impossible to change in the short run. Ultimately, school effectiveness may depend on the discovery of organizational variables that are both amenable to change and improve student performance—a formidable challenge.

A second study by Goddard and colleagues (Goddard, Salloum, & Berebitsky, 2006) used a path analysis to examine the direct and indirect effects of faculty trust in clients (students and parents) on mathematics and reading achievement. This study used a stratified random sample of all Michigan elementary schools to get a representative sample of elementary schools. Completing two paths (one each for math and reading achievement), the authors found that faculty trust in clients was a significant, positive predictor of both mathematics achievement (explaining about two-thirds of the variance) and reading achievement (explaining more than half the variance explained). Other contextual variables in the models, including SES and proportion of minority students, were not significant direct predictors of achievement. Most important, economic and racial disadvantage were directly related to faculty trust in clients, which strongly predicted achievement. Thus, faculty trust in clients mediated the relationship between school disadvantage (SES and proportion minority) and academic achievement.

Consistent with these studies, Tschannen-Moran (2004) did a comparative study of faculty trust in the principal and faculty trust in clients, and not surprisingly, it was the faculty trust in parents and students, not trust in the principal, that was strongly related to school achievement on the Virginia Standards of Learning tests.

Finally, in another study of faculty trust and achievement, this one of high schools, Hoy (2002) demonstrated that faculty trust in clients was related to school achievement and had a stronger influence on achievement than SES. The strength and power of collective trust in facilitating school achievement was stunning.

AN EXPLANATION. Just how does collective faculty trust function to influence student achievement? Hoy proposed two plausible and complementary explanations.

First, trusting others is an important element of human learning because learning is often a cooperative process. Distrust makes cooperation virtually impossible, so teachers must trust students and parents if they are to cooperate with them to achieve common learning goals. We believe, and the evidence supports the conclusion, that cooperation between teachers and students and between parents and students sets the stage for effective learning in schools. Such trust and cooperation are ingredients that improve teaching and learning.

Second, the link between collective trust and student achievement is also indirect because student achievement is mediated by collective efficacy of the school. Teacher self-efficacy is the teacher's belief in his or her ability to organize and execute actions to accomplish a specific teaching task (Bandura, 1997). When teachers believe they can be effective at a specific task, they typically are.

Collective efficacy is the shared perception of the teachers that the faculty as a whole has a strong capability to be effective with students. When collective efficacy is high, teachers believe they can reach their students and overcome such negative external influences as poor living environments. Consequently, teachers exert more effort, are persistent, set high but achievable goals, plan more, and accept responsibility for student achievement. Efficacious teachers are resilient: they do not become easily discouraged by setbacks and failure; they overcome them (Bandura, 1997; Hoy, 2002).

Strong collective efficacy not only enhances individual teacher performance but also affects the shared beliefs held by organizational members. For example, a teacher with average self-efficacy beliefs is likely to exhibit even more effort when joining a faculty having strong collective efficacy. The normative effect of the school's collective efficacy and collective trust positively influences its individual members (Goddard, Hoy, & Woolfolk Hoy, 2000). Collective efficacy and collective trust in students and parents are strongly and inextricably related to each other (Hoy, 2002), and both school properties facilitate learning and achievement independently and in concert.

This second explanation of improved student performance is summarized as follows:

- Strong faculty trust in students and parents leads to high levels of collective efficacy in schools; teachers come to share the belief that their school can have positive effects on students regardless of external problems.
- High collective efficacy, in turn, stimulates teachers to set challenging student goals, to work harder, to persist longer in their teaching, to be resilient when they confront difficulties, and to seek and use constructive feedback.
- Student achievement reinforces both collective efficacy and collective trust in parents and students.

Figure 6.1 depicts the integrated relationships among collective faculty trust, collective efficacy, and student achievement.

Academic Optimism and School Achievement

Academic optimism is a general construct that includes faculty trust in clients but also collective efficacy as well as academic emphasis. All three of these collective properties are similar in both nature and function and also in their potent and positive effects on school outcomes, especially on achievement.

ACADEMIC OPTIMISM: A LATENT CONSTRUCT. Academic optimism is a collective set of beliefs about strengths and capabilities in schools in which optimism is the overarching idea that unites collective efficacy and collective trust with academic emphasis. The composite elements of academic optimism are the following:

- Collective efficacy, the shared belief that the faculty can make a positive difference in student learning; the faculty believes in itself.
- Faculty trust in students and parents, the belief that teachers, parents, and students can cooperate to improve learning; that is, the faculty believes in its students.
- Academic emphasis, the enacted behavior of these beliefs; that is, *the* faculty focus is on student success in academics.

Figure 6.1. Theoretical explanation for the influence of collective trust and collective efficacy on student achievement.

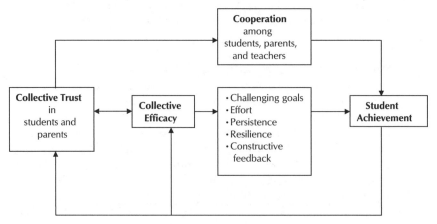

Unlike many conceptions of optimism that treat it as a cognitive property, our conception of academic optimism includes cognitive (efficacy), affective (trust), and behavioral (academic emphasis) components. Moreover, academic optimism is a collective property, not an individual one. A school with strong academic optimism defines a culture in which the faculty believes:

- It can make a difference.
- Students can learn.
- Academic performance can be achieved (Hoy, Tarter, & Woolfolk Hoy, 2006a; Hoy et al., 2006b).

These three aspects of collective optimism interact in a reciprocal way with each other (see Figure 6.2).

For example, faculty trust in parents and students increases a sense of collective efficacy, but collective efficacy in turn reinforces collective trust. Similarly, when the faculty trusts parents, teachers believe they can demand higher academic standards without fear that parents will undermine them, and emphasis on high academic standards in turn strengthens the faculty trust in parents and students. Finally, when the faculty as a whole believes it can organize and execute actions needed to have a positive effect on student achievement, it will stress academic achievement, and academic emphasis will in turn support a strong sense of collective efficacy. In brief, all three aspects of academic optimism are in transactional relationships with each

Figure 6.2. Reciprocal relationships between the three components of academic optimism.

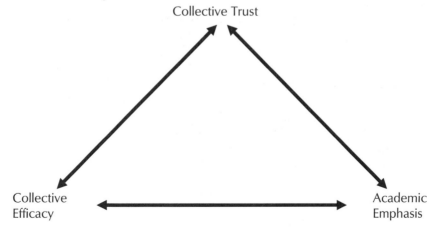

other and interact to create a culture of academic optimism in the school workplace.

POTENTIAL OF ACADEMIC OPTIMISM. A number of factors underscore the utility of a culture of academic optimism (Hoy & Hoy, 2009). Optimism suggests learning possibilities; a pessimistic school workplace can change. Faculty can learn to be optimistic. Academic optimism gains its name from the conviction that its composite properties all express an optimistic and malleable perspective.

Administrators and teachers have reason to be optimistic; they are empowered to make a difference in the lives of their students. Neither the faculty nor students need be irretrievably trapped by socioeconomic factors that breed a sense of hopelessness and cynicism. Optimism trumps hopelessness and pessimism.

THE EVIDENCE. As expected, academic optimism can and does have a strong, positive effect on school achievement, even controlling for socioeconomic factors, previous success, and other demographic variables (Hoy et al., 2006b; Kirby & DiPaola, 2009; McGuigan & Hoy, 2006; Smith & Hoy, 2007; Wagner & DiPaola, 2009).

The results of these studies are compelling; they all offer strong empirical evidence for the positive connection between academic optimism and school achievement at all levels of schooling. That is, the optimism-achievement relationship holds regardless of whether the school is an elementary, middle, or high school. Remember that academic optimism has three facets: collective efficacy is the thinking and believing side; collective faculty trust in students and parents is the affective and emotional side; and academic emphasis is the behavioral side—the enactment of the cognitive and affective.

Perhaps the strongest *single* piece of evidence for the optimism-achievement relationship is the study of high schools (Hoy et al., 2006b). This study had more controls (including controls for SES, previous achievement, and demographic variables) than others, had a large diverse sample, multiple measures of student achievement, and used structural equation modeling to test the theory. The evidence was convincing; the theoretical model was supported (see Figure 6.3). Moreover, using hierarchical linear modeling (HLM), interclass correlations demonstrated that our measure of academic optimism was indeed a collective one rather than merely an aggregate of individual perceptions.

AN EXPLANATION. The common view of achievement in schools is that success is a function of talent and motivation; the talented and motivated

Figure 6.3. Theoretical model explaining the relationship between academic optimism and student achievment.

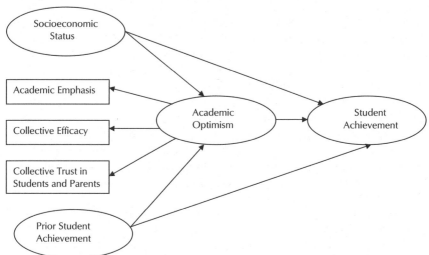

excel. Seligman (1998), however, offers a third factor for success—optimism. He maintains that optimism matters as much as talent or motivation in achievement. Further, optimism can be learned and developed. Seligman views learned optimism as an individual variable, but we conceive of academic optimism as a collective property, which may be an even more powerful force for achievement because it has the power of the group and taps into both the social structure and potent norms of the school. Thus, we anticipated that many of the conclusions about individual learned optimism applied to the collective, and the results supported those expectations.

Seligman (1998) argues and provides evidence that learned optimism gets people over the "wall of learned pessimism" and not just as individuals but also as organizational participants. In the same way that students and parents can develop learned helplessness, schools can be seduced by pervasive pessimism. Pessimism communicates the general message, These kids can't learn, and there is nothing I can do about it, so why worry about academic achievement? Such a view is reinforcing, self-fulfilling, and defeating. Academic optimism, in stark contrast, is a collective view of teachers as capable, students as willing and able, parents as supportive and reliable, and the learning as achievable. Norms of confidence, optimism, and efficacy are powerful motivators of achievement.

Why is academic optimism such a strong force for achievement? Consider the functions of the three underlying elements. Collective efficacy gives teachers confidence that they can be successful working with students regardless of the difficulties. It motivates teachers to set challenging academic goals and persist until they are attained (Goddard et al., 2000; Hoy, Sweetland, & Smith, 2002). Collective faculty trust in parents and teachers liberates teachers to experiment with new techniques without fear of retribution if things do not go as planned, and perhaps even more important, it encourages cooperation and support between teachers and parents (Bryk & Schneider, 2002; Goddard et al., 2001).

Further, an emphasis on academics is enacted because students and parents trust the teachers. Not only do both teachers and parents push for academic success, but students also come to value working hard, succeeding, getting good grades, and achieving. In the end, academic optimism produces a powerful synergy that engenders motivation, creates hope, encourages persistence, promotes resilience, and channels behavior toward the accomplishment of high academic goals.

In sum, academic emphasis, faculty trust, and collective efficacy form a general latent construct called *academic optimism*. The construct draws from a number of different theories. Collective efficacy comes from Bandura's work (1997) in social cognitive theory; trust emerges as an important concept in Coleman's (1990) analysis of social interaction and social capital; academic emphasis evolves from Hoy and his colleagues' research on the organizational health of schools (Hoy et al., 1991) with its theoretical underpinnings from Parsons and his colleagues (Parsons, Bales, & Shils, 1953).

Bringing these streams of theory and research together gives a richer and yet more direct explanation of how schools enhance student learning. Further, knowing the composite elements of collective academic optimism has the added benefit of providing a wider set of possibilities for improving optimism in the school. One might even argue that collective optimism in schools provides social capital for success in the form of informal norms and structures that support and enhance the teaching-learning process.

McGuigan and Hoy (2006) argue that collective efficacy gives teachers confidence that they can be effective and motivates them to act to achieve challenging goals and persist until they are successful (Goddard et al., 2000; Hoy et al., 2002). Collective trust increases cooperation and support between parents and teachers (Bryk & Schneider, 2002; Goddard and Tschannen-Moran, 2001). Academic emphasis is enacted in behavior, in part, because students and parents trust the teachers. Not only do teachers and parents stress academic success, but students also learn to value hard work and academic success.

In the end, efficacy, trust, and academic emphasis produce a powerful combination that engenders motivation, creates optimism, and channels behavior toward the accomplishment of high academic goals (Hoy et al., 2006b).

THE UNIVERSITY OF CHICAGO STUDIES

The impetus for the University of Chicago study of trust was quite different from that of The Ohio State Studies. As explained in Chapter 5, Anthony Bryk and Barbara Schneider (2002) didn't set out to study trust; their focus was on school effectiveness. During the course of their research, they discovered, quite accidentally, the salience of trust.

The Evidence

As pointed out in Chapter 5, Bryk and Schneider's (2002) general finding was that composite teacher trust is highly predictive of school productivity trends (i.e., improving math and reading performance). "Schools reporting strong positive trust levels in 1994 were three times more likely to be categorized eventually as improving in reading and mathematics than those with very weak trust reports" (p. 111). The effects of trust on math and reading improvement persisted, even when controlling for teacher background, student demographics, and other school contextual factors.

Relational Trust: An Indirect Force

Bryk and Schneider (2002) found that, as has been the case in other organizational contexts, trust enhanced school effectiveness indirectly. They discovered that trust fostered the set of organizational conditions listed in Chapter 5:

1. A positive orientation to innovation (teacher "can do" attitude and internalized responsibility)
2. Outreach to parents
3. Professional community (collaborative work practices, personal commitment to improve teaching and school operations)
4. High expectations and high academic standards

Consistently, improving relational trust was associated with higher levels of school commitment, positive orientation to innovation, parent outreach, and professional community. These conditions, in turn, made the initiation and sustenance of school improvement by teachers more likely.

A Convergence: A Theoretical Model of School Achievement

What is striking about Bryk and Schneider's school conditions that promote learning is their remarkable similarity with Hoy and his colleague's latent construct of academic optimism (see Figure 6.4).

Figure 6.4. Social conditions that promote learning.

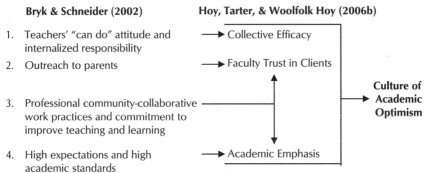

The University of Chicago and The Ohio State Studies converge and support each other in terms of both the importance of collective faculty trust of clients as well as its relationship to organizational conditions that foster student achievement.

A culture of academic optimism is composed of three interacting elements: collective trust in parents and students, collective efficacy, and the enactment of academic emphasis. Moreover, relational trust between parents and teachers enhances and supports a culture of academic optimism and promotes a spirit of cooperation among students, parents, and teachers. Together academic optimism and relational trust foster a learning environment in which students embrace challenging goals, are motivated to exert strong effort, persist in difficult tasks, and are resilient in the face of setbacks as they receive feedback on their progress. The positive motivation and cooperative effort lead to high levels of student achievement, which in turn reinforce academic optimism and relational trust. These school factors and the positive dynamics that influence student achievement are demonstrated pictorially in Figure 6.5.

THE OKLAHOMA STATE UNIVERSITY AND UNIVERSITY OF OKLAHOMA STUDIES

Until early 2000, for the most part, the collective trust research was on faculty trust, that is, the degree to which faculty trusted various referent groups such as parents, students, teachers, and administrators. Forsyth and Adams and their colleagues (Adams, 2008; Adams & Forsyth, 2009b; Adams & Forsyth, 2007a, 2007b, 2009; Adams et al., 2009; Forsyth, 2008), however, began to examine the formation of parent trust as well as student trust. This

Figure 6.5. Model of the dynamics of school properties that promote student achievement.

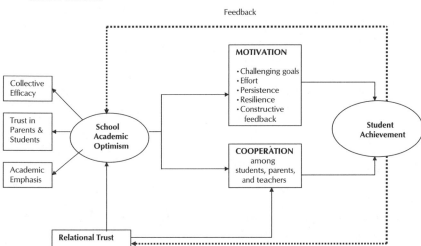

work is in its early stages, but once again the significance of trust as a predictor of student achievement is clear. The development of the measures of student trust in the principal and in faculty, and parent trust in school and the principal, has already been explicated in Chapter 3. Here we examine the beginning research that tests the influence of parent trust and student trust on student achievement.

With a stratified random sample of elementary, secondary, and high schools in Oklahoma, Forsyth, Barnes, & Adams (2005) used canonical correlation analysis to examine the combined effects of parent trust and faculty trust on a set of school outcome measures. In particular, the researchers were interested in how the trust variables worked together with SES to influence school structure, collective efficacy, and student achievement as measured by the state's standardized test scores. The first set of independent variables was composed of parent trust in the principal, parent trust in the school, faculty trust in colleagues, faculty trust in the principal, and SES, whereas the criterion set of variables included collective efficacy, enabling school structure, and academic performance.

The results were consistent with the other findings on collective trust and student achievement. The school community's trust environment was a strong predictor of school consequences; in fact, patterns of school success seem dependent on a variety of contextual conditions, including parental wealth, parental trust, collective efficacy beliefs, and enabling school structure. The dominant canonical factor revealed a strong classic pattern of the effective school: High parent trust and high faculty trust together with high socioeconomic conditions predict high teacher expectations for efficacy, enabling school structure, and high academic performance. The results again demonstrate that trust is an important lubricant for effective school functioning.

In a second analysis of the Oklahoma data, Forsyth and Adams (2004) attempted to refine the measure of collective trust by introducing a more complex measure that they called *reciprocal trust*, which occurs when two groups have high levels of trust for each other. Consistent with the earlier studies (Bryk & Schneider, 2002; Goddard et al., 2000, 2001, 2006; Hoy, 2002; Tschannen-Moran, 2004), teacher-parent reciprocal trust was strongly related to school performance controlling for the socioeconomic status.

In another study of collective student trust, Adams and Forsyth (2009), not only demonstrated the validity of a measure of student trust in teachers, but also showed that such trust predicted the achievement growth of students and positive identification of students with school whereas student trust was unrelated to the gender, experience, and ethnicity of the faculty. In yet another analysis of collective parent trust, Adams and colleagues (2009) found that parent collective trust was not inherently deficient in poor schools with large proportions of minority students. It appears that, regardless of poverty, school size, ethnic composition, and school level, school leaders can build and sustain parent trust by aligning policies and practices to address the needs of parents.

Finally, Mitchell and Forsyth (2004, 2005) have demonstrated the importance of student identification in predicting student achievement. Schools with high levels of student identification are higher-performing schools academically. Although both collective parent and faculty trust explain school-level academic achievement, even controlling for SES, student identification with school not only is in part a function of such trust, it also has a direct, independent influence on academic performance.

In sum, these more recent studies in Oklahoma support the extant research on the importance of collective trust in promoting student achievement. Moreover, they add to our understanding of collective trust by exploring two additional role groups—parents and teachers. They also begin to grapple with the extent to which collective trust is reciprocal and suggest that reciprocity increases the practical and productive power of trust. For example, when both parents and teachers trust each other, the force of the trust increases and has even more potency for improving student achievement.

SUMMARY

We began this chapter with a broad definition of school effectiveness that included a myriad of indicators. Then we narrowed our analyses primarily to two basic frameworks: objective measures of effectiveness in terms of school standardized achievement scores and subjective measures of trust that included the extent to which schools adapt to their environment, achieve their goals, maintain solidarity, limit conflict, and motivate their participants. Using these two perspectives on school effectiveness, we examined four major research programs on school trust and school effectiveness, which have spanned four decades: the Rutgers University Studies, The Ohio State University Studies, the University of Chicago studies, and the Oklahoma State University and University of Oklahoma Studies.

The Rutgers Studies were concerned with defining and measuring three forms of collective trust in schools: faculty trust in colleagues, in the principal, and in the school. The initial findings were encouraging in that faculty trust in colleagues and faculty trust in the principal were both related to subjective measures of effectiveness. Furthermore, the leadership of the principal, especially of an authentic and supportive principal, promoted trust. All attempts, however, to connect faculty trust directly to student achievement failed when SES was included in the analysis. In other words, SES was the only independent predictor of academic success; it simply overwhelmed the other variables.

After a brief hiatus, a renewed effort to link collective trust to school effectiveness started at The Ohio State University. The definitions of collective trust were refined, improved, and expanded to include faculty trust in parents and in students. Surprisingly, faculty trust in parents and in students turned out to be a single unidimensional aspect of collective trust; when the faculty trusted parents, the faculty also trusted students and vice versa. Moreover, faculty trust in parents and student (clients) emerged as the key aspect of collective trust that was consistently related to student achievement, even controlling for SES, previous achievement, and other demographic variables. In addition, The Ohio State University Studies also demonstrated that faculty trust in parents and students was a crucial ingredient of a more general construct called *academic optimism*, which helped to explain the dynamics and operation of school conditions in improving student performance.

Concurrently with The Ohio State Studies, researchers at the University of Chicago (Bryk & Schneider, 2002) were engaged in a long-term study of achievement in the urban schools of Chicago. In their attempt to explain differences in school capacity and improvement, they discovered the key variable to success was relational trust. They argued that although trust was critical for achievement, it did not directly affect academic performance. Instead, relational trust in school fostered the organizational conditions that directly affected learning: an "I can do" attitude and internalized responsibility in teachers, outreach to parents, a professional community of collaboration, and high expectations and high academic standards. These school conditions are strikingly similar to those embodied the Ohio State description and research on academic optimism (Hoy et al., 2006); in fact, the conditions suggest how academic optimism enables high levels of student performance. The two sets of findings led to a theoretical model for explaining the role of trust in promoting school conditions that foster achievement.

The Oklahoma State and University of Oklahoma Studies by Forsyth and Adams and their colleagues are the latest inquiries into collective trust. They have advanced the school trust research one step further because they use students and parents in addition to teachers to describe the trust relations of different role groups (e.g., parent trust of teachers and student trust of teachers). Their studies are just beginning, but findings are consistent with the earlier trust research that related collective trust and student performance. Furthermore, these new studies add the intriguing perspective of examining and comparing internal and external collective trust. Finally, Forsyth and Adams (2004) have begun to look at reciprocal trust, that is, the extent, for example, to which there is strong trust between parents and teachers. Not surprisingly, such reciprocal trust is also related to student performance even controlling of socioeconomic conditions.

CHAPTER 7

Collective Trust, Control, and Leadership in Schools

Most of the difficulties in leading and managing organizations are due to resistance to change. One of the factors that make organizational change possible and palatable is trust.
—John Bruhn, *Trust and the Health of Organizations*

This chapter uses collective trust theory and research in schools to address long-standing dilemmas about how schools can be held accountable, managed, and led. Focusing on the particular contextual conditions of schools as organizations, an ideal type of school can be described in terms of collective trust, control, and leadership. The argument is based, not on a philosophical commitment to principles of democracy, or on what works in commercial enterprises, but rather on a structural-functional understanding of organizational effectiveness within the context and mission of public education.

THE PROBLEMS OF COOPERATION AND PREDICTABILITY

McEvily, Perrone, and Zaheer (2003) assert that managing "interdependence among individuals, units, and activities in the face of behavioral uncertainty constitutes a key organizational challenge" (p. 92). Similarly, Bachmann (2003) points out that "the question of how to integrate different actors' expectations and interaction lies at the heart of any organization's identity" (p. 58). As discussed earlier, some organizations are faced with the complication of achieving the cooperation of multiple, interdependent groups. Public schools, which depend for their success on the cooperation of teachers, parents, students, and administrators, all groups that are integral to the achievement of school core goals, are exemplary of this type of organization. We are particularly interested in the role that collective trust might play in achieving necessary cooperation in the public schools.

CONTROL OR TRUST

The need for achieving predictable or certain cooperation in organizations is not much disputed. What is less clear is how to achieve cooperation and whether or not the various means to achieve it are compatible or mutually exclusive, and under what conditions. The literature appears to favor two avenues for achieving predictable cooperation. The first is to reduce uncertainty or risk through control mechanisms. The second is to reduce uncertainty by increasing trust, which replaces uncertainty with willingly embraced risk (Bachmann, 2006). Möllering (1998) has noted the dearth of research addressing both control and trust simultaneously; however, there are several approaches emerging.

Organizational theorists have argued that the confidence partners have in cooperative relationships is rooted in either control or trust (Aulakh, Kotabe, & Sahay, 1997; Forsyth et al., 2006; Leifer & Mills, 1996; Zaheer & Venkatraman, 1995). Das and Teng (1998) describe control as regulatory processes that make predictable the mutual interests of partners; rules, policies, and procedures are common examples employed by organizations. Trust, on the other hand, is not a process but a belief or attitude about a partner's goodwill and reliability in high-risk situations (Gambetta, 1988; Nooteboom, Berger, & Noorderhaven, 1997; Ring & Van de Ven, 1992). At first glance, it would appear that both control and trust can enhance confidence in partner cooperation. The questions appear to be whether and how control and trust function together.

As Das and Teng (1998) note, the relationship between control and trust is complex and not well understood. One interpretation is that since both control and trust enhance confidence in partner cooperation, they are alternative, substitute, or complementary mechanisms (Aulakh et al., 1997; Sitkin & Roth, 1993; Zaheer & Venkatraman, 1995). The evidence in support of a complementary relationship between control and trust is mixed (Beamish, 1988; Creed & Miles, 1996; Inkpen & Currall, 1997), suggesting an incomplete understanding of the phenomenon. Das and Teng (1998) propose instead that a more realistic dynamic is a supplementary relationship. That is, confidence in partner cooperation is the joint product of trust and control.

Although Argyris (1952) argued that the presence of control mechanisms implies distrust, most contemporary scholars agree that control mechanisms are not invariably destructive of trust in partner relationships (Das & Teng, 1998; Goold & Quinn, 1990; Sitkin, 1995). Because we are most interested in a specific type of organization, public schools, it is important to explain the conditions under which control and trust allow predictable teacher-parent cooperation, for example, to flourish. Scholars have suggested that organizational outcomes may differ based on the type of control used (Aulakh et al., 1997; Eisenhardt, 1985; Hoy & Sweetland, 2000; Kirsch, 1996; Ouchi, 1979). Thus, some argue that trust is only diminished when the type of control used is not appropriately matched with the organization's complexity, outcome uncertainty, or behavior observability (Kirsch, 1996). Or the type of control mechanism used (output, process, or social) has inherently specific consequences for trust as hypothesized by Aulakh and colleagues (1997).

Das and Teng (1998) provide a set of control concepts that we see as particularly useful for examining the relationship between groups in schools. They distinguish formal control from social control. The former they describe as employing "codified rules, goals, procedures, and regulations that specify desirable patterns of behavior" (p. 501). The latter they describe as using "organizational values, norms, and cultures to encourage desirable behavior" (p. 501). There is evidence that formal controls can produce distrust, especially if they are not appropriate to the cooperative task (Sitkin & Stickel, 1996). In contrast, social control, in the form of soft control mechanisms such as influence and persuasion, is consistent with confidence in a partner's competence and judgment, laying a foundation for trust (Larson, 1992). In addition to the theoretical argument explaining the supplementary nature of control and trust, explanations for the formation of trust suggest that cross-group boundary cooperation processes that embed soft social control mechanisms are nearly identical to the processes that spawn collective trust (Das & Teng, 1998; Larson, 1992).

Thus, we take the position, based on the theoretical work of Das and Teng (1998), that successful partnerships between organizational groups are the joint product of control and trust as supplementary; that is, control and trust additively contribute to productive and reciprocal cooperation between an organization's various groups. However, because schools are organizations having relatively low outcome measurability and task programmability, the appropriate supplementary control mechanisms for the enhancement of cooperation between groups should be primarily soft, built on communication and expressed as influence and persuasion rather than prescription.

Control processes can enhance behavioral predictability (Leifer & Mills, 1996), supplementing collective trust in the facilitation of cooperation. But in addition, the very processes that make up social or soft control simultaneously provide opportunities for the social construction of participating group beliefs about the trustworthiness of the cooperating group. Thus, in the cooperation between a school's groups, social control serves first to provide straightforward predictability, by its very nature. The processes of social control are often the same processes involved in the formation of collective trust, thereby creating a second and less direct enhancement of trust.

Control and trust, then, are not mere alternatives substituting for each other at the whim of organizational leaders seeking predictability and cooperation. There are many ways to conceptualize control, but one useful way is to distinguish between impersonal and personal control mechanisms. Impersonal control mechanisms include such things as rules, policies, laws, procedures, and hierarchy, to mention some. They are "impersonal" in the sense that they regularize behavior without face-to-face contact. They make expectations explicit and performance public. In the extreme case, their use would seem to eliminate nearly all uncertainty, uncooperative action, and risk. At the same time, as Gouldner (1954) points out, these prescriptions may prove dysfunctional, eliciting the minimum expected level of cooperation and predictability.

Personal control mechanisms include face-to-face control through supervision, management, performance monitoring, and work evaluation. Both personal and impersonal control mechanisms are effective because of implicit or explicit sanctions that may be used to reward cooperation and punish uncooperative behavior. It is obvious how these manifestations of control make performance and cooperation more predictable. Quite different from control, the establishment of trust is another way to enhance the likelihood of cooperation.

THE VARIETIES AND IMPORTANCE
OF ORGANIZATIONAL CONTEXT

It is instructive to contrast contextual elements of our collective trust model across public and elite private schools to demonstrate the importance of context and its relationship to collective trust formation. Elite private schools tend to reduce uncertainty in their goal attainment by controlling inputs; that is, they tend to admit high-achieving children who have few or no special educational requirements and whose families hold high expectations for their academic achievement. This selective-admission approach produces what organizational scholars sometimes refer to as standardizing inputs.

In addition to demographic homogeneity, this narrowed band of admitted students generally shares social values, and thus cooperation is more predictable. Standard inputs permit standard process (in this case, the instructional system) and outcomes are usually predictable. Forsyth and colleagues (2006) found examples of schools that were badly organized with poor organizational climates and structures, yet whose academic performance was high because of the benefits provided by family affluence. Thus, by the single standard of academic performance, these schools were successful primarily because their standard inputs were homogeneously possessed of orientations and past experiences that ensured their high performance on standardized tests, despite the school's relative dysfunction.

In contrast, relatively few American public schools have admission criteria that result in a uniform, high socioeconomic clientele and dispositions predictive of academic success. In addition, public schools are legally bound to serve students with disabilities of all kinds, as well as non-English-speaking children. Public schools are exceptionally diverse in urban areas with respect to culture, race, and SES. Shared values are not as likely, nor are they presumed. This diversity produces high levels of potential conflict and misunderstanding among groups whose cooperation is essential for school success. To be successful, diverse inputs require a nonstandard process, and even then, the results are unlikely to be uniform or predictable.

Task context has implications for the formation of collective trust and organizational effectiveness. The contrast between public and elite private schools illustrates the importance of the task context. We situate schools in a typology of task contexts using the dimensions of task complexity and group interdependence (see Figure 7.1). Schools have task contexts that are relatively complex and require cooperation among interdependent groups.

Standardization

Organizations generally take in raw material, enact some process to change it, and then return the changed material to the environment. Thompson

Figure 7.1. Typology of task contexts.

Task Complexity

	Complex	Simple
Interdependent	1 Complex Task Context	2 Mixed Task Context (Interdependent and Simple)
Group Interdependence **Independent**	3 Mixed Task Context (Independent Complex)	4 Simple Task Context

(1967) sees long-linked technologies as those classic assembly line operations that take in standard raw material and use a set of routines or processes to produce a standardized product for return to the environment as output. Tin can manufacturing, for example, takes in rolls of fabricated metal sheeting, runs it through a mechanical shaping mill, and produces for shipment cans of nearly identical specification. At the other end of the spectrum from long-linked technologies are intensive technologies. They take in nonstandard raw material such as students; enact a variety of nonstandard processes to bring about change (such as instruction); and emit an altered, but far from standardized, product (educated students), all the while monitoring feedback garnered from the raw material itself during processing and adjusting the process accordingly. The latter intensive technologies are of course applied to schools metaphorically, but this conceptual analysis comes close to what we mean by complex tasks.

What goes on in organizations that use intensive technologies, like schools, is inimical to standardization. Students arrive with varying degrees of motivation, energy, acuity for abstract thinking, verbal skill, social skill, tactile skill, and background knowledge. Ideally, schools take students where they are and move them forward toward a set of social and educational goals. The process may involve some effort to "even out" learning across a student cohort, but inevitably the schools release into the environment students with different abilities and skills. Through this reasoning, we argue that the school's mission and goals require the achievement of complex tasks, whereas tin can manufacturers perform simple tasks. It all has to do with the possibility and appropriateness of standardization. Complexity is also increased when measurement is imprecise or difficult or the assessment of success or the quality of the enacted processes and outputs cannot be done credibly. All these sources of complexity tend to be problematic for schools.

Interdependence

The other criterion of interest for typing task context is group interdependence. *Interdependence* refers to the condition wherein the organization's success hinges on the efforts of two or more groups. Under conditions of interdependence, one group will want to predict the cooperation, expertise, and efficacy of another group because the other group's success is essential to the first group's success and ultimately that of the organization (Whitener, Brodt, Korsgaard, & Werner, 1998). The predictability of another group's work can often be enhanced by formal and informal contract, by organizational structures, by rules and regulations, or by other traditional control mechanisms such as supervision. These all have the purpose of standardizing work and thus making its outcomes predictable. But complex tasks do not standardize easily. Here enters trust and its importance in organizational life, especially the life of organizations performing complex tasks.

Thus, when we say schools are complex, we are calling attention to the fact that the school tasks require the flexible application of its technologies (for example, a variety of instructional techniques). In addition, the tasks are accomplished through active cooperation among interdependent role groups. The tasks of the schools would be significantly less complex if all children arrived at school performing at grade level in all subjects, backed up by supportive families with high expectations for their achievement, well fed, motivated, and so on. We know this is not the case, and therefore it makes little sense to design an education process that treats children as if it were.

The complexity of schooling is exacerbated by the difficulty of measuring accurately whether or not schools are succeeding in their task. Standardized tests help to some extent, but student performance on them is affected by many threats to their validity, including variation in test coaching, differences in test-taker experience, student reading and writing levels, motivation, family situation, culture, and literally hundreds of other issues. Answering questions about whether and how much a child has learned is like answering a complex health question such as (after extensive chemotherapy), Is a patient cancer free? It is not at all like answering a question such as, What does a child weigh? In the latter case, the answer, given an agreed upon metric, is accurate, objective, and easily reproducible. It is more like the former question in that it is difficult to attribute a test score gain or loss to the school, since there are many relevant contributors, many outside the school, that affect the academic performance of individual children, classes, and schools. The situation is made worse when we attempt to interpret "average" changes in scores across student cohorts.

Teacher performance is also a key variable in school success, one that is not easily examined in all but the grossest of categories. Teachers rightly object to the use of simplistic outcome measures related to student performance, when students are not equivalent across classes. Bureaucratic indicators of teacher performance based on rare and brief observations of teacher behavior by principals are certainly no better than standardized tests.

THE NEED FOR TRUST IN ORGANIZATIONS

We argue that a general understanding of the need for collective trust can be predicted from the typology of task context described above. In a simple task context (Type 4 in Figure 7.1), there is relatively little need for collective trust. Work is highly controlled by precise management-labor contracts that outline working conditions and responsibilities. Typically, detailed rules and procedures for work are well established, and they are often perceived as clearly necessary and acceptable to both management and workers. The quality and quantity of production are patently, and in many cases immediately, obvious, and the lines of responsibility for success are clear as well. Trust under these conditions is relatively unnecessary because there is little or no risk. Because relationships between primary groups, labor and management, are spelled out in contracts, policies, and procedures, and outcomes are objectively and accurately measurable, there is less importance for the groups to trust each other because there is relatively little uncertainty in the organization's process and performance measurement. Keep in mind that we are not arguing that trust under these conditions is undesirable, only that it is not as critical to goal achievement as it is in other task contexts.

The mixed types of task context (Types 2 and 3 in Figure 7.1) hypothetically require more collective trust to achieve their organizational goals than simple task contexts. Type 1, complex task context, is of course most important to this discussion. In schools the consequences of task complexity are everywhere apparent. Teachers are dependent on school administrators, especially principals, to provide safe, clean and orderly schoolwide environments in which teaching and learning are possible. Teachers rely on principals to provide resources, defend their interests with other groups like the school board and parents, coordinate and integrate the schoolwide instructional and curriculum systems, and so on. Without this support, the likelihood of teacher success would be minimal (Bryk & Schneider, 2002). On the other hand, the primary work of the school—teaching—goes on in many classrooms simultaneously. Principals depend on teachers' acting autonomously across the school, to design and deliver competent instruction that meets established learning objectives with diverse learners. Principals rely on teachers to motivate and instruct in such a way that students will meet or exceed learning expectations. If these tasks are not addressed in terms of the needs of learners, the principal and the school cannot succeed in its mission.

Teachers and parents also have an interdependent relationship (Bryk & Schneider, 2002). The work of the teacher as cited above is certainly dependent on the actions of the school's administrators, but this same work is also highly dependent on the behaviors and attitudes of parents. Without a parent culture that values education and holds high expectations for children and teachers, sustained learning is unlikely. Without parents who show interest in their children's school activities, provide children with study time and place, help children with their homework when necessary, and ensure their children's regular attendance, teachers are unlikely to succeed.

Reciprocally, few parents have the capacity, patience, time, or inclination to educate their own children. Parents who value education are most interested in their children's teachers because they know just how critical having competent and likeable teachers is to learning and the educational persistence and life chances of their children. Parents depend on effective teachers and principals.

Our model of collective trust formation does not suggest that task context is the only variable that influences the need or formation of trust; however, it certainly is an important one. Clearly both external context (the characteristics and conditions of the community) and internal context (the characteristics and conditions of the larger organization in which the group functions) also have important and discernable consequences for collective trust formation and school success.

In summary, the need for trust in organizations is determined by a number of conditions, but especially important are the complexity of the organization's primary task and the interdependence of groups whose efforts are essential to addressing the task (Costa, 2003). The more complex the task and the greater the interdependence of groups, the greater is the need for collective trust.

TRUST, CONTROL, AND LEADERSHIP

What do we know about complex task contexts and the roles that formal and informal control, leadership, and collective trust can play in them? We have described complex task contexts as those requiring cooperation among highly interdependent work groups, performing tasks that cannot be standardized, and involving processes and outcomes whose measurement is difficult. What are the implications of these conditions for trust, control, and leadership?

Control

The theory and research related to the use of organizational control to reduce uncertainty and increase cooperation has gradually clarified these relationships. While there continues to be disagreement (Argyris, 1952; Luhmann, 1979), it would appear that context in its various forms provides the answers as to whether and what kinds of control contribute to an organization's effectiveness.

First we consider formal control and its likely function in complex task environments. As explained earlier in the chapter, the purpose of formal control is to make behavior preferences and requirements explicit, thereby setting behavioral boundaries (Das & Teng, 1998). Formal control includes policies, procedures, rules, hierarchy, forms, direct supervision, and evaluation. Both the theoretical and empirical literature appears to support the argument that formal control mechanisms are effective when the primary task is programmable and outcomes are credibly measured (Eisenhardt, 1985; Ouchi, 1979). Das and Teng (1998), however, note that when formal controls are not suited to the task, they may be destructive of trust.

The purpose of informal control mechanisms in organizations is similar to that of formal control, but the mechanisms are quite distinct. Informal or social control focuses on norms as a way of influencing behavior (Das & Teng, 1998). Social control, by shaping and promoting common group norms, elicits appropriate behavior through soft approaches (Leifer & Mills, 1996). Examples of social control mechanisms include recruitment and selection, socialization, training, and leader persuasion. Social control, because it relies on norm formation, best fits a long-term view of organizations and change. As we mentioned earlier, there is evidence that social control and trust are related (Aulakh et al., 1997); in fact, there seems to be significant overlap in the ways that social control is implemented and trust is built (Das & Teng, 1998).

How trust works with control, predictability, and cooperation is quite complex. There are those who claim that the mere presence of control suggests the absence of trust (Argyris, 1952; Creed & Miles, 1996; Rousseau, Sitkin, Burt, & Camerer, 1998). On the other hand, Goold and Campbell (1987) and Goold and Quinn (1990) claim that control under the right circumstances can increase trust. Others claim that only formal control is at odds with trust or obviates its need (Bachmann, 2006). Still others argue that formal control increases the likelihood of trust (Sitkin, 1995) or that informal or social control increases trust (Das & Teng, 1998). What is most important is the recognition that trust does function quite differently from control mechanisms in enabling cooperation. Control constrains uncertainty, thereby promoting a predictable and secure environment in which cooperation can thrive; on the other hand, trust absorbs uncertainty, transforming it into risk (Bachmann, 2006). So trust does not constrain uncertainty; rather, it enables groups and individuals to cooperate, having accepted a certain amount of risk.

The general hypothesis that might be drawn from this work is that when the group's task is complex (not programmable, unable to be standardized, and with difficult-to-measure outcomes), social control appears to be more compatible with success because it can be supplemented with trust formation. When the group's task is simple (programmable, standardized process, easily measured and evaluated outcomes), then formal control may be quite effective. As Eisenhardt (1985) summarizes:

The task characteristics determine which control strategy is appropriate. The key insights of the organizational approach to control are: (1) the role of task characteristics, especially task programmability, in the choice of control strategy through impact on measurement costs and (2) social control as an alternative to control based upon performance evaluation. (p. 136)

Leadership

We move to leadership and its relationship to control and trust in work that is complex. Leadership may, of course, exhibit itself through the leader's efforts to control uncertainty and build trust. The complexity of the task environment constrains a leader's potential use (or at least effective use) of these tools.

The Dirks and Ferrin (2002) meta-analysis of research on subordinate trust confirms that trust in the leader is related to important organizational outcomes, including organization commitment, commitment to leader decisions, intent to leave the organization, organizational citizenship, and job performance. Clearly trust is important, and as we have argued, it is even more important when the task context is complex because controls that work in more programmable organizations may be ineffective or even counterproductive. Studying work teams, Costa (2003) found that task ambiguity and functional dependence were positively related to trust. One interpretation of this research is that we find trust where we find task ambiguity and interdependence because under this dual condition, trust provides an effective means to achieve cooperation. Trust is the glue that holds the organization together.

To summarize, when an organization is complex, the probable best means to achieve cooperation and predictability is for leaders to use social controls and trust building. That is, when the task context is complex, effective leaders will emphasize socialization to a common mission and goals, preferring soft means such as persuasion to shape culture, and for the most part, avoid forms of control based on unnecessary behavioral constraint. Leaders will build trust by acting in ways that reveal them as trustworthy to others in the organization. That is, they will act in ways consistent with the criteria for judging trustworthiness: benevolence, honesty, openness, reliability, and competence.

Strategies for enhancing cooperation and predictability in complex organizations take time to implement. This fact is often at odds with the popular belief that accountability and effectiveness is achieved only through hard controls and outcome measurement. We turn next to the specific case of how control, collective trust, and leadership can function together in public schools to produce effective achievement of their goals.

LEADERSHIP AND TRUST IN SCHOOLS: A MODEL OF SOURCES

We have portrayed the tasks that produce learning and that make up the core technology of public education as complex. To succeed, the processes of schooling (curriculum design, instruction, assessment, etc.) must be adjusted to differences among individual learners, classes, grades, and schools. These same processes are also subject to constant and radical revision or replacement as a result of administrator succession, fad, political upheaval, dictates of charitable foundations, and other outside pressures (Miller, 2004). With a long history of unexplained and often unsuccessful changes, public confidence in the technical knowledge related to teaching and learning (pedagogy) is understandably low. Credible approaches to evaluating teacher performance are uncertain, time consuming, costly, and hence, rarely used effectively.

The evaluation of student performance is likewise surrounded by controversy and skepticism. Cultural, linguistic, class, and value diversity in communities has dampened the cooperation between parents and schools (Webber, 2002). These conditions also add complexity to the school's task. Efforts to reform schools, especially those emerging from business-inspired solutions, have often emphasized formal control as a means to program the education function and achieve predictably high levels of universal student achievement. Our work in collective trust and the general organizational-trust literature suggest that this approach is unlikely to succeed.

Complex tasks make trust and its consequence, voluntary cooperation, necessary because complex work is not easily controlled by bureaucratic rules (which simplify choices) and hierarchy (which monitors and emphasizes work outcomes and process). In contrast, process flexibility permits those performing complex tasks to adjust their actions to the immediate evolving task and context, consistent with their professional expertise and experience. Bureaucratic and other formal controls can constrain the ability of organizations and those who work in them to respond to constant change and diversity of conditions. In highly bureaucratized schools, for example, the instructional system rests on the assumption that all learners are alike. Moreover, high degrees of centralization and formalization deter the emergence of trustworthy behaviors such as delegation and open communication (Creed & Miles, 1996).

Before discussing the sources of principal leadership, we should note that the focus of this discussion is the relationship of the principal to one of the primary groups whose cooperation is necessary to achieve predictable success of schools, the faculty. The decision to focus on teacher-principal cooperation is based on the critical importance of that cooperation and also the traditional employer-employee relationship that exists between

principals and teachers. The relationship between other role groups important to the school (parents and students) and principal leadership requires
a separate analysis, one that takes into account the characteristics of those
groups and the specific basis for those relationships.

Our theory of collective trust and our examination of research on control
and trust allow us to offer a general model of school leadership directed at producing predictability and effective results. Like any general model, it includes
the silent caution "all things being equal," which of course they never are. That
is, we argue that the weight of the evidence suggests this is an optimal approach
to school leadership, assuming as we do that schools have relatively complex
tasks. Essential to our theory are the concepts of internal organizational context
and external context (introduced in Chapter 2), which, among other things, as-
sure us that all things are not equal in any particular case.

Our model of school leadership is based on the utility of control mechanisms and trust as guarantors of predictable cooperation among groups
and, ultimately, predictable results. The model is based on three sources of
principal leadership: formal control, informal control, and collective trust.
Figure 7.2 depicts graphically the essential elements. Each of these leadership sources will be discussed in turn.

Formal Control and School Leadership

Is formal control by the principal a likely effective means of eliciting cooperation and predictable goal-related behavior of teachers? Formal control
mechanisms, such as centralization (hierarchy) and formalization (rules and
policies), have been a source of predictability and an essential part of social

Figure 7.2. Model of the sources of principal leadership.

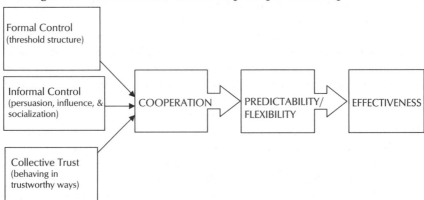

organization throughout the history of human cooperation. The modern study of organizations, however, has found formal control somewhat problematic. Weber's (1947) work initiated a debate related to expertise rather than tradition as a source of leader authority. This conceptual shift in understanding the sources of authority for leadership accompanied the historical shift from a primarily agrarian society to an industrial and bureaucratic one based, not on family, but on larger, specialized forms of organization.

Sociologist Robert Merton (1952), building on Weber's ideal type of bureaucracy, developed the argument that the essential mechanisms of bureaucracy could as easily be dysfunctional as functional. Merton's student Alvin Gouldner (1954) demonstrated in his classic study of industrial bureaucracy exactly how rules designed to control and guide the work of employees could easily destroy worker initiative and commitment, providing, as they do, management's expectations about minimal acceptable performance. Thus formal structures for guaranteeing cooperation seem to be less useful in organizations that depend on expertise and its application to complex work.

It could be asked why formal control should be included as a resource for school leadership when there is evidence that it is destructive of collective trust formation—which, we have argued, is essential for leadership of complex organizations like schools. The truth is, scholars disagree about whether formal control destroys trust or is necessary for trust, and there is some interesting empirical evidence related to formal control in the education literature. It is likely that Bachmann's (2003) observation about personal trust in organizations is true for groups as well: "Where the structural inventory of the organization is fuzzy and unreliable, it is likely that individual actors will be less inclined to invest trust in their relationships with each other" (p. 62). That is, the absence of clear, formal structure can undermine trust formation.

Consistent with this observation, Hoy and Sweetland (2000, 2001) found, in multiple school studies, that formalization (use of rules and policies) and centralization (concentration of power in pyramidal hierarchy) are not always detrimental to school success. When regarded by teachers as supportive of their work, rules and hierarchy actually increased teacher trust of the principal (see also Forsyth et al., 2006). Thus those bureaucratic structures teachers regard as enabling their work rather than hindering it appear compatible with trust.

We argue, then, that enabling formalization and centralization, while clearly formal control mechanisms, are likely to facilitate cooperation, trust, and ultimately predictability and goal accomplishment in schools. Scholars have asserted that a certain amount of formal control increases the perception that another person or group will cooperate (Bachmann, 2006; Luhmann, 1979). It is likely that enabling rules and hierarchy provide a comfort threshold for collective trust formation in schools. Enabling structures do not restrict the capacity of, for example, teacher flexibility to meet student needs. In this case formal control is a source of principal leadership, which promotes cooperation and trust rather than undermining them.

Informal Control and School Leadership

Is informal control an appropriate and effective source of principal leadership? Informal control, also called social control, is an indirect way of eliciting cooperation and predictable results in an organization (Das & Teng, 1998). Informal control does not restrict behavior using rules and other organizational structures. Rather, where there is informal control, individuals and groups choose to act in ways that are cooperative and consistent with the organizational mission as a result of genuinely "shared goals, values and norms" (Das & Teng, 1998, p. 502). Organizational theorists talk about the ways leaders can exert informal control through soft measures including leader influence, persuasion, vision building, and professional development, all techniques that socialize individuals and groups to shared beliefs, norms, and values.

Teachers need flexibility and discretion in sculpting instruction to fit the needs of learners (Darling-Hammond & Goodwin, 1993; Hallinger, 1992; Maeroff, 1988; Schlechty, 1990; Sykes, 1990). It seems clear that informal control is quite compatible with the flexibility needed to perform complex tasks. That is, in doing their work, groups and individuals are not required to do something in a particular way. Instead, sharing an understanding of the organization's objectives and a common set of norms, they make choices and behave in ways that are consistent with a shared set of goals and objectives, as modified by relevant conditions and context.

In brief, those leader behaviors and activities that are directed to enhancing social control are often the same behaviors that elicit collective trust. Both collective trust, as we noted in Chapter 2, and social control emerge out of repeated social exchange and communication. The more people interact, the more alike they become in their beliefs, attitudes, and eventually their behaviors. Or, as Schein (2004) would say, they are creating an organizational culture through the recognition of shared successes.

In schools, clearly principals can use formal controls in an effort to create compliance and predictability of teacher behavior. Indeed, the use of formal controls is alluring because, rules, for example, are quickly enacted and precise in their intended effects. But while rules are often effective at bringing about immediate compliant behavior, their long-term effects are often counterproductive in complex organizations like schools because they constrain choices to a few anticipated categories and sets of circumstances. Informal control, in contrast, is a more effective long-term strategy and an enabler of choice, but its dependence on the formation of norms and culture make its implementation a continuous and long-term project.

So what do we know about how informal control might be used in schools to enhance predictable success? It has to do with shared goals, values, and norms. A good deal of contemporary business literature counsels the rushed and artificial establishment of an organization's vision, mission, and core values, often through a superficial set of activities orchestrated by consultants in a brief workshop. But a common vision, mission, and set of core values are distilled through genuine and repeated interaction over time. The principal and other school leaders' roles here are more likely those of influence and persuasion, shaping vision and mission dialectically in the context of the organization's daily work. Nurtured in this way, school visions are not mere placards displayed in the foyers of buildings, but, rather, espoused subtly and consistently in the relationships and behaviors of the school's teachers and leaders.

Early in the history of modern scholarship, efforts to define leadership prominently included the exercise of influence and persuasion. In his famous *Handbook of Leadership*, Stogdill (1974) cites Nash (1929), Tead (1935), and a host of others who define leadership essentially as influence. In the same volume, Stogdill cites early scholars (e.g. Cleeton & Mason, 1934; Copeland, 1944; Koontz & O'Donnell, 1955) who are equally convinced that leadership is in fact a form of persuasion. In large part, we think that shared goals, values, and norms emerge inductively from myriad acts of influence and persuasion contained in the relationships, behaviors, and words of school leaders. This understanding is consistent with the role that informal control plays in shaping predictable school success.

Hoy and Smith (2007), building on the work of Cialdini (2001), have outlined 10 principles of persuasion and influence derived from the literature, which might serve as basic strategies in the school leader's repertoire for enacting informal control. Interestingly, these strategies overlap significantly with behaviors that demonstrate leader trustworthiness and ultimately elicit collective trust. They are also consistent with transformational leadership (Leithwood & Jantzi, 2000; Podsakoff, MacKenzie, & Bommer, 1996) and servant leadership (Joseph & Winston, 2005; Russell, 2001).

Collective Trust and School Leadership

What is the role of collective trust as a source of principal leadership? In the general organizational literature, a significant amount of research has been done on leadership and trust. Dirks and Ferrin (2002) completed a rigorous meta-analysis of 3 decades of research related to trust in leadership. The analysis demonstrates that trust in leadership has multiple significant and positive outcomes, including its ability to elicit from employees altruism, civic virtue, conscientiousness, courtesy, organizational commitment, job satisfaction, belief in information provided by the leader, and commitment to decisions. These findings concur with Tyler and Degoey's (1996) assertion that "attributions about trustworthiness are central to the willingness to accept decisions" of leaders (p. 335). Dirks and Skarlicki (2004) similarly concluded after reviewing three recent studies that "trust is related to 'bottom-line' effects in terms of group and organizational performance" (p. 26). It should be kept in mind that this research is based on interpersonal trust between leaders and individual employees.

There is very little research on collective trust outside education (McEvily, Weber, Bicchieri & Ho, 2006). Currall and Inkpen (2006), exploring the possible configurations of trust, do portray collective trust theoretically as a situation where the trustor is a group and the trustee or referent is a group or individual, but empirical studies of group trust in the organizational literature outside of education are rare.

In education, however, there is a long history of studying the relationship between the faculty trust in the principal and its positive consequences. As presented in Chapter 5, the collective trust of teachers for the principal is positively related to faculty trust in colleagues and in the school system. Faculty trust in the principal is also related to structural features of the school, namely enabling rather than hindering rules and centralized control. Faculty trust is associated with teacher perceptions of increased influence on school decisions. Collective faculty trust of the principal is also related to positive organizational climate and health of the school, student identification with the school, collective teacher efficacy (teacher confidence that the faculty can be successful with these students), and the principal's transactional leadership and authenticity.

Faculty trust in principal is consistent with positive cultural features of a school and structures perceived as enabling. Louis (2007) notes that faculty trust in the principal expands the zone of acceptance for principal decisions. That is, when teachers trust the principal, they are more likely to embrace decisions made by the principal and less likely to subject the day-to-day choices of the school's leaders to suspicious scrutiny. Perhaps contrary to intuition, trust appears to expand the principal's control over school outcomes.

SUMMARY

Refer to our model of the sources of principal leadership (Figure 7.2). Cooperative behavior of teachers is portrayed as the product of three leadership sources. The principal will rely on these sources unequally, depending on context. First and most important, we argue, the principal will elicit and rely on faculty trust in the principal by behaving in trustworthy ways (being benevolent, reliable, competent, honest, and open). Second, the principal will use informal and soft control to stoke the positive feelings and attitudes of teachers through influence, persuasion, and championing the school vision and goals. Finally, the principal will draw on the comfort provided by a threshold of minimal rules, policies, and procedures that teachers at the school regard as enabling their work.

We have argued, and demonstrated, that in response to these three sources of principal leadership, teachers will cooperate, acting predictably, yet flexibly, in consonance with the commonly shaped and embraced goals of the school. Ultimately, of course, this cooperation is to achieve school effectiveness, learning, and development for all students.

CHAPTER 8

Collective Trust as a Condition of Social Capital and Academic Optimism

Social capital is an instantiated informal norm that promotes cooperation between two or more individuals. The norms that constitute social capital can range from a norm of reciprocity between two friends . . . to complex and elaborately articulated doctrines like Christianity or Confucianism.

—Francis Fukuyama, *Trust*

In this chapter we compare and contrast two theoretical approaches to social action and examine the role that collective trust plays in each. The first approach, social capital theory, explains social action at nearly all levels of human society, from national governments to the local bridge club. It describes the potential emergence of cooperative social action in terms of social norms and social structures. In contrast, academic optimism theory, introduced in Chapter 6, reveals the potential effectiveness (dependent on cooperation) of educational organizations in terms of collective forms of trust, efficacy, and academic focus. The point of interest is that both these conceptual perspectives on social action have at their cores a form of collective trust, making our case for the importance of trust, not only for society, but quite specifically for schools.

SOCIAL ACTION

Individuals act purposively—that is, individual actions are motivated by their anticipated consequences—however, purpose cannot be attributed to systems. Instead, actions of systems are an emergent consequence of the interdependent actions of the human actors who constitute the system. In other words, system behavior is at times appropriately conceived of as being simply a system of actors whose actions are interdependent. With Coleman (1990), we define social action as system-level behavior, such as the collective behavior of groups, organizations, or social movements, which emerges out of the combined purposive actions of individuals (Coleman, 1986).

Social Action in Schools

Social action in schools is embodied in successful school reform, professional learning communities, and organizational learning. To illustrate, school reforms often fail during implementation if the collective force of teachers and parents is not behind the purpose of the reform (Berman & McLaughlin, 1975; Borman, Hewes, Overman, & Brown, 2003; Blakely, et al., 1987). Professional learning communities are more myth than reality if teachers operate independently and in isolation from one another (Hord, 1997). And organizational learning depends on school members embracing common goals and working collectively to produce a common good (Senge et al., 2000).

It is one thing to identify the preceding phenomena as outcomes of social action in schools and quite another to explain how school-level phenomena emerge. This latter task has eluded many social theorists. Coleman (1986) explains that a theory of action is a functional theory at the individual level, but not at the systems level. He elaborates:

> Purpose and goal directedness are useful in theory construction, but not if they characterize the entity or system whose behavior is to be explained. They must instead characterize elements of the system, which in the case of sociology can be regarded as actors in the system, either actors or corporate actors. The central theoretical problems then come to be two: how the purposive actions of the actors combine to bring about system-level behavior, and how those purposive actions are in turn shaped by the constraints that result from the behavior of the system. (p. 1312)

Our work and analyses are primarily at the collective or system level; hence we are also confronted with the problem of making the transition from the micro (individual) level to the macro (system) level; that is, from purposive action of individuals to the functioning of the social system as a whole. In this chapter, social action refers to system action, not individual behavior.

The Micro-Macro Dilemma

Explanations of social action in schools must overcome the micro-macro problem that is associated with making school-level generalizations based on individual data. Conceptual and analytical methods to examine the movement from individual to system-level actions tend to capture either individual patterns of behavior at the expense of organizational-level consequences or group outcomes at the expense of individual behavior (Coleman, 1986). Our use of social capital and academic optimism theories to understand school-level behavior addresses this dilemma by specifying school norms as conditions that mediate purposive individual behavior and social action.

We argue that social action in schools is dependent on two types of relational connection: (1) social ties that unite individuals within schools groups and (2) relational bridges that link interdependent groups to a common vision. These two types of relationships can facilitate normative conditions that regulate individual and group behavior. Figure 8.1 is a simple model of the micro-macro transition whereby individual behavior leads to norms in schools and norms in schools lead to social action at the school level. The individual-to-norm-to-social-action relationship is not unique to schools; in fact, this triadic relationship is found in most social systems (Coleman, 1990).

When social relationships within school groups and across role boundaries are strong, normative conditions become the antecedents of both individual and group behavior. Norms mediate individual behavior and system behavior, correcting for the aggregation problem (Coleman, 1986, 1990) associated with making inferences about groups from individual behavior (Hox, 2002). Inferences based on group norms, as opposed to individual behavior, reflect the shared orientations of group members.

Collective trust is a group norm that mediates individual behavior and the systemic actions of a school community. Its capacity to influence both individual actions and system behavior comes from its mediating effect on other social conditions. Dirks and Ferrin (2001) argue that "instead of proposing that trust directly results in desirable outcomes . . . trust provides the conditions under which certain outcomes, such as cooperation and higher performance, are likely to occur" (p. 450). This is consistent with Cummings and Bromiley's (1996) claim that trust affects social processes and social structures of organizations.

Figure 8.1. Relationship between individual behavior and social action in schools.

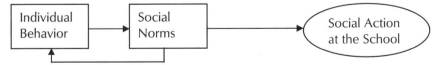

Some forms of collective trust in schools, such as faculty trust in clients, influence school performance directly (Goddard & Tschannen-Moran, 2001; Hoy, 2004), but an environment of trust also has indirect effects on school performance by lessening the dependence on hindering control mechanisms (Forsyth et al., 2006). Collective trust, as an alternative to social control, spawns robust normative conditions like social capital and academic optimism that in turn lead to system-level behaviors associated with high performing schools. The nature of the relationship between collective trust, social capital, and academic optimism, as illustrated in Figure 8.2, has implications for school effectiveness. We turn to these relationships next.

COLLECTIVE TRUST AND SOCIAL CAPITAL

The concept of social capital is well established in sociology and economics, and more recently educational scholars have studied the phenomenon as well (Forsyth & Adams, 2004; Goddard, 2003; Uekawa, Aladjem, & Zhang, 2005). Yet there is significant disagreement over the theoretical properties of social capital (see Lin, 1999; Woolcock, 1998). Our objective is not to enter this debate; instead, it is to illustrate the relationship between collective trust and the formation of social capital in schools.

We begin with a definition of *social capital* that incorporates the theoretical elements described by Loury (1977), Coleman, (1986, 1990), Bourdeau (1985), Putnam (2000), and other scholars: social capital is a set of "resources embedded in a social structure which are accessed and/or mobilized in purposive actions" (Lin, 1999, p. 35). Resources embedded in interpersonal relationships emerge from social ties that connect individuals to opportunities (Granovetter, 1985). A similar benefit results from relationships that connect schools to other organizations (Sheldon, 2002). To

Figure 8.2. The relationship among individual behavior, collective trust, and norms of social capital and academic optimism.

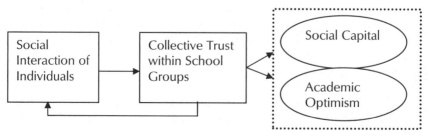

illustrate, a school's relationship with a local foundation can provide funding for specialized programs that address specific needs of individual students. As beneficial as external partnerships can be for schools, these are not the type of connections that lead to social action within schools.

Situating Social Capital in Schools

To understand how collective trust shapes social capital and social action, it is necessary to first specify the type of social capital that we believe is fundamental for schools. As previously noted, one view of social capital defines relationships that bridge the space between schools and external organizations, such as university-school partnerships, as functional resources for schools (Portes, 1998). The expanding social and emotional needs of students make cooperation with external agencies an attractive resource for schools. But what effect, if any, do these relationships have on the internal social networks of schools? The internal social network of schools is the nucleus of social action at the school level.

School-community partnerships can expand access to resources and opportunities for public schools, but the effects of these collaborations are conditioned on the degree of social cohesion within the school itself. Social capital within schools grows out interdependent relationships that align with the shared expectations and responsibilities of school groups. Collaborations with external partners can provide access to additional networks, but the social resources needed for effective teaching and learning are found in the interactions among teachers, parents, students, and administrators. System-level behavior is not a by-product of services supplied through external partners; it is a function of a robust social network and supportive norms that make cooperative relationships among school members and school role groups possible.

COOPERATIVE RELATIONSHIPS. Our belief that social ties among school members are more valuable for school effectiveness does not imply that we view collaboration with external organizations as unimportant. To the contrary, we view collaboration as vital. Partnerships are necessary for schools, but their effectiveness depends on the strength of cooperative relationships among school members. Internal connections determine the degree to which resources and opportunities provided through external collaborations can be diffused within schools. Ultimately, the potential of partnerships to meet the needs of the school community is dependent on the connectedness of school members.

Evidence from major lines of inquiry in education, such as parent involvement, school community, transformational leadership, and instructional leadership, support our claim that social capital within schools inheres in cooperative relationships among members of the school community. Effective parent involvement depends on school-family relationships that make shared responsibility for the learning and development of children normative (Epstein, 2001; Sheldon, 2002). Similarly, in reference to school community, Bryk and Driscoll (1988) write, "Within the school community, adults are linked to one another by a common mission and by a network of supportive personal relations" (p. 4).

Transformational leadership also is based on relational processes centered on building a vision, stimulating inquiry, providing support, fostering decisional influence, and valuing high expectations (Leithwood & Jantzi, 2000). Instructional leadership requires frequent communication and regular interactions between principals and teachers as well as among teachers (Quinn, 2002). Each of the above constructs is often extolled as a property of effective schools, and the shared feature across them is their dependence on quality social relationships among school actors.

Schools can benefit from cooperation across role boundaries and external partnerships, but social ties that connect the school with other organizations in the community do not necessarily change the internal social dynamics of schools, nor are they always aligned with the goals or needs of the school. Cohesion among members of the school community is the foundation for social action. Harnessing the power of relationships to reform schools involves supporting cooperative interactions within school social networks.

RELATIONAL GAPS IN SCHOOLS. Some scholars (Burt, 2000; Lin, 1999) view relational gaps positively. We are skeptical that this is the case for schools where gaps can be seen to hinder the flow of information to individuals, reduce the frequency of reciprocal behavior across role groups, and limit the cohesiveness of a school community; all such outcomes are detrimental to school-level social action.

The agency inherent in cooperative relationships within schools emerges from what Portes (1998) called *bounded solidarity*. Effective schools are often characterized as ones where teachers, administrators, parents, and students are bound together by a shared vision, shared responsibilities, and common expectations (Edmonds, 1979; Hallinger & Murphy, 1986). Where social interactions are fragmented, relational gaps can dilute the social action of school members. Take, for example, schools where parent attendance at school events is minimal or schools where teachers have little contact and limited conversations about teaching and learning. In the first example, parents and teachers operate independently of each other, and in the second, instructional practice lacks a cohesive focus. Cooperative action is infrequent and episodic when relational gaps exist in school social networks.

Not all social structures in schools foster effective interactions across school groups. However, social structures characterized by high collective trust (Adams & Forsyth, 2007a, 2007b; Forsyth et al., 2006; Tschannen-Moran, 2001) mediate effective school performance by facilitating cooperative interactions and minimizing relational gaps. Efforts to convert the natural social structures of schools into sources of social action depend on the establishment of collective trust within school groups. Collective trust is both a property of social capital (Coleman, 1986, 1990; Fukuyama, 1996; Putnam, 2000) and a norm that enables the formation of other requisite conditions of social capital, including reciprocity and cohesion.

Collective Trust and Reciprocity

The norm of reciprocity is exemplified by Putnam's (2000) illustration of the construct, "I'll do this for you now . . . confident that down the road you or someone else will return the favor" (p. 134). Underlying reciprocal behavior are social obligations and expectations (Coleman, 1990). In Putnam's example, the function of obligation and expectation is easy to detect. It is similar to a quid pro quo: Person A does something for person B, obligating B to do something for A at a later date. If A does not expect reciprocation from B (in other words does not trust B), A is unlikely to help B in the first place.

This example is sensible in a social setting where specific roles and responsibilities are not defined or in a contractual arrangement in which outcomes are controlled through instrumental means. But in schools, roles and responsibilities are indeed defined, making reciprocal action less dependent on returning favors and more dependent on fulfilling the responsibilities associated with one's role. In the relationship between teachers and parents, for example, teachers are expected to carry out their obligations and fulfill their responsibilities for promoting student learning. Parents also have socially defined obligations and responsibilities related to student learning. When both teachers and parents behave according to their mutual expectations, reciprocity is visible in their cooperative actions.

If, in a contrasting example, one role group is perceived as consistently neglecting its responsibilities, while the other group fulfills its responsibilities, the potential of the social network to produce social action is diminished. Collective trust is the missing social condition in this case. Without trust, social interactions are often fragmented and episodic, two characteristics injurious to social action. Reciprocity in all social systems, not just schools, hinges on trust (Coleman, 1986, 1990; Putnam, 2000).

EMPIRICAL EVIDENCE. Because empirical evidence on the relationship between collective trust and reciprocity is scarce, we look to the effects of trust on observable factors in reciprocal behavior. First, from the organizational literature we find that trust directly produces positive attitudes, cooperation, risking taking, and better team processes (Dirks & Ferrin, 2001). Trust also mediates other psychosocial states and behavior. Dirks (1999) found that in groups with high levels of trust, group-member motivation was directed toward collective goals, as opposed to group members being motivated by individual self-interest. Kimmel and colleagues (1980) found that trust mediated the relationship between high aspiration levels and information exchange. In particular, the presence of trust among group members led to stronger aspirations and more frequent and transparent exchanges. In low-trust groups, aspiration levels and information exchanges both depreciated; in high-trust groups reciprocal behavior was enhanced.

Similar findings appear in the educational literature. Forsyth et al. (2006) examined the effects of trust on school consequences and found that trust produced structures that facilitated reciprocal action as well as beliefs, such as collective teacher efficacy, that underlie such behavior. Adams and Forsyth (2009b) found a positive relationship between parent trust in the school and faculty trust in clients, suggesting that the collective action of teachers has consequences for the collective behavior of parents and vice versa. A norm of reciprocal trust between school role groups was necessary for cooperative action to emerge.

SCHOOL DESIGN AND RECIPROCITY. School designs that enable social action support reciprocal interactions among school members and encourage the open and regular exchange of ideas and practices. Creating opportunities to examine teaching and learning promotes collaborative inquiry (Wagner, 1998, 2001), cooperation (Fullan, 2005) and teacher leadership (Silins & Mulford, 2004). These social mechanisms are supported by trust and leveraged for social action. Schools that have transformed traditional structures to become more collaborative and open have done so with a culture of professional behavior that emerges from positive, reciprocal actions among the faculty (Rowan, 1990). This professional behavior, as described by Tschannen-Moran (2009), is sustained by a faculty's shared understanding that "their colleagues take their work seriously, demonstrate a high level of commitment, and go beyond minimum expectations to meet the needs of students" (p. 232).

School designs supportive of professional cultures are able to balance formal control with teacher autonomy and creativity. Organizational structures, such as school size or instructional roles, are often the target of reform strategies, but structural manipulation by itself is insufficient to create a culture of professional behavior that supports social action. As Tschannen-Moran (2009) found, collective trust is also needed. Faculty trust in colleagues enables teachers to teach and act in ways that reinforce their obligations and responsibilities to student learning.

Examples of collaborative and professional behavior abound in schools, but effective system-level behavior depends on a pervasive pattern of collaborative and professional interactions among faculty, parent, student, and administrator groups. Isolated cases of collaboration are not enough to transform schools. The collective nature of behavior is what has the power to produce the most good in schools, not episodic examples of exemplary practice. Certainly a healthy reciprocal relationship between a teacher and a parent benefits the child, but positive outcomes at the school level depend on a consistent pattern of reciprocal action between teachers and parents that benefit all students. School designs can enable or hinder cooperative action depending on the consonance between structures and norms (Hoy & Sweetland, 2001).

In schools, collective trust makes social action possible because it helps to sustain the effective performance of all parts of a system. As mentioned in Chapter 1, solidarity among different parts of a system is a criterion of organizational effectiveness (Parsons, 1960). Effective systems simultaneously maintain group solidarity as they meet individual needs. Balancing the needs of the system against the needs of its parts is the role of leaders (Knoop, 2007). Such leadership starts by building a culture of trust (Bryk & Schneider, 2002; Kochanic, 2005; Tschannen-Moran, 2004).

Collective Trust and Network Cohesion

Another property of social capital has to do with the density or closure of relationships within the social network (Bourdieu, 1986; Coleman, 1990; Putnam, 1995). Coleman (1990) argues that closure (the direction and frequency of interactions in a relational network) adds value to a social network by facilitating group norms, but other social network theorists caution against closed networks for their potential exclusivity (Burt, 2000; Lin, 1999). The value of a closed network should be considered within the context of the particular social system (Lin, 1999). School contexts, as described in Chapter 2, consist of interdependent groups and complex processes. Closure within groups in school settings, where cooperation across group boundaries is essential, can impede student learning by reinforcing role divisions within the school community and limiting social action. Strong social bonds can improve the density of relationships within a school group, but social bridges across groups are needed to coalesce school actors around a common purpose. In the network vernacular, social bonds and bridges (Jordan, 2006) are two types of relational connections than can minimize isolation in schools and make the work of teaching and learning a collective responsibility.

We argue that, instead of closure, the strength of social ties lies in their ability to galvanize a group of individuals around a common set of beliefs. The degree to which a social network is connected and inclusive depends on the level of agreement among members (Forrest & Kearns, 2001). We believe that network cohesion is a better specification for social capital in schools than closure because cohesion accounts for the thoughts and feelings of parents, teachers, and students that undergird their purposive behavior. Whereas closure defines the direction and frequency of interactions, cohesion captures the social norms that make individuals feel like they belong to the school community. A sense of belonging that is shared among school members is a potent motive of social action.

Forrest and Kearns (2001) argue that common values, social order, and social solidarity are domains of social cohesion, and Friedkin (2004) defines social cohesion as positive attitudes, behaviors, and interactions that reinforce group attachments. The examples of social action provided at the beginning of the chapter support the belief that system-level behavior is a product of relationships that promote a visceral attachment to the school. Because the normative environment mediates individual behavior and social action, feelings of belonging and identification are important for collective action.

EMPIRICAL EVIDENCE. The relationship between collective trust and cohesion is best documented through the qualitative accounts of social capital building provided by Putnam and Feldstein (2003). They studied 12 communities throughout the United States to take stock of mechanisms that drive the creation of social capital. Of importance in their work is the distinction between bonding and bridging mechanisms, two concepts introduced earlier. As they discovered, trust brings individuals together within a social system by forming intragroup bonds; trust links a social system to other social networks through intergroup bridges. Extrapolating their findings to schools, trust can form bonds that unite individuals within school role groups and relational bridges that form connections between groups. Together, these two types of relational ties create social capital within schools.

Social bonds and bridges need to be balanced to foster cooperation between school groups. Many school practices centered on collaboration attempt to create relational bonds or bridges, but not both. As our theory of collective trust suggests, a shared understanding among members within groups (i.e., social bonds) is a precondition for establishing sustainable social connections across groups. Bridges connecting different school groups are ineffective if groups are not bound together by a shared understanding, a critical element of social action. Similarly, strong bonds within school groups, without bridges among groups, limit individual and groups access to additional resources and opportunities.

Parent-involvement strategies are a classic example of how establishing strong social connections between parents and schools is incongruent with network theory. The problem is greatest in low-income communities where Auerbach (2007) and others (Lopez, 2001; Prins & Toso, 2008) note that school-based parent-involvement models are misaligned with the needs of low-income families. School-based models primarily attempt to develop social bridges between teachers and parents before assessing the level of social cohesion among parents. Without social cohesion social action is improbable.

The problem with school-based parent involvement approaches has to do with the variability of parent role construction (Auerbach, 2007; Hoover-Dempsey & Sandler, 1995, 1997). Parents who view their role as the primary educator of their child are more likely to participate in school-based involvement activities (e.g., parent-teacher organizations, parent-teacher conferences, and back-to-school nights). In contrast, parents who do not perceive themselves as the primary educator are less likely to engage in school-based activities. A dense parent network that has established common values, a social order, and social solidarity (Forrest & Kearns, 2001) is more persuasive for the latter group of parents than school-based involvement activities.

Evidence from the Comer Development Program supports the importance of developing social cohesion among parents. Program evaluators found that parent involvement on the parent team, in the school-planning process, and on the student and staff support team increased through meetings being held in neighborhood and community centers, parent volunteers being used to connect with other parents, and carpools being formed to and from school events (Comer, 1996). Each of these activities increased the level of social cohesion within the parent group, creating a foundation for stronger social action among parents and teachers.

Social Capital Summary

Collective trust emerges from the shared understanding among individuals within groups and facilitates cooperative relationships across groups. Trust enables cohesion to form through its effects on interactions and the flow of communication within all structures of the relational network. If trust exists among colleagues in organizations or among individuals in a social system, the exchange of information tends to be open and frequent (Coleman, 1990; Grootaert & Van Bastelaer, 2002; Lin, 2001). Not only is communication flow improved when trust is present within a social network, but trust is also likely to increase a sense of psychological safety among individual members of the social network (Edmondson, 2004). In contrast, distrust leads to the antithesis of psychological safety—suspicion (Deutsch, 1958). The effects of trust on other indicators of a cohesive network include team satisfaction and commitment (Costa, Roe, & Taillieu, 2001).

In short, collective trust is a core resource for school improvement (Bryk & Schneider, 2002) partly because it undergirds social bonds, social bridges, and reciprocity, each of which is needed to produce effective social action within schools. Like human and physical capital, relationships among school members can be a resource for schools if they are based on collective trust. Low levels of trust, or even distrust, can lead to gaps in the social network that disrupt the cohesiveness of a school community and erect structural barriers reinforcing role boundaries. Collective trust, on the other hand, facilitates cooperative interactions across role boundaries and unites individuals around a common vision. Both effects need to be leveraged in order to achieve the level of reform necessary to make schools responsive to the changing needs of a global and information-based society.

COLLECTIVE TRUST AND ACADEMIC OPTIMISM

Thus far in this chapter, we have explained how collective trust mediates social action in schools through its direct effects on social capital. Social capital theory explains how trust, reciprocity, and cohesion collectively unite individual school members for a common purpose. Social action brought about by trusting and reciprocal relationships may take the form of collective processes like professional learning communities, school reform, and organizational learning. Academic optimism is a more specific source of social action in that its existence is directly linked to student and school achievement. As with social capital, collective trust is a necessary property of academic optimism.

Academic optimism, like social capital, is another important aspect of a school's culture, which consists of the shared beliefs among teachers about the potential of their students to succeed in school. This notion of optimism encompasses faculty trust in parents and students; that is, collective trust is a critical component of academic optimism.

The construct was developed fully in Chapter 6, so here we briefly review its critical elements. Academic optimism is a latent construct that includes not only faculty trust in clients but also collective efficacy and academic emphasis. All three of these collective properties are similar and have a potent and positive effect on school outcomes, especially on achievement. Hence, it should come as no surprise that the three properties work together in a unified way to produce a strong general construct of optimism.

In brief, academic optimism includes cognitive (efficacy), affective (trust), and behavioral (academic emphasis) elements. Moreover, it is a collective property, not an individual one. A school with high academic optimism defines a culture in which the faculty believes: (1) It can make a difference, (2) students can learn, and (3) academic performance can be achieved (Hoy et al., 2006a, 2006b). These three aspects of collective optimism interact in a reciprocal way with each other (refer to Figure 6.2).

At least four trust studies have supported the collective and general nature of academic optimism (Hoy et al., 2006a, 2006b; McGuigan & Hoy, 2006; Smith & Hoy, 2007). All these empirical analyses demonstrated either through exploratory factor analysis or confirmatory factor analysis that academic optimism is a constellation of the collective properties of trust, collective efficacy, and academic emphasis. We hasten to add that the kind of trust that is instrumental in academic optimism is of one variety—faculty trust in parents and students. Further, the elements of academic optimism are the same regardless of the school level—elementary, middle, or high school. Figure 8.3 demonstrates the relationships between academic

Figure 8.3. The basic elements of academic optimism.

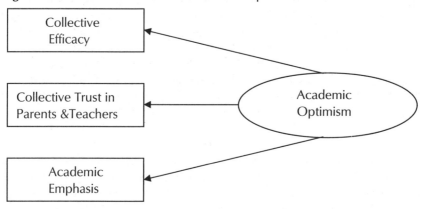

Note: The arrows in this diagram do not represent paths; rather they demonstrate that academic optimism is a general and latent construct composed of the three elements of efficacy, trust, and academic emphasis.

emphasis and its three elements; academic optimism is saturated with all three of these elements.

As we saw earlier in this chapter, social capital is embodied in social networks, especially social structures that serve as resources to facilitate productive action. Academic optimism in schools is a dynamic group property that undergirds individual and collective action. We insist that academic optimism influences and is influenced by many organizational properties, including norms, beliefs, leadership, power, communications, and policy and practices in schools. Just as collective trust is inextricably related to social capital, so too is it with academic optimism; hence, we anticipate many of the same outcomes as we found for social capital.

We view academic optimism as a strong social resource that should lead to effective functioning of schools. In brief, it is not surprising that academic optimism is directly related to school success, particularly student achievement and overall school effectiveness (Hoy et al., 2006a, 2006b; McGuigan & Hoy, 2006; Smith & Hoy, 2007).

A SYNTHESIZING MODEL: SOCIAL CAPITAL, ACADEMIC OPTIMISM, AND SOCIAL ACTION

The goal of this chapter was to provide a conceptual framework for illustrating the emergence of social action. We used social capital and academic optimism to illustrate the development of social action and to demonstrate the central importance of collective trust in both theoretical formulations. As illustrated in Figure 8.4, collective trust is a core property of both social capital and academic optimism, two broader perspectives that combine to explain social action.

As individuals interact in a group context, they inevitably engage in social exchanges that have the potential to produce both social capital and academic optimism. In the top panel of Figure 8.4, we have illustrated how collective trust is capable of producing social capital through its relationship with reciprocal behavior and social cohesion. That is, collective trust promotes relational connections within and between school groups that motivate collective behavior. Similarly, in the bottom panel collective trust fosters both academic emphasis and collective efficacy, giving rise to beliefs and feelings about the collective agency of the school.

The existence of social capital and academic optimism are mutually reinforcing and together influence both the collective beliefs and social actions that are possible and necessary for effective school-level performance, as summarized in Figure 8.4.

Figure 8.4. Social action in school organizations.

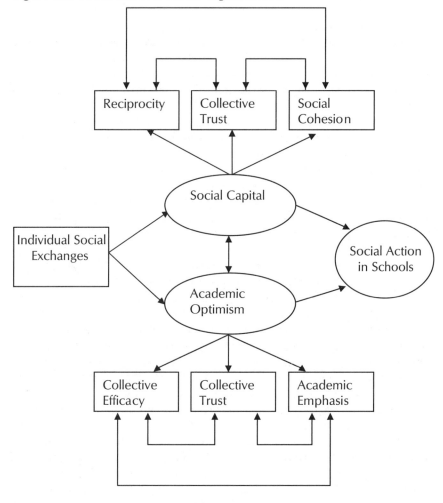

SUMMARY

We began this chapter with the challenge of explaining how individual behavior in schools evolves into social action at the school level. System-level behavior is not easily reduced to an aggregation of individual actions where the sum of individual behavior leads to quality school performance. Its antecedent mechanisms are social structures and processes that culminate in normative conditions within the school. In particular, we demonstrated how collective trust mediates individual and system behavior serving as a conduit for social capital and academic optimism, two generative norms linked to effective performance.

Collective trust is a requisite factor of both social capital and academic optimism as well as a lubricant that facilitates the production of other core elements: reciprocity, cohesion, academic press, and collective efficacy. Social action at the school and systems level is needed to achieve the elusive educational change that many policy makers, educators, and researchers envision. As we illustrated in this chapter, establishing such a critical mass, a tipping point, if you will, begins by building collective trust within school role groups. Collective trust is the keystone that regulates individual actions and undergirds other vital social norms like social capital and academic optimism.

Collective trust is a socially created phenomenon, which enables relational networks to produce collective and individual capital. It is a core resource within the social environment of schools that functions as a catalyst for the formation of social capital. The natural social resources found within schools cannot be converted into capital without collective trust. In its absence, control mechanisms are used to reduce teaching and learning to a narrowly defined set of behaviors and actions, resulting in isolated and fragmented instruction. For school organizations, a cohesive social structure depends on both the bonding and bridging mechanisms that unite individuals within their role group and connect the group to other critical school groups.

Collective trust is not only a necessary condition within a social network, but is also a critical affective factor of academic optimism, which is an important cultural and school property that enhances the operation of schools. Academic optimism is a latent construct that includes not only collective trust but also collective efficacy and academic emphasis. All three of these collective properties are similar in both nature and function but also in the potent and positive effects they have on school outcomes, especially achievement. Just as collective trust is inextricably related to social capital, so too is it to academic optimism. We view academic optimism as a strong social resource that leads to the effective functioning of schools.

PART III

Practice and Synthesis

In Part III we explore implications of collective trust in its various forms for schools. Although it can be argued that collective trust affects nearly all aspects of school life, here we examine the theoretical, empirical, and practical ways collective trust formation is important for school policy and school leadership, with special attention to the practical and policy implications.

In Chapter 9 we explore what meaning collective trust has for policy-making around goals of school accountability. We advance the argument that the fundamental purpose of education policy is to support teachers and school conditions that enable human development rather than legitimating intervention and control. Four specific guidelines consistent with this perspective are proposed to policy-makers and education practitioners.

In the final chapter the importance of collective trust for effective leadership is highlighted. We examine transactional and transformational leadership behaviors and their specific consequences for academic performance as mediated by organizational citizenship. Three guidelines for practice suggest a dispositional and behavioral framework for principal leadership.

We conclude with a brief epilogue and a summary of nine basic principles gleaned from the research and theory on trust in schools as well as with a set of practical suggestions for school principals to enhance trust.

CHAPTER 9

Education Policy and Collective Trust

> Only when we have something to value, will we have something to evaluate . . . and we cannot value something that we cannot share, exchange, and examine.
>
> —Lee Shulman, *Counting and Recounting*

Two converging realities make this chapter an important resource for policy makers and school leaders. The first is the increased press for educational reform coming from federal and state governments. Calls to improve schools have sounded for decades (Levin, 1998; McLendon & Cohen-Vogel, 2008), but today's alarm is accompanied by a funding framework that attaches federal dollars to innovative programs (Hanushek, 2009), making policy change inevitable. The second concerns the nature and function of contemporary education policies. Current regulations continue to advance control mechanisms, for example teacher evaluation models, that reinforce traditional organizational structure and culture. Significant change in schooling is not likely as long as the structural conditions that many researchers identify as the sources of poor performance remain intact (Cantrell, 2009; Chubb, 2001; Ogawa, 2009).

The primary source of school improvement will not be new curricular standards, governance structures, or teacher quality policies; rather, improvement in the culture of teaching and learning has the most potential to improve school performance (Spillane, Gomez, & Mesler, 2009). The problem with viewing policies as change mechanisms is that genuine change does not emerge from formal regulation; it grows out of the actions and interactions of individuals who interpret and make sense of policies within the context of their local environments (Spillane, 2004). Agreement among school members on outcomes and processes facilitates the change process (Christensen, Horn, & Johnson, 2008), but how can education policies formulated at a macro level, where beliefs and values are diffuse, facilitate agreement among individuals within schools or districts? We believe a focus on collective trust is the key.

137

Education policies that support collective trust adjust to the idiosyncratic needs of schools and districts, whereas, policies that attempt to control teacher quality and performance from outside schools are often wedded to standardized designs. This is not to suggest that teacher quality and school performance are inappropriate targets of improvement policies, but to point out that pressure applied through external regulations, a common approach of education policy (Sykes, O'Day, & Ford, 2009), is misaligned with improvement and reform needs. Historically, the reach of policies has been confined to inputs (e.g., teacher quality) or outcomes (e.g., test performance), not the social conditions within schools that affect the use of inputs or the quality of outputs (Cantrell, 2009). Controlling inputs or outputs ignores social conditions, like collective trust, that connect policies to school outcomes (Forsyth, Barnes, & Adams, 2006; Goddard, Tschannen-Moran, & Hoy, 2001). In the absence of healthy social conditions, policies are likely to be anemic resources for improvement.

Collective trust facilitates the effective functioning of schools, and thus examining its responsiveness to education policy makes sense. In this chapter, we use the collective trust framework to deduce guidelines that leaders and policy makers can employ as they explore school improvement and reform. The guidelines address the question, How can externally imposed policies support a culture of collective trust? We confine our analysis to accountability and school reform because policies related to these themes have far-reaching effects on social interactions within schools.

ACCOUNTABILITY POLICY AND COLLECTIVE TRUST

Accountability is a core policy lever for school improvement, and its effects have transformed how districts and schools manage the performance of teachers and administrators. Public disclosure of achievement results and corrective action linked to low school performance (O'Day, 2002) have changed both instructional practice and the coordination of teaching and learning (Darling-Hammond, 2004; Webb, 2005). Under current accountability frameworks, instruction has become standards based (Darling-Hammond, 2004), test scores have become the primary indicator of teacher effectiveness and school performance (Goe, 2007; Wong, 2008), and school choice has become a market force driving innovation (Cullen, Jacob, & Levitt, 2005; Wong, 2008).

The term *accountability* is used pejoratively by many, but its function, promoting improvement, is neither bad nor harmful to teaching. Problems can result from its application and use. Yet accountability can be an asset to communities and schools (Block, 2008) if it emerges from the actions, interactions, and attitudes of school members as they work collectively to improve performance. When accountability measures and collective trust are mutually reinforcing, human and social capacity can maximize performance, but when accountability measures are applied autocratically, regulations are likely to erode or destroy relational networks critical to school effectiveness.

We offer four guidelines for designing accountability policies to support collective trust. Our guidelines are predicated on three elements of trust formation: (1) conditions of cooperation, vulnerability, and interdependence; (2) socially defined expectations and responsibilities; and (3) social interactions that embody facets of trustworthiness. Specifically, we call attention to how policies are framed and the use of control.

Guideline I: Frame Problems as Opportunities for Progress

Conventional policy making starts by identifying problems and the factors contributing to them. Problem definition may seem routine and innocuous, but it can lead to the demise of well-intended policies if rhetoric is preoccupied with indicting teachers. Teachers are the indispensable resources of school improvement, and like all resources they need nurturing and support, not blame. Generalized claims of incompetent teaching used to justify accountability measures place teachers in a defensive position and evoke emotional states that restrict openness, cooperation, and risk taking, the very essence of trust. Even well-designed policies will fail during implementation if teachers feel threatened and unappreciated. It is bad practice to demean those who are being called upon to implement changes and harmful for collective trust.

If accountability is the objective, policies legitimized by fear and blame are incapable of promoting responsible and professional teaching behavior. Blame alienates teachers, undermines professional practice, and evokes feelings of powerlessness (Cox & Wood, 1980), all of which fuel distrust and lead to noncompliance. What we know about optimal human and organizational behavior stands in stark contrast to the use of blame and fear as motivating devices. Operational capacity is greatest when organizational conditions support relatedness, competence, recognition, involvement, and autonomy (Herzberg, 1966; McGregor, 1960; Ryan & Deci, 2000). Words without action cannot create these conditions, but the language used during policy making sets the tone for future interactions.

Instead of teachers being singled out as the source of achievement problems, framing policies as investments in teachers, students, and communities suggests a collective commitment and responsibility for school improvement (Gagne, Koestner, & Zuckerman, 2000). Visions for a better future prompt interactions and conversations on expectations, responsibilities, dreams, and innovation. These interactions are the basis of trust formation in schools; they bring individuals together to co-create conditions that will lead to better outcomes. Trust-sensitive policies start by recognizing the complexity of teaching and learning and by framing school improvement as the collective responsibility of all school members, not just improved performance from one role group.

Guideline II: Use Social Control to Stimulate Improvement

Conflict surrounding control of teachers can be minimized, and school improvement enhanced, if accountability policies rely on social controls to stimulate change. Whereas hard control is embodied in rigid regulations, coercion, and punitive sanctions (Das & Tang, 1998), social control elicits commitment, influence, identification, and persuasion (Etzioni, 1964; Shapiro, 1987), natural properties of collective trust. Eztioni (1964) warned against the use of hard control to force compliance of organizational participants, such as teachers, who are characterized as being highly committed to the mission of the organization or the profession. When moral commitment is strong, the application of hard controls alienates and reduces motivation by removing meaningful improvement incentives like professional autonomy and responsibility (Ryan & Deci, 2000). Trust cannot survive in environments where autonomy and responsibility are restricted (Knoop, 2007).

Evidence from research on schools in corrective action, an element of No Child Left Behind that epitomizes hard control, validates Etzioni's concern. The professional autonomy and authority of school members diminishes if schools fail to meet annual yearly progress for 4 consecutive years (Mintrop & Trujillo, 2005). New programs, interventions, and regulations supplant social controls like responsibility and trust as the primary tools to regulate teaching and learning in corrective-action schools. It is unconscionable to allow failure to persist; it is also unacceptable to promote practices that contradict what we know about performance. The use of hard control to impose accountability from outside the school generally has not produced the level of improvement that is needed (Ravitch, 2010).

Empirical support for the long-term effectiveness of hard controls is difficult to find. Fullan (2005), for instance, argues that rigid accountability policies are detrimental to sustainable improvement. Mintrop (2003) found that coercive pressure applied to probation schools in high-accountability states resulted in initial achievement changes, but long-term effectiveness was not sustained. In a study of first-generation corrective-action policies from seven states and two urban districts, Mintrop and Trujillo (2005) discovered that rigid regulations prompted action by school leaders, but their actions failed to produce any significant performance changes. Similarly, Malen and Rice (2009) concluded that threats of reconstitution prompted changes that contradicted school improvement and ultimately diminished the capacity of schools to improve.

Some schools in corrective action have turned around performance, but in general the evidence does not support the use of hard controls to facilitate sustainable improvement (Fullan, 2005; Ravitch, 2010). So, what conditions underlie sustainable reform? Contemporary policy research (Bryk et al., 2010; O'Day, 2002; Ogawa, 2009; Spillane, Gomez, & Mesler, 2009) underscores the following factors:

- Positive teacher and administrator behaviors
- Constructive interactions among school members
- Social conditions that support teaching and learning
- Instructional or professional capacity, rather than specific interventions or programs

Fullan (2005) sums up the evidence: "Capacity building must become a core feature of all improvement strategies" (p. 180).

We offer a few examples of accountability policies based on social control. Our examples draw on ideas from Fullan, Bertani, and Quinn's (2004) study of district policies and school capacity; McLaughlin and Talbert's (2006) elements of district support for learning systems; and Kenney's (2008) study of quality improvement in medicine. By no means are these the only school-improvement mechanisms that are consistent with social controls, but they are processes and organizational behaviors associated with collective trust.

HIGH, BUT ACHIEVABLE, STANDARDS. The standards movement has been effective at raising the bar of academic expectations. Too often, though, high academic standards are reflected in vision statements that resemble marketing slogans, like "Every child can learn," instead of viable strategies for achieving goals. High standards supportive of continuous improvement need to be attached to a theory of action that enables school members to monitor performance and to make necessary adjustments on a regular and continuous basis (Guerra-Lopez, 2008). Theories of action, in contrast to vision statements, present the conceptual blueprint for how the interdependent elements of schools work together to produce intended outcomes.

Instead of relegating academic standards to vision placards, theories of action provide a concrete performance framework through which standards are reflected in practices and conditions that shape the teaching and learning environment. Theories of action originated within the evaluation field, but their application has utility for organizational development in general and school improvement in particular. Figure 9.1 is an example of a theory of action. It reflects the vision of school readiness, family readiness, and child readiness that was developed between an urban district and a partnering community organization. The program's vision is not couched in an idyllic phrase; it is visible in the program mechanisms (i.e., leadership, community, and transition mechanisms) and mediating conditions (i.e., dense social network) used to achieve the outcomes of higher school attendance, increased parent responsibility, positive transitions, and ready children. Explicit theories of action place greater emphasis on the processes and practices that bring visions to life.

Not only does a theory of action establish a road map to carry out a vision, it forms the architecture of a performance-measurement plan that can provide to decision makers continual feedback on processes and outcomes. Collective trust benefits from the clear expectations and responsibilities that theories of action delineate. The absence of shared understanding and cohesion among school members is often the source of trust violations and the reason why it is critical to establish clear expectations about practices, mediating conditions, and outcomes.

TEACHER QUALITY. Teacher quality has attracted significant attention over the past decade (Darling-Hammond, Chung Wei, & Johnson, 2009). Podgursky and Springer (2006) capture the prevailing logic behind many teacher-quality policies in their discussion of reading and math achievement distributions in New York City. They argue,

> Any policy that can retain and sustain the performance of teachers in the upper tail of the distribution, and enhance the performance of or counsel out teachers in the lower-tail, possesses potential for substantial impact on student growth. (p. 23)

If the actual achievement remedy were a simple linear function of changing a policy (X) to cause a comparable change in teacher effectiveness (Y), we would have solved the achievement problem decades ago.

Two findings from the teacher effects literature are clear: Teachers matter for student achievement and teacher effects are larger on low-income students (Darling-Hammond, 2006). Less clear is the best policy approach to improve teacher quality. Tightening teacher preparation and licensure requirements, improving mentoring programs, increasing alternative licensure options, making it easier to fire ineffective teachers, using new pathways to teaching (e.g., Teach for America or the New York City Teaching Fellows), and adopting performance-based evaluation models are some of the many policies and approaches being advanced by states and districts.

Figure 9.1. Theory of action example.

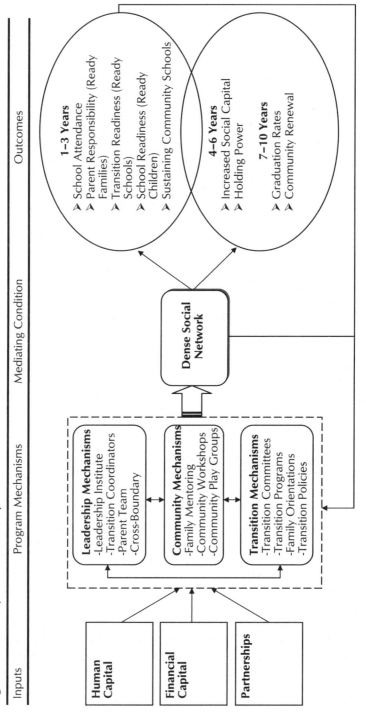

Inputs   Program Mechanisms   Mediating Condition   Outcomes

Human Capital

Financial Capital

Partnerships

Leadership Mechanisms
-Leadership Institute
-Transition Coordinators
-Parent Team
-Cross-Boundary

Community Mechanisms
-Family Mentoring
-Community Workshops
-Community Play Groups

Transition Mechanisms
-Transition Committees
-Transition Programs
-Family Orientations
-Transition Policies

Dense Social Network

1–3 Years
➤ School Attendance
➤ Parent Responsibility (Ready Families)
➤ Transition Readiness (Ready Schools)
➤ School Readiness (Ready Children)
➤ Sustaining Community Schools

4–6 Years
➤ Increased Social Capital
➤ Holding Power

7–10 Years
➤ Graduation Rates
➤ Community Renewal

Much of the policy debate has neglected a strategy that holds great promise for building collective trust and improving teaching and learning: an effective model of instructional supervision (DiPaola & Hoy, 2008; Zepeda, 2006). Supervision is not evaluation. Whereas evaluation is more of a bureaucratic tool for employment decisions, the purpose of supervision is to improve instruction through shared inquiry, reflective dialogue, collaboration, and professional development (Blasé & Blasé, 2000; DiPaola & Hoy, 2008; Hoy & Hoy, 2009). The distinction between evaluation and supervision is captured by Acheson and Gall (2003): "Supervision is interactive rather than directive, democratic rather than authoritarian, teacher-centered rather than supervisor-centered" (p. 15). The potential convergence of a supervisory culture with collective trust is evident in this contrast. Interactive, democratic (shared influence and responsibility), and teacher-centered behaviors make up the behavioral, cognitive, and affective sources of collective trust. In contrast, directive and authoritative behaviors deter trust formation (Adams, 2008).

Evidence on the effects of direct assistance to teachers (Blasé & Blasé, 2000) and learning communities (McLaughlin & Talbert, 2006) supports the performance benefits of supervisory practices that address teachers' need for professional autonomy, relatedness, and competence. Supervision improves teaching by addressing the social conditions that maximize teacher performance. An effective model of instructional supervision can address the teacher-quality problem that many high-poverty schools face, but onerous regulations in these schools often leave principals with little time and support to build cultures of supervision.

Unlike external approaches to teacher quality, supervision is compatible with social conditions, like collective trust and academic optimism, which promote student and school achievement. Moore Johnson (2001) found that cultures of supervision offer support for teachers, develop professional capacity, and promote continuous dialogue around instructional issues. These social norms build and sustain trust within the internal and task structures of schools as teachers work cooperatively to achieve collective goals. Collective trust is likely to suffer if performance-evaluation models lead to the abandonment of supervisory practices. Supervision is so valuable to teacher quality that Zepeda (2006) claims that evaluation without supervision is akin to professional malpractice.

STUDENT ASSESSMENT. Controversy surrounding student assessment can be very polarizing, but despite different viewpoints, no credible position advocates for the elimination of assessments. Contention centers on what skills and knowledge to assess, the validity and reliability of standardized tests, and the legitimacy of using test scores to judge the effectiveness of teachers and schools. Achievement indicators are necessary to cultivate collective trust within schools, but the misuse of achievement data has harmful consequences for collective trust and sustainable improvement.

We offer four assessment policy characteristics that support conditions and interactions linked to collective trust. These elements reflect Shulman's (2007) four principles of effective assessment:

- Accountability policies should be clear about what is and what is not being measured and why particular assessments were selected.
- Given the limitations of tests, accountability frameworks should draw on multiple measures to provide a more comprehensive picture of individual students and schools.
- Assessments should be embedded in instruction and occur throughout the school year. Regular performance feedback promotes learning, yet accountability policies often place testing late in the academic year when achievement data are unlikely to be available to teachers.
- Performance results should be used formatively to improve instruction through regular conversations and reflection on instruction.

Taken together, these elements of effective assessments help to define outcomes that are valued and shared by school members, provide a more complete picture of performance, encourage interactions and feedback on assessment data, and make assessments an active element of teaching and learning. Many current high-stakes approaches have had the opposite effect. They measure narrow competencies and knowledge domains, use results for summative evaluations, and turn annual yearly progress into a statistical game that distorts the reality of teaching and learning.

The Case of Connecticut

A belief in the importance of trust for effective school performance shifts the purpose of external regulation from control of school resources and outputs to a focus on processes and practices that facilitate collective action and accountability. External policies aligned with collective trust do not mandate what they cannot control, namely, the actions and interactions of people; instead they support structures that enable local administrators and school members to work collectively toward sustainable school improvement. What follows is an account of school-improvement legislation in Connecticut during the late 1980s that parallels our guidelines.

State-level reform in Connecticut spurred by the 1986 Education Enhancement Act (EEA) illustrates the potential performance effects of aligning state policies with sources of collective trust. Contrary to the prevailing design of performance-based incentives for teachers and high-stakes accountability, Connecticut increased standards in a way that valued the contribution of teachers. The EEA legislation raised teacher salaries across the board to attract and retain quality teachers while also improving teacher quality by focusing on teacher preparation, licensure standards, support for new teachers, and improved professional development (Baron, 1999). Connecticut also addressed funding and resource inequities between schools and school districts and used publicly reported performance data to monitor school progress toward goals, not to reward or punish teachers or schools (Darling-Hammond, 2004). Darling Hammond commented, "Rather than pursue a single silver bullet or a punitive approach . . . Connecticut has made ongoing investments in improving teaching and schooling through high standards and high supports" (p. 1063).

Connecticut more than closed the achievement gap during the 1990s; data from the Third International Math and Science Study (TIMSS) placed the state's students second behind Singapore in science achievement (Baron, 1999; Darling-Hammond, 2004). Fisk (1999) found that EEA fostered a climate supportive of innovation, group problem solving, cooperation, and technical capacity. Darling-Hammond (2004) and Baron (1999) note that district administrators credit the legislation for establishing coherence around instructional improvement while allowing for professional autonomy and local decision making, all of which are linked to collective trust.

SCHOOL REFORM POLICY AND COLLECTIVE TRUST

School reform policies primarily use an incentive-and-threat approach to improve school performance. Part F of No Child Left Behind is an example of how financial incentives encouraged school systems to adopt externally developed comprehensive reform models (Rowan, Correnti, Miller, & Camburn, 2009). More recent examples of incentives are contained in the federal grant program Race to the Top. This policy approach calls for low-performing schools receiving federal reform grants to adopt one of four turnaround models: transformation, turnaround, restart, or school closure model (U.S. Department of Education, 2010). The threat approach is visible in the corrective action provision of NCLB (Malen & Rice, 2009).

Our concern with the incentive-threat model is that it trivializes school reform. Massive increases in federal funding for comprehensive school reform models (Rowan et al., 2009) have partly contributed to the belief that school reform means the adoption of external interventions. Adoption and actual changes in practice are unrelated processes. Reform cannot be reduced to packaged programs or external prescriptions that are forced on schools; it is a social process. Not attending to the reform process is a reason why many interventions fail to change traditional instructional practices (Spillane, 2000; Tyack & Cuban, 1995), leadership behaviors, or instructional values and beliefs (Coburn, 2003).

Established views toward the purpose of reform policy need to be adjusted in order to support the formation of collective trust. Greater attention to implementation and collective action can stimulate authentic and sustainable change. It is true that interventions and programs are often linked to student achievement, but their performance effects are mediated by the degree to which interaction patterns among school members and social norms change (Coburn, 2003; Ogawa, 2009). Instead of defining *reform* as a noun, as in the case of comprehensive reform models, it needs to be viewed as a verb, suggesting the purposive action of school members. A shift in meaning alters the focus of reform policy from incentives and threats to support for local efforts to bring about authentic reform. This brings us to our third and fourth guidelines: Make the school the unit of improvement and make trust the linchpin of reform diffusion.

Guideline III: Make the School the Unit of Improvement

Improvement in one failing school is challenging, but reforming the performance of an entire educational system is daunting. It is naive to view external accountability policies as the most effective vehicle to transform an entire system. Evidence from the 1988 Chicago School Reform Act supports our claim. Some Chicago schools made significant academic progress under this legislation, while many others did not. For those schools that improved, social conditions like trust, collective responsibility, professional accountability, and motivation made the difference, not the reform policy itself (Bryk & Schneider, 2002; Bryk et al., 2010).

The federal or state level is the wrong place to control school reform. We have learned from major social movements like women's suffrage and the resistance to apartheid that sustainable change starts with the purposive actions of a few individuals at a local level that gradually diffuse throughout society as the actions, interactions, and stories began to spread. Small groups are the origin of large-scale transformation (Block, 2008), not external policies set at the federal or state levels. For educational improvement purposes, the small group is the school, and the behaviors, practices, and interactions of school members are the determinants of performance.

Instead of attempting to control school-level behaviors and interactions at the federal and state level, policies hold more promise if they support schools as they work to develop and sustain human and social capacity around their unique needs and contexts (Spillane, Gomez, & Mesler, 2009).

Professional culture is an alternative policy approach that supports capacity building (Adams & Kirst, 1999; O'Day, 2002). In contrast to external strategies, a professional culture empowers school members to take collective responsibility for effective teaching and learning. For example, teacher quality in a professional culture is regulated through norms of shared inquiry, mentoring, collaboration, and information sharing (O'Day, 2002). Accountability that comes from the immediate social environment is more proximate to teaching and learning and more compatible with collective trust formation.

When an educational practice is perceived to work, there is a tendency to mandate it everywhere. Collective trust, though, emerges from social environments; it is not responsive to external mandates. Policies can support trust's emergence with a vision for improvement that is linked to a theory of action, a commitment to shared influence and choice, and a system of performance measurement that includes continuous feedback. Next, we describe each of these examples in some detail.

IMPROVEMENT AGENDA. Support for school improvement starts with a clear agenda. The agenda needs to be broad enough to allow for school-level interpretation and flexibility, but specific enough to delineate common outcomes, essential learning conditions, and mechanisms to bring about improvement. The point is to identify processes, conditions, and outcomes that link to effectiveness while appreciating and valuing different approaches schools can take to arrive at common goals. The purpose of an improvement agenda is to establish shared expectations and responsibilities and to provide a framework for the improvement process.

Unlike the traditional 3-to-5-year strategic plan, improvement agendas should be dynamic and responsive to changing conditions but stable enough to establish consistency and trust in the improvement process. New practices, processes, or other tools to carry out the agenda need to emerge from evidence coming directly from the field, not from external prescriptions or programs. The needs and outcomes explicated in the improvement plan remain stable, but practices need support to evolve as new performance data and information emerge.

SHARED INFLUENCE AND CHOICE. Influence and choice are effective strategies for building collective trust and motivating school members to take responsibility for performance goals. Learning theorists point to the importance of shared influence, relationships, and the social environment for motivating student learning (Zimmerman, 1990; Zimmerman & Martinez-Pons, 1988). It is not a stretch to believe these same processes have utility for organizational performance. However, influence and choice in schools with lagging performance are the first professional controls to be removed from teachers and administrators. This approach stands in contrast to evidence on effective performance. An alternative is to balance controls with an instructional design that coheres around instructional practices and goals while facilitating cooperative interactions, shared inquiry, and autonomy.

PERFORMANCE MEASUREMENT AND FEEDBACK. The practice of medicine is an informative example for thinking about performance measurement and feedback systems. When physicians examine patients, they gather multiple indicators of patient health, including taking a medical history, to diagnose plausible causes of complaints. This information is used to isolate the root cause of the problem before interventions are recommended. If symptoms do not abate after the initial treatment, more diagnostics are performed, and new treatments prescribed. Performance measurement and information use in schools do not often follow a similar diagnostic-treatment process; in many cases they overrely on relatively crude achievement indicators that are incapable of locating sources of problems and tracking the health of a student or school.

Federal, state, or district policies can support improvement at the school level by designing measurement systems that track, longitudinally, multiple diagnostic indicators of school health over time. The specific measures used by a district or school should be determined by the improvement agenda (theory of action). For example, if instructional capacity is a mediating condition in a theory of action, it can be measured by faculty trust in colleagues, collective efficacy, instructional leadership, and student trust. Simply collecting data is not enough. School leaders must understand the concepts being measured, how to interpret results, and how data can be used to improve the culture of a school. Timely and readily available data are also critical. A comprehensive system of performance measurement and feedback can facilitate meaningful conversations that support trust formation and lead to improvement.

Guideline IV: Make Trust the Linchpin of Reform Diffusion

Diffusion is defined as "the process by which an innovation is communicated through certain channels over time among the members of a social system" (Rogers, 2003, p. 35). Reform diffusion follows a growth model that is based on the Sigmoid Curve. Diffusion starts slowly as individuals make sense of the reform and how it works. Gradually the rate of change increases as new practices are tested and improved. A tipping point is reached when a critical mass of individuals embraces new beliefs and practices. Once a reform has spread throughout the system, the final phase is sustainability

Figure 9.2. Reform diffusion.

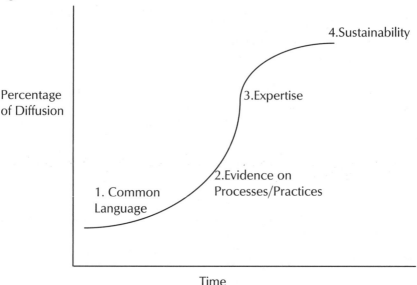

and continuous improvement (Rogers, 2003) (see Figure 9.2). As natural as this process seems, reforms do not diffuse throughout systems by chance. Conditions that influence the formation of collective trust also affect the rate of diffusion and consequently the effectiveness of the reform itself.

SOCIAL INTERACTIONS. Social interactions are the first element of reform diffusion. Reforms capable of changing practice filter down to the beliefs and orientations that underlie behaviors (Spillane et al., 2009). Rogers (2003) notes that early interactions center on the relative advantage of planned change, the compatibility between reform and school needs, and reform logic. Initial conversations to design a reform agenda or to adopt a specific reform lay a foundation for collective trust.

Not establishing a common framework, or excluding teachers and other school members from the design, can have harmful consequences on reform diffusion and trust. The rate of diffusion partly depends on the degree of agreement on processes and outcomes among individuals in organizations (Christensen, Horn, & Johnson, 2008). When agreement exists in school cultures, conflict and distrust among members is low (Bryk & Schneider, 2002), and cooperative interactions and collective responsibility are likely to be high.

COMMUNICATION CHANNELS. Communication channels are a second element of reform diffusion. Both formal and informal structures make up communication channels in schools, but it is the informal environment that is more deterministic of diffusion than formal structures. Informal conversations and observations of practice are ideal communication channels to socialize reform. Rogers (2003) suggests, "Diffusion is a very social process that involves interpersonal communication" (p. 19). Formal structures provide opportunities for interactions, but without norms, such as trust and cooperation, positive relationships are difficult to sustain.

TIME. Time is the third element of reform diffusion. As much as society values quick fixes to complex problems, school improvement takes time, a clear vision, a flexible plan, and persistence. Capacity for effective reform and performance builds over time. This is true for individual and organization performance. Malcolm Gladwell (2008) attributes the success of individuals at the pinnacle of their careers, such as Bill Gates, to the 10,000-hour principle, which suggests a threshold of time coupled with practice contributes to the accomplishments of highly successful individuals. An example of the relationship between time and school-community renewal comes from Geoffrey Canada and the Harlem Children's Zone; he notes that it took approximately 10 years to build an infrastructure and culture to support the organization's vision (Tough, 2008).

LEADERSHIP. Leadership is a fourth element that shapes the rate of reform diffusion. Without supportive leadership, reforms die on the vine. Leadership is often seen as the responsibility of central office administrators or school principals, but leadership for reform diffusion is less positional and more interactional (Heller & Firestone, 1995; Spillane, 2006). Leaders build capacity for diffusion by leveraging the social ties of school members who interact at the boundaries of role groups (Greenhalgh, Robert, MacFarlane, Bate, & Kyriakidou, 2004). Boundary spanners have influence over their own and other role groups. These individuals are change agents who can slow down, speed up, or stop reform by tapping into their social network and informal authority. Examples of boundary spanners include teachers who have developed respect and trust from their peers for their effectiveness in the classroom or parents who serve on parent-teacher councils or site leadership teams.

In summary, full diffusion does not happen until planned change has been socialized to a point where past organizational culture has been disrupted. Social interactions, communication channels, time, and leadership are essential variables in the process. These conditions are sources of collective trust as well. Lewicki and Bunker's (1996) stages of trust suggest that trust evolves over time as the intentions of others become more familiar. Bryk and Schneider (2002) argue that trust emerges from repeated social exchanges that are consistent with defined expectations and obligations. Kochanec (2005) and Tschannen-Moran (2004) point to the important role of leaders in supporting relational trust. Just as social interactions, communication channels, time, and leadership are critical sources of diffusion, they are also necessary for trust (Adams, 2008). Reform policies that support reform diffusion have positive consequences for the formation of collective trust.

SUMMARY

We based this chapter on the claim that people and relationships, not policies or interventions, reform and improve schools. Our assumption changes the fundamental purpose of education policy from control over teachers to support for conditions that enable human and social capacity to flourish. The four policy guidelines presented in this chapter challenge the prevailing notion that improvement and reform result from pressure, punitive consequences, and external accountability. We advocate instead a set of policy guidelines capable of leveraging collective trust to improve performance. We restate these guidelines and their underlying assumptions for clarity and simplicity.

1. *Frame Problems as Opportunities for Progress.* Policies framed as *opportunities* to create a better future provide a foundation for cooperation, supportive interactions, collective trust, and risk taking by appealing to the motivational needs of teachers. Given the importance of implementation for effective improvement and reform policies, initiating change with language that devalues teachers and overly simplifies achievement creates friction in the relational network that often leads to the premature demise of school reform policies.

2. *Use Social Controls to Foster Commitment and Stimulate Change.* Theories of action, instructional supervision, and formative assessments are three examples of social controls that are capable of facilitating collective trust and responsibility and, consequently, encouraging social action guided by an improvement agenda. High-performing schools are often defined by the social conditions of collective trust and instructional capacity as well as by coordination based on cooperation and shared inquiry. Social controls, as

opposed to hard controls, are consistent with and facilitate the operational environment of high-performing schools.

3. *Treat the School as the Unit of Improvement.* Small groups are the unit of change. An alternative to improving schools at federal or state levels is to promote large-scale change one school at a time. Federal, state, and even district policies that establish an improvement agenda, encourage influence and choice, and rely on a comprehensive and dynamic performance measurement system can support improvement efforts at the local school level.

4. *Make Trust the Linchpin of Reform Diffusion.* Effective school reform is not an external program or intervention, but rather a process that is affected by dynamic relationships among school members. Social interactions, communication, time, and leadership affect the rate of reform diffusion within schools, and all evolve from collective trust.

With achievement scores at the national level continuing to lag behind those of other industrial countries, and an unchanged achievement gap, it is understandable that federal and state policies would intercede where many schools have failed. Such failures, however, should not be viewed as an indictment of practices that align with the science of human behavior and organizational performance. Individuals who work in complex organizations are at their best when structures and cultures promote identification, self-regulation, reflection, trust, professional autonomy, ingenuity, collective responsibility, and motivation. Performance and innovation are jeopardized by a culture of control and enhanced by a culture of collective trust. Whereas control was a dominant policy model of the past, support needs to be the policy framework of the future. In short, our guidelines suggest a different route to school reform and improvement, one that goes through collective trust.

CHAPTER 10

The Practice of School Leadership and Collective Trust

Leaders create and maintain a trusting culture through the example they set and through listening. The culture of an organization and its leader are mutually reinforcing.
—John G. Bruhn, *Trust and the Health of Organizations*

In this chapter, we follow Dirks' (2006) lead in addressing fundamental questions regarding trust in leaders: "Why is trust in leaders important? What factors build or undermine trust in leaders? What can leaders do to try to repair trust after it is damaged?" (p. 15). These questions, with adjustments for the school setting, school research, and collective trust theory developed in this book, structure our discussion of the implications of collective trust for the practice of school leadership. Our discussion focuses on principal, rather than district, leadership. Trust in the principal is somewhat distinctive, depending as it does on face-to-face judgments that can be made about the reciprocal trustworthiness of principals and various school role groups.

WHY IS TRUST IN THE PRINCIPAL IMPORTANT?

Simply put, trust in the principal is important if it is related to school effectiveness. However, the research evidence on the relationship between trust in leaders and effectiveness is somewhat mixed (Dirks, 1999, 2006; Dirks & Skarlicki, 2004). Williamson (1993) denies a relationship between trust in leaders and effectiveness; others have found it to be a critical predictor of effectiveness. When an empirical research record contains contradictory findings, as this one does, it can often be traced to a misspecification of the variables included in the causal model or the absence of some important mediating variables. In Chapter 7, we identified two such variables, group interdependence and task complexity, that together mediate an organization's need for trust or control as sources of effective leadership. That is, the effective use of leadership sources (formal control, informal control, and collective trust) is mediated by the task complexity and interdependence of work groups.

When an organization is complex, it is generally true that low levels of formal control; high levels of informal, or "soft," control; and collective trust are the effective means to achieve cooperation. Schools are complex organizations because they are composed of highly interdependent groups, which must cooperate to complete highly complex tasks. Effective school leadership, then, relies on low levels of formal control (rules, regulations, and procedures), high levels of informal control (influence, persuasion, and commitment to a common set of goals), and high levels of collective trust (willingness to act in the presence of risk).

There is a historical tension with respect to the claim that the tasks of schooling are complex. Schools can choose to define their tasks narrowly and simply. For example, schools might say their task is to have 90% of children perform at a specific level on a criterion- referenced test. Articulating the task in this way permits schools to script instruction quite precisely. It allows them to mobilize their resources to achieve a precisely defined and measured outcome.

Simplifying the instructional and other tasks of education may seem reasonable when considering some subject matter, less so when thinking about creative writing, history, citizenship, or the schoolwide instructional task. Performance and mastery of the latter is less reliably measured and evaluated; the scripting of effective instruction is less possible and the very definition of target outcomes seems more arbitrary. Defining school tasks simply is also more defensible when students are homogeneous with respect to culture, socioeconomic status, mobility, adult support, and so on, but less so when schools, teachers, families, students, and conditions are diverse.

Rejecting the notion that school tasks are complex secures the argument for establishing precise and universal performance requirements and a model of schooling that approaches manufacturing. Such a view, however, is simplistic and ultimately ineffective. Much of what our society holds schools responsible for is not easily tested or measured. Even if we focus solely on instructional outcomes, cognitive facility and higher-order thinking skills would be severely constrained by the assumption that their mastery could be gauged adequately by standardized tests.

We favor an understanding of schools as having complex tasks. This view limits hope in policy solutions; canned programs; and comprehensive reform efforts based on testing, scripting of instruction, and assumptions that we can or have the will, validly and reliably, to distinguish levels of teacher performance with much precision. School leadership should generally favor the form we have described as appropriate for organizations having complex tasks, wherein schools build the capacity of individuals and teams of teachers to address learning needs in context. Such schools would be flexibly organized and managed and promote risk taking, experimentation, and collaboration. Intense teacher commitment to shared goals provides the cohesion; choices of teachers are guided by those goals but are responsive to the learners they face each day.

Effective, complex organizations have been associated empirically with high trust and trustworthy leaders. Dirks and Ferrin (2002) summarized effects of trust in the leader, finding it to be related to individual job performance, organizational citizenship, intent to leave the organization, job satisfaction, commitment to the employing organization, and commitment to leader decisions. In fact, Dirks (2006) concluded, "Trust is related to bottom-line effects in terms of group and organizational performance" (p. 19).

There are two other findings that suggest the importance of leadership that can be extrapolated to schools. The first is that trust in the immediate supervisor is more important to job-related outcomes such as job performance and organizational citizenship than is trust in the organization's senior leadership (Dirks & Ferrin, 2002). As applied to schools, this finding suggests the importance of trust in the principal for school effectiveness, perhaps over and above trust in the superintendent. A second relevant finding is that trust in the leader is greater when an organization is doing well, but the relationship between trust and performance is stronger when the organization is doing poorly (Dirks, 2000). Ironically, schools and principals under stress may often resort to formal control and close supervision rather than trust building.

As related in Chapter 6, collective trust of faculty in the principal is related to teacher perceptions of the school's effectiveness. Bryk and Schneider (2002) found that collective trust had positive and direct consequences for reading and mathematics performance, with additional, indirect effects on school effectiveness through the improvement of school commitment, orientation to innovation, outreach to parents, and the vitality of the teacher professional community. These direct and indirect effects of collective trust, evident in the trust research of The Ohio State studies, the University of Chicago studies, and the Oklahoma State and University of Oklahoma studies, are powerful even when accounting for the often-overwhelming effects of poverty.

In sum, the ambiguity surrounding the relationship between trust in leadership and organizational performance is clarified when we view schools as having complex tasks and highly interdependent subgroups. As with many organizations, trust is essential to a school's task achievement.

For schools, trust in the principal is predicted to have direct and indirect benefits for both individual and organizational performance. Trust in the principal maximizes teacher effort and performance and helps to focus collective energy on what is important. Moreover, the principal's role as teacher-supervisor makes collective trust in the principal undeniably critical, especially when conditions are difficult.

In our model of collective trust we claim that trust is especially important in the creation of cooperation and success in schools. We turn to the work of the school principal in creating a climate of trust and harvesting its benefits. We interpret and apply current leadership models and evidence as they apply to the school principal and the role that collective trust plays in helping schools become effective.

COLLECTIVE TRUST, LEADERSHIP, AND ORGANIZATIONAL CITIZENSHIP

Although there is empirical evidence that trust in the leader/supervisor has significant consequences for an organization's productivity and effectiveness, exactly why this is so is not as clear. One way to understand how trust functions in schools is to recognize that trust is nested within a complex system of attitudinal, structural, and other contextual variables that make up the environment that conditions behavior. We begin our discussion with an overview of principal behaviors and teacher behaviors by exploring the research literature on transformational leadership and organizational citizenship, especially as these are intertwined with trust in the leader.

Leadership Behavior

For over 30 years, scholars have made the useful distinction between *transactional* and *transformational* leadership (Burns, 1978). Transactional leadership, as the name implies, describes a leader-follower relationship based on a quid pro quo, or exchange of performance for monetary or other rewards. In contrast, transformational leadership (sometimes called *charismatic* or *inspirational*) describes leadership that focuses on fostering an awareness and commitment to an ever emerging common mission. While Burns (1978) described these types of leadership as polar opposites, scholars now view them as potentially supplementary (Bass, 1985; Hater & Bass, 1988; Den Hartog, 2003), or as augmenting each other (Judge & Piccolo, 2004; Waldman, Bass, & Yammariono, 1990). Transactional leadership, as discussed by Bass (1999), refers to the exchange relationship between leader and follower to meet their own self-interests. It may take the form of contingent reward in which the leader clarifies for the follower through direction or participation what the follower needs to do to be rewarded for the effort. It may take the form of active management-by-exception, in which the leader monitors the follower's performance and takes corrective action if the follower fails to meet standards. Or it may take the form of passive leadership, in which the leader practices passive managing-by-exception by waiting for problems to arise before taking corrective action or is laissez-faire and avoids taking any action. (pp. 10–11)

The two measurement scales most used to study transactional leadership behaviors are part of Bass's (1985) Multifactor Leadership Questionnaire:

1. *Contingent Reward:* The leader rewards followers if they perform in accordance with contracts or expend the necessary effort.
2. *Management-by-Exception:* The leader avoids giving directions and allows followers to do their jobs as always if performance goals are met. (Bass, 1985; Bass, Avolio, & Goodheim, 1987)

In stark contrast with transactional leadership behavior, Bass describes transformational leadership as

the leader moving the follower beyond immediate self-interests through idealized influence (charisma), inspiration, intellectual stimulation, or individualized consideration. It elevates the follower's level of maturity and ideals as well as concerns for achievement, self-actualization, and the well-being of others, the organization, and society. Idealized influence and inspirational leadership are displayed when the leader envisions a desirable future, articulates how it can be reached, sets an example to be followed, sets high standards of performance, and shows determination and confidence. Followers want to identify with such leadership. Intellectual stimulation is displayed when the leader helps followers to become more innovative and creative. Individualized consideration is displayed when leaders pay attention to the developmental needs of followers and support and coach the development of their followers. The leaders delegate assignments as opportunities for growth. (p. 11)

A slightly different understanding of the concept emerges from the comprehensive literature review of Podsakoff, MacKenzie, Moorman, and Fetter (1990), who distilled six key transformational leadership behaviors:

- Identifying and articulating a vision
- Providing an appropriate model
- Fostering the acceptance of group goals

- Developing high performance expectations
- Providing individualized support
- Stimulating intellectual stimulation

Yet another understanding of transformational leadership behaviors is provided when we examine how it is most often measured, again, using Bass's (1985) Multifactor Leadership Questionnaire. The three scales used to measure transformational leadership include

1. *Charisma:* The leader instills pride, faith and respect, has a gift for seeing what is really important, and transmits a sense of mission which is effectively articulated.
2. *Individualized Consideration:* The leader delegates projects to stimulate learning experiences, provides coaching and teaching, and treats each follower as a respected individual.
3. *Intellectual Stimulation:* The leader arouses followers to think in new ways and emphasizes problem solving and the use of reasoning before taking action (Bass, 1985; Bass et al., 1987).

These perspectives on leadership behavior suggest that, on the one hand, the leverage leaders have can be situated in their formal authority and control over the distribution of rewards, monetary or symbolic. When this leverage is used, there is an explicit or implicit "transaction" or exchange of employee behavior for reward, thus, transactional leadership. Transactional leadership appears to elicit employee behaviors that are easily and accurately measured.

On the other hand, leader leverage can also be situated in personal behavior and interactions that call attention to the higher purposes of an organization, transforming organizational life from a system of self-interested exchanges to the pursuit of future accomplishment, hence, transformational leadership. Transformational leadership elicits employee cooperation and vision-directed behavior even when the need for such behavior cannot be predicted or even clearly articulated, formally agreed to, measured, or precisely rewarded. As with other leaders, principal behavior can be discussed as transformational or transactional. Both, in proper balance, have implications for school success.

Organizational Citizenship Behavior

We use the concept of organizational citizenship to discuss the behavior of teachers. Organizational citizenship behavior (OCB) is a useful way to conceptualize teacher behavior because it has a significant literature that links collective trust in the leader with organizational performance, providing a bridge for our analysis. Organ and colleagues introduced the OCB concept in 1983; it has its origins in the work of Chester Barnard, who drew attention to the importance of employee "willingness to cooperate" in his classic book *The Functions of the Executive* (1938). There is a significant amount of empirical and theoretical work related to organizational citizenship, and it is a concept that resonates with the experience of both school principals and education scholars.

Organ (1988) defined OCB as:

> individual behavior that is discretionary, not directly or explicitly recognized by the formal reward system, and that in the aggregate promotes the effective functioning of the organization. By discretionary, we mean that the behavior is not an enforceable requirement of the role or the job description, that is, the clearly specifiable terms of the person's employment contract with the organization; the behavior is rather a matter of personal choice, such that its omission is not generally understood as punishable. (p. 4)

In this book we have claimed that education is a complex task that cannot effectively be achieved through prescription, rules, or policy; effective schooling requires teacher flexibility and autonomy. It is easy to see how important organizational citizenship behaviors might be under conditions that are not easily routinized but still require high levels of cooperation. The causal chain we are proposing is as follows: Certain leadership behaviors elicit trust in the leader; trust in the leader, in turn, elicits organizational citizenship behaviors (OCBs), which are by their nature cooperative, aligned with common goals, and result in organizational effectiveness (MacKenzie, Podsakoff, & Ahearne, 1996; Podsakoff, Ahearne, & MacKenzie, 1997; Podsakoff & MacKenzie, 1994; Podsakoff, MacKenzie, Paine, & Bachrach, 2000; Walz & Niehoff, 1996).

Although there is disagreement about the best way to conceptualize and measure organizational citizenship behaviors (Organ, 1997; LePine, Erez, & Johnson, 2002; Van Dyne, Cummings, & Parks, 1995), there is a great deal of evidence that they have powerful consequences for performance (DiPaola & Hoy, 2005a; LePine et al., 2002; Organ & Ryan, 1995; Podsakoff et al., 1990; Smith, Organ, & Near, 1983; Wang, Law, Hackett, Wang, & Chen, 2005). This is especially true of relationships between leader behavior, organizational contexts, and effectiveness.

What are organizational citizenship behaviors? There have been several efforts to create a taxonomy of OCBs that follow taxonomic rules. It seems that the approach of Podsakoff et al. (2000) is useful for our purposes. In their review of the research, they organized OCBs under seven categories and defined these behaviors as follows:

1. *Helping behaviors* involve freely helping others or preventing work task-related problems.
2. *Sportsmanship* includes the disposition to accept inconveniences without complaint (Organ, 1990). Leaders displaying sportsmanship are positive even when disappointed, are not offended when others don't accept their suggestions, sacrifice their interests for the group, and don't take personally rejection of their ideas.
3. *Organizational loyalty* involves promoting, protecting, and defending the organization and staying committed to it.
4. *Organizational compliance* refers to an individual's acceptance and internalization of the rules, regulations, and procedures, even when not monitored.
5. *Individual initiative* includes creativity and innovation used to improve one's own or the organization's performance, as well as enthusiasm for the job, willingness to accept additional responsibilities, and encouragement of others to as well.
6. *Civic virtue* has to do with commitment to the organization as a whole and a willingness to participate in governance and actively contribute to organizational decisions.
7. *Self-development* includes a willingness to improve one's work-related knowledge and skill.

Originally these OCBs were described as being above and beyond contractual job responsibilities, managerial expectation, or enforcement (Organ, 1988). In fact, often these behaviors cannot easily be written as job tasks, but they do seem, more and more, to be a part of managerial expectation for acceptable job performance. At any rate, it should be clear that citizenship behaviors are essential for organizations whose processes and outcomes are somewhat ill defined and difficult to measure.

Because the work of schools is necessarily unpredictable, as it responds to the diverse and changing needs of learners, and because many outcomes of schooling are the consequence of conditions outside school or teacher control, teaching cannot be scripted, monitored, or even evaluated easily by simple outcome measures, gain scores, or sampled observation. Ideally, teachers practice their profession and craft with a great deal of autonomy, the essence of professionalism (Forsyth & Danisiewicz, 1985). Critical, then, is organizational citizenship behavior, which when present, substitutes for close managerial supervision and organizational formalization (Dirks & Ferrin, 2001). Not only does organizational citizenship stand in for performance and outcome monitoring, but it is also the appropriate mechanism for developing successful schools because it supports risk taking, flexibility, creativity, and reflective teacher response to learners (DiPaola & Hoy, 2005a, 2005b; DiPaola & Tschannen-Moran, 2001).

PUTTING IT TOGETHER

Figure 10.1 depicts a simplified version of research findings that link leader behaviors with collective trust, organizational citizenship, and task performance. This set of relationships will be integrated with our theory of collective trust to tease out implications for the practice of school leadership. Some generalizations about effective principal leadership can be drawn quite clearly because of our focus on research related to principal and teacher behavior.

We are most interested in how principal behaviors produce teacher cooperation and high performance. Some leadership behaviors have direct consequences for performance, whereas the evidence suggests that others affect performance primarily through collective teacher trust in the principal, the production of teacher citizenship behaviors, or both. It seems useful to assume that all these variables act both directly and indirectly on performance.

The Effects of Leadership Behaviors

As we show in Figure 10.1, we move from leadership behaviors to organizational performance, with collective trust in leaders and organizational leadership behaviors mediating the process. Our discussion and analysis also move from findings reported in the broader organizational literature to school research findings and, eventually, to implications for the principal's leadership practice.

The Dirks and Ferrin (2002) meta-analysis consistently found high correlations between transformational leadership and trust in leadership. Podsakoff and colleagues (1990) studied the effects of transformational and transactional leadership behaviors on trust in leader, employee job satisfaction, and organizational leadership behaviors and found that transactional leadership behaviors did not affect OCBs directly, but indirectly through collective trust in the leader. However, transactional leadership behavior, specifically contingent reward behavior (measured as the extent to which a leader provides rewards in exchange for follower effort), did affect organizational citizenship positively. The finding is consistent with the reasoning behind our collective trust model, which recognizes the control function

Figure 10.1. General model of evidence related to leadership behavior, collective trust in leader, organizational citizenship, and cooperation/task performance.

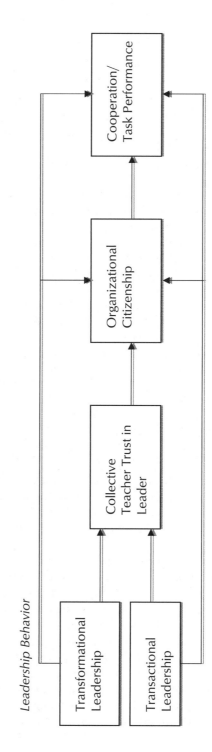

of contingent reward as part of a necessary threshold of formal structure underpinning trust formation.

Transformational leadership behaviors enhance employee trust in leader, and through this trust, increase the levels of cooperative employee behaviors that complex/professional organizations depend on. The Podsakoff and colleagues (2000) meta-analysis, summarizing the research of the previous decade and a half, found a strong relationship between all transformational leadership behaviors and all OCBs.

In addition to affecting both collective trust of the leader and OCBs, the Lowe, Kroeck, and Sivasubramaniam (1996) meta-analysis concluded that transformational leadership behaviors reliably and consistently predict the effectiveness of work units, leader charisma being most strongly related to effectiveness. The relationship between transactional leadership behaviors and effectiveness was less reliable. Interestingly, there was a consistently stronger relationship between two transformational leader behaviors (charisma and intellectual stimulation) and effectiveness in public organizations, especially educational institutions. Lowe and colleagues (1996) explain:

> Introducing employees to appreciate, dissect, ponder and discover what they would not otherwise discern is perhaps the basis of behavior that comes closest to our prototypical abstractions of "true leadership." The leader who intellectually stimulates subordinates is teaching subordinates "how to fish for themselves rather than simply giving them the fish" (Bass, 1988). When leaders actually engage in such behavior, they appear to engender not only subordinate acclamations, but productive ardor as well. The transformational leader through intellectual stimulation instills feelings of power in followers to attain higher goals through socialized power rather than the "pure" charismatic leader who attempts to exert dominance and subjugate followers through personalized power. (Waldman, 1987, as cited in Lowe et al., 1996, pp. 415–416)

Before we leave the subject of leadership behavior, we should highlight the similarity between behaviors predictive of high levels of employee performance and those behaviors that reveal the leader as trustworthy. In constructing their framework for initiating trustworthy leader behavior, Whitener, Brodt, Korsgaard, and Werner (1998) identify behaviors (behavioral consistency, behavioral integrity, sharing and delegation of control, communication, and demonstration of concern) that closely parallel the antecedents of perceived trustworthiness (honesty, openness, reliability, benevolence, and competence). Fortuitously, these behaviors are also consistent with transformational leadership (identifying and articulating a vision, providing an appropriate model, fostering the acceptance of group goals, high performance expectations, providing individualized support, and intellectual stimulation) and certain transactional behaviors as well. The overlap in these behavioral sets suggests that there are a few critical leader behaviors that directly and indirectly produce a succession of outcomes eventually resulting in the high performance levels in organizations.

Some school leadership research supports the claim of a direct relationship between transformational and certain aspects of transactional leadership and academic performance as well (Geist & Hoy, 2004; Koh, Steers, & Terborg, 1995; Marks & Printy, 2003; Somech & Ron, 2007). It is not clear, however, why this happens. Our model begins to explain how the principal's leadership behavior promotes teacher trust in the principal and organizational citizenship.

The Effects of Collective Trust in the Leader

The preceding discussion establishes particular leader behaviors as antecedents of collective trust in the leader. The level of collective teacher trust in the principal becomes normative in the teacher group. Keep in mind that, in addition to principal behavior, the faculty as a group plays an important role in the formation and sustenance of this norm. We turn now to the relationships between normative trust in the leader, organizational citizenship, and task performance.

There is strong evidence that trust in the leader affects task performance directly as well as indirectly through employee OCBs (Dirks, 2000; Dirks & Ferrin, 2002; Forsyth & Adams, 2010; Jung & Avolio, 2000; Konovsky & Pugh, 1994; Wech, 2002). Relevant to our interest in collective trust, Wech (2002) notes that a "group's global perception of the trustworthiness of its supervisor is affected by each member's personal experiences with the supervisor, as well as observations or communications about the supervisor's interactions with other group members" (p. 358).

There is also evidence that collective teacher trust in colleagues is strongly and positively related to the emergence of OCBs (DiPaola & Hoy, 2005a). Data from that same study are consistent with other studies showing that collective trust in the principal is positively related to OCBs (Dirks & Ferrin, 2002; Podsakoff et al., 2000). For teachers, as well as employees in general, organizational citizenship behaviors are enhanced by leader behavior and the trust that individuals and the collective work group have for leaders. The ways in which these leadership and trust effects come about vary, but the consequences for OCBs are clear and strong.

The Effects of Organizational Citizenship

The assumption of Organ (1988, 1990) and his colleagues (Bateman & Organ, 1983; Smith et al., 1983) was that organizational citizenship behaviors would contribute positively to organizational performance. As late as 2000, however, Podsakoff and his colleagues complained that little evidence verified that assumption; however, after completing a review of emerging research, Podsakoff and colleagues (2000) concluded that organizational citizenship behaviors are related to organizational effectiveness. Additional support for this claim can be found in Allen and Rush (1998), Bell and Menguc (2002), Podsakoff and colleagues (1997), and Wang and colleagues (2005).

The school literature, like the general organizational literature, focuses on the antecedents of organizational citizenship behaviors rather than their consequences (Bogler & Somech, 2004, 2005; Somech & Ron, 2007). In one of a few school studies, DiPaola and Hoy (2005a) found that organizational citizenship was related to 12th-grade proficiency in reading and mathematics. The weight of organizational and school evidence favors a conclusion that organizational citizenship behaviors of teachers will have positive consequences for school performance.

In sum, we can understand the interactive roles of collective trust of the principal, together with leadership and organizational citizenship in this way. Leadership behaviors of principals, directly and through their enhancement of trust and organizational citizenship, elicit cooperation and high teacher performance levels. The functional motives of these leadership behaviors are not sinister or manipulative; rather they are to create a work environment facilitating the mission and tasks of the school. In the complex arena of teacher and principal behavior, trust is pivotal to nuture a culture of optimism. The advice of Whitener and colleagues (1998) to managers in general is as appropriate for principals: "We propose that managers and organizations interested in establishing trust must take the first step" (p. 527). Even more to the point: "In general, trust in the principal is directly influenced by the behavior of the principal" (Geist & Hoy, 2004, p. 13).

GUIDELINES FOR LEADERSHIP PRACTICE

We turn finally to an interpretation and application of what research and theory have to tell us about how principals can foster trust and organizational citizenship behavior in teachers. While leader behavior is not the only antecedent of collective teacher trust in the principal and organizational citizenship, it is an important one, and one that is under the direct control of the principal.

The guidelines we propose are not particularly novel, but they are essential and basic. The evidence is clear that the success of organizations depends on trusting interpersonal relationships. That is, successful leadership is not as mysterious as we might have thought; it has simply a great deal to do with trusting relationships. The theory of collective trust is an important way of thinking about, talking about, and acting on these relationships in a school community. Unless there is utter chaos in a school, which threatens the basic safety of students and teachers, a first priority of principals should be to establish a trusting environment, and to start with, that means trust in the person and leadership of the principal.

Guideline 1: Establish Trust in the Principal by Being Trustworthy

Trust in the principal makes teacher cooperation with the principal more likely and it elicits from teachers citizenship behaviors that make school success more likely. Trust serves as a central catalyst that energizes optimistic beliefs and hopeful behaviors by teachers and other members of the school community.

Early in this book we established that trust means taking action even when there is risk. When the principal is perceived as trustworthy, teachers are willing to take the risks inherent in innovative and creative efforts to address learner need, important especially in the face of great challenge. Trustworthiness and the establishment of collective teacher trust in the principal take time; there are no quick fixes. The formation of collective teacher beliefs that the principal is trustworthy emerges from repeated teacher discernment of the principal's behavior that it consistently meets expectation.

Principals are more likely to be perceived as trustworthy if they are mindful of the criteria that will be used to judge their trustworthiness, namely, honesty, openness, reliability, competence, and benevolence. Trusted principals will reflect on these criteria frequently, examining how their behavior appears to teachers and others in the school community. Teachers and others, of course, can only discern the principal's trustworthiness if they have opportunity to observe the principal in action and through frequent, personal communication. For principals, being in the presence of teachers and creating opportunities for interaction around the central work of the school are essential for teacher perceptions of principal trustworthiness to emerge as normative.

It is nearly impossible to fake authenticity in the long term. So, for example, to be perceived as authentically benevolent, it is necessary for principals to show genuine care about the people they work with. To be perceived as competent, it is necessary that principals be knowledgeable about the core technology of schools and instruction and to be visibly and intensely interested in the teaching challenges and experiments of teachers. To be perceived as genuinely honest, it is necessary that principals be equitably transparent with everyone about the challenges that face the school, bad news and good news. Principals should not have an informal clique of favorites, real or imagined.

The principal's challenge to be trustworthy is one that never ends and requires constant reflection, vigilance, and effort. Fortunately, many of the behaviors that elicit trust are also effective leadership behaviors and ones that evoke organizational citizenship. Trustworthiness, among all the characteristics of effective school leaders, is not optional; it is a necessity.

Guideline 2: Be Mostly a Leader, Sometimes a Manager

As Bruhn (2001) notes, "Most of the difficulties in leading and managing organizations are due to resistance to change. One of the factors that make organizational change possible and palatable is trust" (p. 50). In at least one sense, leadership is about the future, and management is about the present. Leadership invests and builds capacity; management monitors the tidiness of the organization in the here and now. The better the leadership, the less necessary the management. Earlier we demonstrated that leadership, especially transformational leadership, elicits the trust and organizational citizenship of teachers and supports high performance and school effectiveness.

How does transformational vision, a collective desired future state, emerge in a school community? Too often leaders use a formulaic process, usually a workshop, for developing the school's formal vision, mission, and core-values statements. The results of this process are then posted prominently for all to see and be inspired by. A vision statement can also be issued by the school board, superintendent, or principal based on what they believe should be the vision of the school. Neither of these approaches is consistent with transformational leadership, nor do they produce a collective, desired future. A vision's certain death and irrelevance is assured when it is framed and hung in the foyer. A vision is a living thing and must emerge dynamically and continuously from the school community.

The transformational leadership of schools is dependent on relationships and interactions that are centered in teaching and learning. Through inspiration and intellectual stimulation, constantly nourished understanding, and insatiable interest in teaching, transformational principals engage teachers constantly in the examination of the present and the building of a collective desired future. The examined work of teachers, together with authentic conversation among teachers, school leaders, parents, and students, produces a shared vision rooted in emergent understandings, experiment, failure, success, and hope. The vision shepherded by transformational principals defies encryption because it lives in the daily reflection, talk, and behavior of teachers and leaders.

The principal's role is to practice a soft vigilance. Expertise, influence, and persuasion are the tools effective principals use in collaboration with all members of the school community to shape the school's vision. This brand of leadership is flexible, fluid, and guided, in a very disciplined way, by a common desired future.

We are, of course, not saying that transactional leadership, management, and structure have no place in schools, but their place is minimal and their role is supportive. Much like rules and hierarchy as discussed in Chapter 7, management practices in schools should *enable* the work of teachers, not hinder it. Management practices, however, can provide a threshold of comfort contributing a basis for a predictable organization.

Guideline 3: Expect, Respect, and Model Organizational Citizenship

Much like collective trust, organizational citizenship behavior works best when it becomes normative within groups and organizations. Like other group norms, it takes time and nurturance to establish. A similar set of context factors enables the development of OCBs and collective trust. That is, the context surrounding the school, the community in all its levels, enters the school through the history and dispositions of teachers, leaders, students, and parents. The climate and history of the school itself affect organizational citizenship, as do the norms, beliefs, and attitudes of the various role groups that make up the school.

We have noted that transformational and trustworthy behaviors of the principal are likely to elicit organizational citizenship behaviors from teachers. Principals should, of course, be the best of organizational citizens—their selfless commitment to the school being always and everywhere evident. But another very critical way that the principal can affect the school's culture, including organizational citizenship, is by extraordinarily careful selection of new teachers. All the characteristics and conditions of school success are affected by the dispositions, competence, and commitment of teachers to the work of the school.

Our experience suggests that the teacher selection process is typically not done well and decisions to employ are often hurried and based on little credible evidence. Seldom are teachers asked to demonstrate teaching skills. Interviews are perfunctory; reference checks are little more than a verification of heartbeat. Yet it is in the selection of new teachers that principals can have dramatic influence on a school's future. Hiring decisions that are fraught with rushed compromise, inadequate tests of instructional competence, unexamined histories of organizational citizenship, and naive assumptions about candidate dispositions can haunt a school for many years.

In contrast, the selection of teachers who are dynamic, knowledgeable, caring, and good citizens of the school community will also influence the school for years to come. To create a trusting and functional school, principals must dedicate adequate time to recruiting and screening effective teachers. In this matter, principals should never compromise—there are few actions that will so directly determine their success or failure.

Guideline 4: Develop and Nurture a Culture of Trust and Optimism

There are at least two ways the principal can nurture a culture of trust in the school. One we have been discussing throughout this chapter targets the fostering of collective teacher trust in the principal through the practice of transformational leadership and through being trustworthy. Such trust elicits teacher citizenship and enhances the organizational predictability necessary for teacher cooperation (Forsyth & Adams, 2010). In this way, the trustworthy and transformational behaviors of principals, indirectly through enhanced organizational predictability and teacher citizenship, affect positive school performance.

The other way principals promote a trusting culture was introduced in Chapter 6 where we demonstrated how collective faculty trust in clients promotes student achievement. The principal's role in this matter is critical but also primarily indirect. The leadership task of the principal is to build social conditions that promote learning: (1) a can-do attitude in teachers; (2) internalized responsibility; (3) outreach to parents; (4) professional community, which focuses on collaborative work practices and commitment to improve teaching and learning; and (5) high expectations and academic standards (Bryk & Schneider, 2002). The one general notion that encompasses *all these conditions* is a culture of academic optimism, which is anchored in trust relationships. Academic optimism serves both as a strong motivational force for achievement as well as a catalyst for cooperative and collaborative relations among students, parents, and teachers, which ultimately reinforce both trust relations in the school and a collective sense of optimism about teaching and learning.

In summary, we have demonstrated the importance of a climate of collective trust for effective schools. In order to explore how trust in the leader is nurtured in schools, we examined principal behaviors as transactional and transformational, showing how these behaviors influence the formation of trust, elicit organizational citizenship behaviors of teachers, and move schools toward a common desired future. Finally, we concluded that the principal's leadership influences student achievement indirectly by nurturing a culture of academic optimism anchored in collective trust.

In this book we have explored quite thoroughly a theory and extant research on collective organizational trust as it functions in schools. Embracing trust, in all its forms, we have examined the ways trust lubricates the processes that make schools effective. We have explored the horizons of trust, holding out for practicing school leaders the trusting environment as a necessary and critical condition of success.

Epilogue

In this volume we have examined more than 3 decades of research on collective trust in schools and have formulated a theory of collective trust. The text provides researchers and scholars with a sound theoretical framework and set of reliable measures to continue the study of trust. It also gives school practitioners a set of tools to assess and develop comprehensive cultures of trust with the goal of long-term development and reform. Finally, the book summarizes what we know about collective trust and how we can use that knowledge to improve schools.

We conclude our analysis with a brief summary that highlights nine important principles gleaned from the research and theory on trust in schools along with a few practical suggestions.

1. Leadership generates collective trust.

   - Make authentic behavior and openness habits of action.
   - Stamp out artificiality and game playing.

2. Organizational structure influences collective trust.

   - Build enabling school structures.
   - Avoid structural features that restrain and hinder.

3. School innovation and reform require collective trust.

   - Make trust the linchpin of school reform.
   - Use social support to create and nurture trust.

4. Trust, efficacy, and academic emphasis create a synergistic sense of academic optimism.

   - Forge a culture of academic optimism.
   - Treat academic optimism as an investment in persistence, resilience, and achievement.

5. Positive and productive social interaction requires collective trust.

   - Infuse trust as a persistent theme in the life of schools.
   - Guard against any action that erodes trust.

6. Collective trust is salient for student achievement.

   - Build collective trust as a platform for efficacy, optimism, parental outreach, professional community, and high expectations.
   - Earn the trust of parents and students.

7. Collective trust requires risk taking and vulnerability.

   - Demonstrate benevolence, reliability, honesty, openness, and competence.
   - Eschew secrecy and deal making.

8. Collective trust enhances cooperation.

   - Establish the community as a partner in school affairs.
   - Confirm collaborative and professional behavior as the norm.

9. Collective trust shapes social capital and social action.
   - Create and support authentic reciprocal interactions: They boost trust.
   - Use social capital to promote school conditions that enhance student achievement.

Hardin (2006) makes the astute observation that the literature on trust barely mentions trustworthiness, even though much of it is primarily about trustworthiness. His observation holds for school trust research as well. As we have demonstrated in this book, a large measure of a school's success depends on the creation of a culture of trustworthiness. Our nine principles and suggestions are first steps on the road to creating such a culture.

Appendixes

APPENDIX 1.1 EARLY COLLECTIVE TRUST SCALES

Directions. Please indicate your degree of agreement with each of the statements about your school from **strongly disagree (1)** to **strongly agree (6)**.

	Strongly Disagree	Disagree	Somewhat Disagree	Somewhat Agree	Agree	Strongly Agree
1. The teachers in this school are suspicious of most of the principal's action.	1	2	3	4	5	6
2. The teachers in this school have faith in the integrity of the principal.	1	2	3	4	5	6
3. The principal takes unfair advantage of teachers in this school.	1	2	3	4	5	6
4. The principal in this school typically acts with the best interests of the teachers in mind.	1	2	3	4	5	6
5. Teachers in this school often question the motives of the principal.	1	2	3	4	5	6
6. Teachers in this school trust the principal.	1	2	3	4	5	6
7. The principal in this school keeps his/her word.	1	2	3	4	5	6
8. Teachers in this school typically look out for each other.	1	2	3	4	5	6
9. Teachers in this school are suspicious of each other.	1	2	3	4	5	6
10. Teachers in this school trust each other.	1	2	3	4	5	6
11. Even in difficult situations teachers in this school can depend on each other.	1	2	3	4	5	6
12. Teachers in this school believe in each other.	1	2	3	4	5	6
13. Teachers in this school take unfair advantage of each other.	1	2	3	4	5	6
14. Teachers in this school have faith in the integrity of their colleagues.	1	2	3	4	5	6
15. Teachers in this school district see no need for job actions.	1	2	3	4	5	6

16. This school district takes unfair advantage of
their teachers.   1   2   3   4   5   6
17. In this school district the teachers association is
unnecessary.   1   2   3   4   5   6
18. This school district typically acts in the best
interests of the teachers.   1   2   3   4   5   6
19. Teachers in this school system are suspicious of
the motives of the district.   1   2   3   4   5   6
20. Teachers in this school system have trust in the
school district.   1   2   3   4   5   6
21. In this school district a strong teachers'
organization is needed.   1   2   3   4   5   6

Scoring Directions:
1. Score Items 1, 3, 5, 9, 13, 16, 19, and 21 in reverse, that is, [1 = 6, 2 = 5, 3 = 4, 4 = 3, 5 = 2, 6 = 1].
2. Faculty Trust in the Principal = Sum of items 1–7.
3. Faculty Trust in Colleagues = sum of items 8–14.
4. Faculty Trust in the Organization = Sum of items 15–21.

All Appendices are available at www.waynekhoy.com

APPENDIX 1.2 EFFECTIVENESS INDEX

Directions: Teachers produce a variety of products such as lesson plans, new curricula, and student learning as well as numerous services, including teaching, advising, counseling, and parent conferences. Think of these products and services as you respond to each item and indicate the degree to which you agree with the following statements about your school.

	Strongly Disagree	Disagree	Somewhat Disagree	Somewhat Agree	Agree	Strongly Agree
1. The *quality* of products and services produced in this school is outstanding.	1	2	3	4	5	6
2. The *quantity* of products and services in this school is high.	1	2	3	4	5	6
3. The teachers in my school do a good job *coping* with emergencies and disruptions.	1	2	3	4	5	6
4. Most everyone in the school *accepts* and *adjusts* to changes.	1	2	3	4	5	6
5. When changes are made in the school, teachers accept and adjust *quickly*.	1	2	3	4	5	6
6. Teachers in this school are well *informed* about innovations that could affect them.	1	2	3	4	5	6

7. Teachers in this school *anticipate* problems and
   prevent them.   1   2   3   4   5   6
8. Teachers in this school use available resources
   efficiently.   1   2   3   4   5   6

APPENDIX 3.1 OMNIBUS T-SCALE

Directions: Please indicate your degree of agreement with each of the statements about your school from **strongly disagree (1)** to **strongly agree (2)**.

	Strongly Disagree	Disagree	Somewhat Disagree	Somewhat Agree	Agree	Strongly Agree
1. Teachers in this school trust the principal.	1	2	3	4	5	6
2. Teachers in this school trust each other.	1	2	3	4	5	6
3. Teachers in this school trust their students.	1	2	3	4	5	6
4. The teachers in this school are suspicious of most of the principal's actions.	1	2	3	4	5	6
5. Teachers in this school typically look out for each other.	1	2	3	4	5	6
6. Teachers in this school trust the parents.	1	2	3	4	5	6
7. The teachers in this school have faith in the integrity of the principal.	1	2	3	4	5	6
8. Teachers in this school are suspicious of each other.	1	2	3	4	5	6
9. The principal in this school typically acts in the best interests of teachers.	1	2	3	4	5	6
10. Students in this school care about each other.	1	2	3	4	5	6
11. The principal of this school does not show concern for the teachers.	1	2	3	4	5	6
12. Even in difficult situations, teachers in this school can depend on each other.	1	2	3	4	5	6
13. Teachers in this school do their jobs well.	1	2	3	4	5	6
14. Parents in this school are reliable in their commitments	1	2	3	4	5	6
15. Teachers in this school can ely on the principal.	1	2	3	4	5	6
16. Teachers in this school have faith in the integrity of their colleagues.	1	2	3	4	5	6
17. Students in this school can be counted on to do their work.	1	2	3	4	5	6
18. The principal in this school is competent in doing his or her job.	1	2	3	4	5	6

19. The teachers in this school are open with each other.   1   2   3   4   5   6
20. Teachers can count on parental support.   1   2   3   4   5   6
21. When teachers in this school tell you something,
    you can believe it.   1   2   3   4   5   6
22. Teachers here believe students are competent
    learners.   1   2   3   4   5   6
23. The principal doesn't tell teachers what is really
    going on.   1   2   3   4   5   6
24. Teachers think that most of the parents do a
    good job.   1   2   3   4   5   6
25. Teachers can believe what parents tell them.   1   2   3   4   5   6
26. Students here are secretive.   1   2   3   4   5   6

APPENDIX 3.2 PARENT TRUST IN SCHOOL SCALE

Directions: The items below permit a range of response from one extreme on the left (strongly disagree) to the other extreme on the right (strongly agree). Please indicate how you feel about your child's school by filling in one circled number in each row. Circled numbers close to the "1" or "8" suggest more intense feelings.

	Strongly Agree	Agree	Somewhat Agree	Slightly Agree	Slightly Disagree	Somewhat Disagree	Disagree	Strongly Disagree
1. This school always does what it is suppose to.	1	2	3	4	5	6	7	8
2. This school keeps me well informed.	1	2	3	4	5	6	7	8
3. I really trust this school.	1	2	3	4	5	6	7	8
4. Kids at this school are well cared for.	1	2	3	4	5	6	7	8
5. This school is always honest with me.	1	2	3	4	5	6	7	8
6. This school does a terrific job.	1	2	3	4	5	6	7	8
7. This school has high standards for all kids.	1	2	3	4	5	6	7	8
8. This school is always ready to help.	1	2	3	4	5	6	7	8
9. I never worry about my child when he/she is there.	1	2	3	4	5	6	7	8
10. At this school, I know I'll be listened to.	1	2	3	4	5	6	7	8

APPENDIX 3.3 PARENT TRUST IN PRINCIPAL SCALE

Directions: The items below permit a range of response from one extreme on the left (strongly disagree) to the other extreme on the right (strongly agree). Please indicate how you feel about your child's principal by filling in one circled number in each row. The closer the circled number is to the "1" or "8," the more clearly and intensely you feel about the item.

	Strongly Agree	Agree	Somewhat Agree	Slightly Agree	Slightly Disagree	Somewhat Disagree	Disagree	Strongly Disagree
1. The principal of this school **is good at his/her job.**	1	2	3	4	5	6	7	8
2. The principal of this school **can be counted on to do his/her job.**	1	2	3	4	5	6	7	8
3. The principal of this school **is well intentioned.**	1	2	3	4	5	6	7	8
4. The principal of this school **is always honest.**	1	2	3	4	5	6	7	8
5. The principal of this school **invites both criticism and praise from parents.**	1	2	3	4	5	6	7	8
6. The principal of this school **is very reliable.**	1	2	3	4	5	6	7	8
7. The principal of this school **has high standards for all kids.**	1	2	3	4	5	6	7	8
8. The principal of this school **is always ready to help.**	1	2	3	4	5	6	7	8
9. The principal of this school **treats everyone with respect.**	1	2	3	4	5	6	7	8
10. The principal of this school **keeps an open door.**	1	2	3	4	5	6	7	8
11. The principal of this school **owns up to his/her mistakes.**	1	2	3	4	5	6	7	8
12. The principal of this school **knows how to make learning happen.**	1	2	3	4	5	6	7	8
13. The principal of this school **is always there when you need him/her.**	1	2	3	4	5	6	7	8
14. The principal of this school **is trustworthy.**	1	2	3	4	5	6	7	8
15. The principal of this school **likes to talk to parents.**	1	2	3	4	5	6	7	8

APPENDIX 3.4 STUDENT TRUST IN FACULTY SCALE

Directions: Please indicate how much you agree or disagree with each of the following statements. Please choose the answer that is closest to how you feel or what you think by filling in one circled number in each row. Please answer all items, even if you are not sure.

	Strongly Disagree	Disagree	Agree	Strongly Agree
1. Teachers are always ready to help at this school.	1	2	3	4
2. Teachers at this school are easy to talk to.	1	2	3	4
3. Students are well cared for at this school.	1	2	3	4
4. Teachers at this school always do what they are supposed to.	1	2	3	4
5. Teachers at this school really listen to students.	1	2	3	4
6. Teachers at this school are always honest with me.	1	2	3	4
7. Teachers at this school do a terrific job.	1	2	3	4
8. Teachers at this school are good at teaching.	1	2	3	4
9. Teachers at this school have high expectations for all students.	1	2	3	4
10. Teachers at this school *do not* care about students.	1	2	3	4
11. Students at this school can believe what teachers tell them.	1	2	3	4
12. Students learn a lot from teachers at this school.	1	2	3	4
13. Students at this school can depend on teachers for help.	1	2	3	4

APPENDIX 3.5 STUDENT TRUST IN PRINCIPAL SCALE

Directions: Please indicate how much you agree or disagree with each of the following statements. Please choose the answer that is closest to how you feel or what you think by filling in one circled number in each row. Please answer all items, even if you are not sure.

	Never	Some of the time	Most of the time	Always
1. The principal at my school **is nice.**	1	2	3	4
2. The principal at my school **likes students.**	1	2	3	4
3. The principal at my school **is fair.**	1	2	3	4
4. The principal at my school **is helpful.**	1	2	3	4
5. The principal at my school **does what he/she says he/she will do.**	1	2	3	4
6. The principal at my school **is there for students when needed.**	1	2	3	4
7. The principal at my school **tells the truth to students.**	1	2	3	4
8. The principal at my school **makes time to talk.**	1	2	3	4
9. The principal at my school **is smart.**	1	2	3	4
10. The principal at my school **can be trusted.**	1	2	3	4
11. The principal at my school **does his/her job well.**	1	2	3	4
12. The principal at my school **treats all students with respect.**	1	2	3	4

References

Acheson, K., & Gall, M. (2003). *Clinical supervision and teacher development*. New York: Wiley & Sons.

Adams, C. M. (2003). The effects of school structure and trust on collective teacher efficacy. Unpublished doctoral dissertation, Oklahoma State University, Stillwater, OK.

Adams, C. M. (2008). Building trust in school: A review of the empirical evidence. In Wayne K. Hoy & Michael DiPaola (Eds.), *Improving schools: Studies in leadership and culture* (pp. 29–54). Greenwich, CN: Information Age.

Adams, C. M. (2010). Social determinants of student trust in high poverty elementary schools. In W. K. Hoy & M. F. DiPaola (Eds.), *Analyzing school contexts: Influences of principals and teachers in the service of students* (pp. 255–276). Charlotte, NC: Information Age.

Adams, C. M., & Forsyth, P. B. (2007a). *Determinants of parent-school trust: A multilevel analysis*. Paper presented at the annual meeting of the American Educational Research Association, Chicago, IL.

Adams, C. M., & Forsyth, P. B. (2007b). Promoting a culture of parent collaboration and trust: An empirical study. *Journal of School Public Relations, 28*(1), 32–56.

Adams, C. M., & Forsyth, P. B. (2009a). Conceptualizing and validating a measure of student trust. In Wayne K. Hoy & Michael DiPaola (Eds.), *Studies in school improvement* (pp. 263–281). Charlotte, NC: Information Age.

Adams, C. M., & Forsyth, P. B. (2009b). The nature and function of trust in schools. *Journal of School Leadership, 19*, 126–151.

Adams, C. M., Forsyth, P. B., & Mitchell, R. M. (2009). The formation of parent-school trust: A multilevel analysis. *Educational Administration Quarterly, 45*(1), 4–33.

Adams, J. E., & Kirst, M. W. (1999). New demands and concepts for educational accountability: Striving for results in an era of excellence. In J. Murphy & K. S. Louis (Eds.), *Handbook of research on educational administration* (2nd ed., pp. 463–489). San Francisco: Jossey-Bass.

Adler, P. S., & Borys, B. (1996). Two types of bureaucracy: Enabling and coercive. *Administrative Science Quarterly, 41*(1), 61–89.

Allen, T. D., & Rush, M. C. (1998). The effects of organizational citizenship behavior on performance judgments: A field study and a laboratory experiment. *Journal of Applied Psychology, 83*(2), 247–260.

Anderson, M. (1971). *Family structure in 19th century Lancashire*. Cambridge: Cambridge University Press.

Angus, L. (2008). The politics of community renewal and educational reform. In E. A. Samier & A. G. Stanley (Eds.), *Political approaches to educational administration and leadership* (pp. 204–219). London: Taylor & Francis.

Argyris, C. (1952). *The impact of budgets on people*. New York: Controllership Foundation.

Argyris, C. (1964). *Integrating the individual and the organization*. New York: Wiley.

Auerbach, S. (2007). From moral supporters to struggling advocates: Reconceptualizing parent roles in education through the experience of working-class families of color. *Urban Education, 42*(3), 250–283.

Aulakh, P. S., Kotabe, M., & Sahay, A. (1997). Trust and performance in cross-border marketing partnerships. In P. W. Beamish & J. P. Killing (Eds.), *Cooperative strategies: Vol. 1. North American perspectives* (pp. 163–196). San Francisco: New Lexington Press.

Bachmann, R. (2003). Trust and power as means of coordinating the internal relations of the organization: A conceptual framework. In B. Nooteboom & F. Six (Eds.), *The trust process in organizations: Empirical studies of the determinants and the process of trust development* (pp. 58–74). Cheltenham, UK: Edward Elgar.

Bachmann, R. (2006). Trust and/or power: Towards a sociological theory of organizational relationships. In R. Bachmann & A. Zaheer (Eds.), *Handbook of trust research* (pp. 393–408). Cheltenham, UK: Edward Elgar.

Baier, A. (1986). Trust and antitrust. *Ethics, 96*(2), 231–260.

Baier, A. (1994). Sustaining trust. In *Moral prejudices: Essays on ethics*. Cambridge: Harvard University Press.

Bandura, A. (1997). *Self-efficacy: The exercise of control*. New York: Freeman.

Bandura, A. (n.d.). *Teacher self-efficacy scale*. Unpublished manuscript.

Barnard, C. I. (1938). *The functions of the executive*. Cambridge, MA: Harvard University Press.

Barnes, L., Adams, C. M., & Forsyth, P. B. (2002, April). *School trust of principal: Instrument development*. Paper presented at the American Educational Research Annual Convention in New Orleans, LA.

Barnes, L. B., Mitchell, R. M., Forsyth, P. B., & Adams, C. M. (2005). *The effects of parental trust on perceived collective influence and school involvement*. Paper presented at the annual meeting of the American Educational Research Association, Montreal, Canada.

Baron, J. B. (1999). *Exploring high and improving reading achievement in Connecticut*. Washington, DC: National Educational Goals Panel.

Bass, B. M. (1985). *Leadership and performance beyond expectations*. New York: The Free Press.

Bass, B. M. (1998). *Transformational leadership: Industrial, military, and educational impact*. Mahwah, NJ: Erlbaum.

Bass, B. M. (1999). Two decades of research and development in transformational leadership. *European Journal of Work and Organizational Psychology, 8*(1), 9–32.

Bass, B. M., Avolio, B. J., & Goodheim, L. (1987). Biography and the assessment of transformational leadership at the world class level. *Journal of Management, 13,* 7–19.

Bateman, T. S., & Organ, D. W. (1983). Job satisfaction and the good soldier: The relationship between affect and employee citizenship. *Academy of Management Journal, 26*(4), 587–595.

Beamish, P. (1988). *Multinational joint ventures in developing countries.* London: Routledge.

Bell, S. J., & Menguc, B. (2002). The employee-organization relationship, organizational citizenship behaviors, and superior service quality. *Journal of Retailing, 78,* 131–146.

Berman, P., & McLaughlin, M. W. (1975). *Federal programs supporting educational change, Vol I: A model of educational change.* Santa Monica, CA: Rand Corporation.

Bigley, G. A., & Pearce, J. L. (1998). Straining for shared meaning in organization science: Problems of trust and distrust. *The Academy of Management Review, 23,* 405–421.

Blakely, C. H., Mayer, I. P., Gottschalk, R. G., Schmitt, N., Davidson, W. S., Roitman, D. B., et al. (1987). The fidelity-adaptation debate: Implications for the implementation of public sector social programs. *American Journal of Community Psychology, 15,* 253–268.

Blasé, J., & Blasé, J. (2000). Effective instructional leadership: Teachers' perspectives on how principals promote teaching and learning in schools. *Journal of Educational Administration, 38*(2), 130–141.

Blau, P. (1955). *The dynamics of bureaucracy.* Chicago: University of Chicago Press.

Blau, P. M. (1964). *Exchange and power in social life.* New York: John Wiley & Sons.

Block, P. (2008). *Community: The structure of belonging.* San Francisco: Berrett-Koehler.

Bogler, R., & Somech, A. (2004). Influence of teacher empowerment on teachers' organizational commitment, professional commitment and organizational citizenship behavior in schools. *Teaching and Teacher Education, 20,* 277–289.

Bogler, R., & Somech, A. (2005). Organizational citizenship behavior in school: How does it relate to participation in decision making? *Journal of Educational Administration, 43*(5), 420–438.

Borman, G. D., Hewes, G. M., Overman, L. T., & Brown, S. (2003). Comprehensive school reform and achievement: A meta-analysis. *Review of Educational Research, 73,* 125–230.

Bourdieu, P. (1985). The social space and genesis of groups. *Social Science Information, 24*(2), 195–220.

Bourdieu, P. (1986). The forms of capital. In J. Richardson (Ed.), *Handbook of theory and research for the sociology of education* (pp. 241–258). New York: Greenwood.

Bromiley, P. (1991). Testing a causal model of corporate risk and performance. *Academy of Management Journal, 34*(1), 37–59.

Bruhn, John G. (2001). *Trust and the health of organizations.* New York: Kluwer Academic.

Bryk , A. S., & Driscoll, M. E. (1988). *The school as community: Theoretical foundations, contextual influences, and consequences for teachers and students.* Madison, WI: National Center for Effective Secondary Schools.

Bryk, A. S., & Raudenbush, S. W. (1992). *Hierarchical linear models.* Newbury Park, CA: Sage.

Bryk, A. S., & Schneider, B. (2002). *Trust in schools: A core resource for improvement.* New York: Russell Sage Foundation.

Bryk, A. S., & Schneider, B. (2003). Trust in schools: A core resource for reform. *Educational Leadership, 60*(6), 40–44.

Bryk, A. S., Sebring, P. B., Allensworth, E., Luppescu, S., & Easton, J. Q. (2010). *Organizing schools for improvement: Lessons from Chicago.* Chicago: University of Chicago Press.

Burns, J. M. (1978). *Leadership.* New York: Harper & Row.

Burt, R. (2000). The network structure of social capital. In R. Sutton & B. Staw (Eds.), *Research in Organizational Behavior.* Greenwich, CT: JAI Press.

Butler, J. K., & Cantrell, R. S. (1984). A behavioral decision theory approach to modeling dyadic trust in superiors and subordinates. *Psychological Reports, 55,* 81–105.

Cameron, K., & Whetton, D. (1996). Organizational effectiveness and quality: The second generation. *The Higher Education Handbook of Theory and Research, 11,* 265–306.

Cameron, K. S. (1984). The effectiveness of ineffectiveness. In B. M. Staw & L. L. Cummings (Eds.), *Research in organizational behavior: Vol. 6* (pp. 235–285). Greenwich, CT: JAI Press.

Cantrell, S. (2009). A call to study action: Lessons from research on policies designed to improve the organization and management of schooling. In G. Sykes, B. Schneider, and D. N. Plank (Eds.), *Handbook of Education Policy Research* (pp. 528–533). New York: Routledge.

Cartwright, E., & Zander, A. (1953). Pressures to uniformity in groups: Introduction. In D. Cartwright & A. Zander (Eds.), *Group dynamics: research and theory* (3rd ed.) (pp. 139–151). New York: Harper & Row.

Chiles, T. H., & McMacking, J. F. (1996). Integrating variable risk preferences, trust, and transaction cost economics. *Academy of Management Review, 21*(1), 73–99.

Christensen, C. M., Horn, M. B., & Johnson, C. W. (2008). *Disrupting class: How disruptive innovation will change the way the world learns.* New York: McGraw Hill.

Chubb, J. E. (2001, Spring). The profit motive: The private can be public. *Education Matters,* 6–12.

Cialdini, R. B. (2001). *Influence: Science and practice* (4th ed.). Needham Heights, MA: Allyn & Bacon.

Cleeton, G. U., & Mason, C. W. (1934). *Executive ability—its discovery and development.* Yellow Springs, OH: Antioch Press.

Coburn, C. E. (2003). Rethinking scale: Moving beyond numbers to deep and lasting change. *Educational Researcher, 32*(6), 3–12.

Coleman, J. S. (1986). Social theory, social research, and a theory of action. *The American Journal of Sociology, 91*(6), 1309–1335.

Coleman, J. S. (1990). *Foundations of social theory.* Cambridge, MA: Belknap Press of Harvard University Press.

Coleman, J. S., Campbell, E. Q., Hobson, C. J., McPartland, J., Mood, A. M., Weinfeld, F. D., & York, R. B. (1966). *Equality of educational opportunity.* Washington, DC: U.S. Government Printing Office.

Comer, J. P. (1996). *Rallying the whole village: The Comer process for reforming education.* New York: Teachers College Press.

Cook, K. S., & Cooper, R. M. (2003). Experimental studies of cooperation, trust, and social exchange. In E. Ostrom and J. Walker (Eds.), *Trust and reciprocity: Interdisciplinary lessons from experimental research* (pp. 209–244). New York: Russell Sage Foundation.

Copeland, N. (1944). *The art of leadership.* London: Allen.

Cosner, S. (2009). Organizational capacity through trust. *Educational Administration Quarterly, 45*(2), 248–291.

Costa, A. C. (2003). Understanding the nature and the antecedents of trust within work teams. In B. Nooteboom & F. Six (Eds.), *The trust process in organizations: Empirical studies of the determinants and process of trust development* (pp. 105–124). Northhampton, MA: Edward Elger.

Costa, A. C., Roe, R. A., & Taillieu, T. (2001). Trust within teams: The relation with performance effectiveness. *European Journal of Work and Organizational Psychology, 10*(3), 225–244.

Cox, H., & Wood, J. R. (1980). Organizational structure and professional alienation: The case of the public school. *Peabody Journal of Education, 51*(1), 1–6.

Creed, W. E. D., & Miles, R. E. (1996). Trust in organizations: A conceptual framework linking organizational forms, managerial philosophies, and the opportunity costs of controls. In R. Kramer, & T. Tyler (Eds.), *Trust in organizations* (pp. 16–38). Thousand Oaks, CA: Sage.

Cullen, J. B., Jacob, B. A., & Levitt, S. D. (2005). The impact of school choice on student outcomes: An analysis of Chicago Public Schools. *Journal of Public Edconomics, 89,* 729–760.

Cummings, L. L., & Bromiley, P. (1996). The organizational trust inventory (OTI): Development and validation. In R. Kramer & T. Tyler (Eds.), *Trust in organizations* (pp. 302–330) Thousand Oaks, CA: Sage.

Currall, S. C., & Inkpen, A. C. (2006). On the complexity of organizational trust: A multi-level co-evolutionary perspective and guidelines for future research. In R. Bachmann & A. Zaheer (Eds.), *Handbook of trust research* (pp. 235–246). Northampton, MA: Edward Elgar.

Currall, S. C., & Judge, T. A. (1995). Measuring trust between organizational boundary role persons. *Organizational Behavior and Human Decision Processes, 64,* 151–170.

Darling-Hammond, L. (2004). Standards, accountability, and school reform. *Teachers College Record, 106,* 1047–1085.

Darling-Hammond, L. (2006). Securing the right to learn: Policy and practice for powerful teaching and learning. *Educational Researcher, 35*(7), 13–24.

Darling-Hammond, L., Chung Wei, R., & Johnson, C. M. (2009). Teacher preparation and teacher learning: A changing policy landscape. In G. Sykes,

B. Schneider, and D. N. Plank (Eds.), *Handbook of Education Policy Research* (pp. 613–636). New York: Routledge.

Darling-Hammond, L., & Goodwin, A. L. (1993). Progress towards professionalism in teaching. In G. Cawelti (Ed.), *Challenges and achievements of American education: The 1993 ASCD yearbook* (pp. 19–52). Alexandria, VA: Association for Supervision and Curriculum Development.

Das, T. K., & Teng, B. (1998). Between trust and control: Developing confidence in partner cooperation in alliances. *Academy of Management Review, 23*(3), 491–512.

Den Hartog, D. N. (2003). Trusting others in organizations: Leaders, management and co-workers. In B. Nooteboom & F. Six (Eds.), *The trust process in organizations: Empirical studies of the determinants and the process of trust development* (pp. 125–146). Northampton, MA: Edward Elgar.

Deutsch, M. (1958). Trust and suspicion. *The Journal of Conflict Resolution, 2*(4), 265–279.

Deutsch, M. (1962). Trust, trustworthiness, and the F Scale. *Journal of Abnormal and Social Psychology, 61,* 138–140.

DiPaola, M. F., & Hoy, W. K. (2005a). Organizational citizenship of faculty and achievement of high school students. *High School Journal, 88*(3), 35–44.

DiPaola, M. F., & Hoy, W. K. (2005b). School characteristics that foster organizational citizenship behavior. *Journal of School Leadership, 15*(4), 387–406.

DiPaola, M. F., & Hoy, W. K. (2008). *Principals improving instruction: Supervision, evaluation, and professional development.* Boston: Allyn & Bacon.

DiPaola, M. F., & Tschannen-Moran, M. (2001, September). Organizational citizenship behavior in schools and its relationship to school climate. *Journal of School Leadership, 11,* 424–447.

Dirks, K. T. (1999). The effects of interpersonal trust on work group performance. *Journal of Applied Psychology, 84*(3), 445–455.

Dirks, K. T. (2000). Trust in leadership and team performance: Evidence from NCAA basketball. *Journal of Applied Psychology, 85,* 1004–1012.

Dirks, K. T. (2006). Three fundamental questions regarding trust in leaders. In R. Bachmann & A. Zaheer (Eds.), *Handbook of Trust Research* (pp. 235–246). Northampton, MA: Edward Elgar.

Dirks, K. T., & Ferrin, D. L. (2001). The role of trust in organizational settings. *Organization Science, 12*(4), 450–467.

Dirks, K. T., & Ferrin, D. L. (2002). Trust in leadership: Meta-analytic findings and implications for organizational research. *Journal of Applied Psychology, 87,* 611–628.

Dirks, K. T., & Skarlicki, D. P. (2004). Trust in leaders: Existing research and emerging issues. In R. M. Kramer & K. S. Cook (Eds.), *Trust and distrust in organizations: Dilemmas and approaches* (pp. 21–40). New York: Russell Sage Foundation.

Earle, T. C., & Cvetkovich, G. T. (1995). *Social trust: Toward a cosmopolitan society.* Westport, CT: Praeger.

Edmonds, R. (1979, March). *Discussion of the literature and issues related to effective schooling.* Paper presented at the National Conference on Urban Education, St. Louis, MO.

Edmondson, A. C. (2004). Psychological safety, trust, and learning in organizations: A group-level lens. In K. M. Roderick & K. S. Cook (Eds.), *Trust and distrust in organizations: Dilemmas and approaches* (pp. 239–271). New York: Russell Sage Foundation.

Eisenhardt, K. M. (1985). Control: Organizational and economic approaches. *Management Science, 31*, 134–149. Entrepreneurship in a state education agency: A case study of Connecticut's education reform initiatives. Dissertation, University of Massachusetts–Amherst.

Epstein, J. L. (2001). *School, family, and community partnerships: Preparing educators and improving schools.* Boulder, CO: Westview Press.

Etzioni, A. (1964). *Modern organizations.* Englewood Cliffs, NJ: Prentice Hall.

Fisk, C. W. (1999). *The emergence of bureaucratic entrepreneurship in a state education agency: A case study of Connecticut's education reform initiatives.* (Doctoral dissertation). Retrieved from http://scholarworks.umass.edu/dissertations/AA19930600

Forrest, R., & Kearns, A. (2001). Social cohesion, social capital and the neighborhood. *Urban Studies, 38*(12), 2125–2143.

Forsyth, P. B. (2008). The empirical consequences of school trust. In W. K. Hoy & M. DiPaola (Eds.), *Improving schools: Studies in leadership and culture* (pp. 1–27). Greenwich, CT: Information Age.

Forsyth, P. B., & Adams, C. M. (2004). Social capital in education: Taking stock of concept and measure. In W. K. Hoy & C. G. Miskel (Eds.), *Educational administration, policy, and reform: Research and measurement* (pp. 251–278). Greenwich, CT: Information Age.

Forsyth, P. B., & Adams, C. M. (2010, May). *Organizational predictability in schools: A latent variable.* Paper presented at the annual meeting of the American Educational Research Association, Denver.

Forsyth, P. B., Adams, C. M., & Barnes, L. (2002, April). *Parental trust of school: Scale development.* Paper presented at the annual meeting of the American Educational Research Association, New Orleans.

Forsyth, P. B., Barnes, L. B., & Adams, C. M. (2005, April). *Dilemmas in the measurement of social capital in education research.* Paper presented at the annual meeting of the American Educational Research Association, Montreal.

Forsyth, P., Barnes, L., & Adams, C. (2006). Trust-effectiveness patterns in schools. *Journal of Educational Administration Quarterly, 44*(2), 122–141.

Forsyth, P. B., & Danisiewicz, T. J. (1985). Toward a theory of professionalization. *Work and Occupations, 12*(1), 59–76.

Forsyth, P. B., & Hoy, W. K. (1978). Isolation and alienation in educational organizations. *Educational Administration Quarterly, 14*, 80–96.

French, J. R. P., & Raven, B. (1968). The bases of social power. In D. Cartwright (Ed.), *Studies in social power* (pp. 150–167). Ann Arbor, MI: University of Michigan Press.

Friedkin, N. E. (2004). Social cohesion. *Annual Review of Sociology, 30*(1), 409–425.

Frost, T., Stimpson, D. V., & Maughan, M. R. (1978). Some correlates of trust. *The Journal of Psychology, 99*, 103–108.

Fukuyama, F. (1995). *Trust.* New York: Free Press.

Fukuyama, F. (1996). *Trust: Social virtues and the creation of prosperity*. London: Hamish Hamilton.

Fullan, M. (2005, Winter). Turnaround leadership. *The Educational Forum, 69*, 174–181.

Fullan, M., Bertani, A., & Quinn, J. (2004). New lessons for districtwide reform. *Educational Leadership, 61*(7), 42–46.

Gagne, M., Koestner, R., & Zuckerman, M. (2000). Facilitating the acceptance of organizational change: the importance of self-determination. *Journal of Applied Social Psychology, 30*, 1843–1852.

Gambetta, D. (1988). Can we trust trust? In D. Gambetta (Ed.), *Trust: Making and breaking cooperative relations* (pp. 213–237). New York: Basil Blackwell.

Geist, J. R., & Hoy, W. K. (2004). Cultivating a culture of trust: Enabling school structure, teacher professionalism, and academic press. *Leading and Managing, 10*(2), 1–17.

Gibb, J. R. (1969). Dynamics of leadership. In F. Carver and T. J. Sergiovanni (Eds.), *Organizations and human behavior: Focus on schools* (pp. 316–324). New York: McGraw-Hill.

Gladwell, M. (2008). *Outliers: The story of success*. New York: Little, Brown.

Goddard, R. (2003). Relational networks, social trust, and norms: A social capital perspective on students' chances of academic success. *Educational Evaluation and Policy Analysis, 25*(1), 59–74.

Goddard, R. D., & Tschannen-Moran, M. (2001, April). *Collective efficacy and faculty trust in students and parents in urban schools*. Paper presented at the annual meeting of the American Educational Research Association, Seattle.

Goddard, R. D., Hoy, W. K., & Woolfolk Hoy, A. (2000). Collective teacher efficacy: Its meaning, measure, and impact on student achievement. *American Educational Research Journal, 37*, 479–508.

Goddard, R. D., Hoy, W. K., & Woolfolk Hoy, A. (2004). Collective efficacy beliefs: Theoretical developments, empirical evidence and future directions. *Educational Researcher, 33*(3), 3–13.

Goddard, R. D., Salloum, S. J., & Berebitsky, D. (2006, April). *An empirical examination of the importance of relational trust to academic achievement*. Paper presented at the annual meeting of the American Educational Research Association, San Francisco.

Goddard, R. D., Tschannen-Moran, M., & Hoy, W. K. (2001). Teacher trust in students and parents: A multilevel examination of the distribution and effects of teacher trust in urban elementary schools. *Elementary School Journal, 102*(1), 3–17.

Goe, L. (2007). *The link between teacher quality and student outcomes: A research synthesis*. Nashville, TN: National Comprehensive Center for Teacher Quality.

Golembiewski, T. T., & McConkie, M. (1975). The centrality of interpersonal trust in-group processes. In C. L. Copper (Ed.), *Theories of group processes* (pp. 131–185). New York: John Wiley.

Goold, M., & Campbell, A. (1987). *Strategies and styles: The role of the centre in managing diversified corporations*. New York: Basil Blackwell.

Goold, M., & Quinn, J. J. (1990). The paradox of strategic controls. *Strategic Management Journal, 11*, 43–57.

Gouldner, A. W. (1954). *Patterns of industrial bureaucracy*. New York: The Free Press.

Granovetter, M. (1985). Economic action and social structure: The problem of embeddedness. *American Journal of Sociology, 91*(3), 481–510.

Greenhalgh, T., Robert, G., MacFarlane, F., Bate, P., & Kyriakidou, O. (2004). Diffusion of innovations in service organizations: Systematic review and recommendations. *The Milbank Quarterly, 82*(4), 581–629.

Grootaert, C., & Van Bastelaer, T. (2002). *Understanding and measuring social capital: A multidisciplinary tool for practitioners*. Washington, DC: The World Bank.

Guerra-Lopez, I. J. (2008). *Evaluation: Proven approaches for improving program and organizational performance*. San Francisco, CA: Jossey-Bass.

Hallinger, P. (1992). The evolving role of American principals: From managerial to instructional to transformational leaders. *Journal of Educational Administration, 30*(3), 35–48.

Hallinger, P., & Murphy, J. F. (1986). The social context of effective schools. *The American Journal of Education, 94*(3), 328–355.

Hanushek, E. A. (2009). The economic value of education and cognitive skills. In G. Sykes, B. Schneider, & D. N. Plank (Eds.), *Handbook of Education Policy Research* (pp. 39–56). New York: Routledge.

Hardin, R. (2006). The street-level epistemology of trust. In R. M. Kramer (Ed.), *Organizational trust: A reader* (pp. 21–47). Oxford: Oxford University Press.

Hatch, T. (2006). *Into the classroom: Developing the scholarship of teaching and learning*. San Francisco: Jossey-Bass.

Hater, J. J., & Bass, B. M. (1988). Superiors' evaluations and subordinates' perceptions of transformational leadership. *Journal of Applied Psychology, 73*, 695–702.

Heller, M. F., & Firestone, W. A. (1995). Who's in charge here? Sources of leadership for change in eight schools. *The Elementary School Journal, 96*(1), 65–86.

Herzberg, F. (1966). *Work and the nature of man*. Cleveland, OH: World.

Hipp, K. A. (1997, March). *Documenting the effects of transformational leadership behavior on teacher efficacy*. Paper presented at the annual meeting of the American Educational Research Association, Chicago.

Hipp, K. A., & Bredeson, P. V. (1995). Exploring connections between teacher efficacy and principals' leadership behaviors. *Journal of School Leadership, 5*(2), 136–150.

Hoffman, J. D., Sabo, D., Bliss, J., & Hoy, W. K. (1994). Building a culture of trust. *Journal of School Leadership, 3*, 484–501.

Homans, G. C. (1950). *The human group*. New York: Harcourt, Brace & World.

Homans, G. C. (1967). *The nature of social science*. New York: Harcourt Brace Jovanovich.

Homans, G. C. (1974). *Social behavior: Its elementary forms* (Rev. ed.). New York: Harcourt Brace Jovanovich.

Hoover-Dempsey, K. V., & Sandler, H. M. (1995). Parental involvement in their children's education: Why does it make a difference? *Teachers College Record, 95*, 310–331.

Hoover-Dempsey, K. V., & Sandler, H. M. (1997). Why do parents become involved in their children's education? *Review of Educational Research, 67,* 3–42.

Hord, S. M. (1997). *Professional learning communities: Communities of continuous inquiry and improvement.* Austin, TX: Southwest Educational Development Laboratory.

Hosmer, L. T. (1995). Trust: The connecting link between organizational theory and philosophical ethics. *Academy of Management Review, 20*(2), 379–403.

Hox, J. (2002). *Multilevel analysis: Techniques and applications.* Mahwah, NJ: Lawrence Erlbaum.

Hoy, A. W., & Hoy, W. K. (2009). *Instructional leadership: A research-based guide to learning in schools* (3rd ed.). Boston: Allyn & Bacon.

Hoy, W., Sabo, D., & Barnes, K. (1996, Spring). Organizational health and faculty trust: A view from the middle level. *Research in Middle Level Education Quarterly,* 21–39.

Hoy, W. K. (2002). Faculty trust: A key to student achievement. *Journal of School Public Relations, 23*(2), 88–103.

Hoy, W. K. (2004). An analysis of enabling and mindful school structures: Some theoretical, research, and practical considerations. In W. K. Hoy & M. DiPaola (Eds.), *Essential ideas for the reform of American schools* (pp. 367–394). Charlotte, NC: Information Age.

Hoy, W. K., & Ferguson, J. (1985). A theoretical framework and exploration of organizational effectiveness in schools. *Educational Administration Quarterly, 21*(2), 117–134.

Hoy, W. K., Gage, C. Q., & Tarter, C. J. (2006). School mindfulness and faculty trust: Necessary conditions for each other? *Educational Administration Quarterly, 42*(2), 236–255.

Hoy, W. K., & Henderson, J. E. (1983). Principal authenticity, school climate, and pupil-control orientation. *Alberta Journal of Educational Research, 2,* 123–130.

Hoy, W. K., Hoffman, J., Sabo, D., & Bliss, J. (1996). The organizational climate of middle schools: The development and test of the OCDQ-RM. *Journal of Educational Administration, 34,* 41–59.

Hoy, W. K., & Kupersmith, W. J. (1984). Principal authenticity and faculty trust: Key elements in organizational behavior. *Planning and Changing, 15*(2), 80–88.

Hoy, W. K., & Kupersmith, W. J. (1985). The meaning and measure of faculty trust. *Educational and Psychological Research, 5,* 1–10.

Hoy, W. K., & Miskel, C. J. (1987). *Educational administration: Theory, research, and practice* (3rd ed.). New York: McGraw-Hill.

Hoy, W. K., & Miskel, C. G. (2008). *Educational administration: Theory, research, and practice* (8th ed.). New York: McGraw Hill.

Hoy, W. K., & Sabo, D. J. (1998). *Quality middle schools: Open and healthy.* Thousand Oaks, CA: Corwin Press.

Hoy, W. K., & Smith, P. A. (2007). Influence: A key to successful leadership. *The International Journal of Educational Management, 21,* 158–167.

Hoy, W. K., Smith, P. A., & Sweetland, S. R. (2002). The development of the organizational climate index for high schools: Its measure and relationship to faculty trust. *The High School Journal, 86*(2), 38–49.

Hoy, W. K., & Sweetland, S. R. (2000). School bureaucracies that work: Enabling not coercive. *Journal of School Leadership, 10*(6), 525–541.

Hoy, W. K., & Sweetland, S. R. (2001). Designing better schools: The meaning and measure of enabling school structures. *Educational Administration Quarterly, 37*(3), 296–321.

Hoy, W. K., Sweetland, S. R., & Smith, P. A. (2002). Toward an organizational model of achievement in high schools: The significance of collective efficacy. *Educational Administration Quarterly, 38*, 77–93.

Hoy, W. K., Tarter, C. J., & Kottkamp, R. B. (1991). *Open schools/healthy schools: Measuring organizational climate.* Beverly Hills, CA: Sage.

Hoy, W. K., Tarter, C. J., & Wiskowskie, L. (1992). Faculty trust in colleagues: Linking the principal with school effectiveness. *Journal of Research and Development in Education, 26*, 38–58.

Hoy, W. K., Tarter, C. J., & Woolfolk Hoy, A. (2006a). Academic optimism of schools. In Wayne K. Hoy & Cecil Miskel (Eds.), *Contemporary issues in educational policy and school outcomes* (pp. 135–156). Greenwich, CT: Information Age.

Hoy, W. K., Tarter, C. J., & Woolfolk Hoy, A. (2006b). Academic optimism of schools: A force for student achievement. *American Educational Research Journal, 43*(3), 425–446.

Hoy, W. K., & Tschannen-Moran, M. (1999). Five faces of trust: An empirical confirmation in urban elementary schools. *Journal of School Leadership, 9*, 184–208.

Hoy, W. K., & Tschannen-Moran, M. (2003). The conceptualization and measurement of faculty trust in schools. In Wayne K. Hoy & Cecil Miskel (Eds.), *Studies in leading and organizing schools* (pp. 181–207). Greenwich, CT: Information Age.

Hughes, L. W. (1947). Achieving effective human relations and morale. In J. A. Culbertson, C. Henson, & R. Morrison (Eds.), *Performance objectives for principals: Concepts and instruments* (pp. 121–151). Berkeley, CA: Scotchman.

Inkpen, A. C., & Currall, S. C. (1997). International joint venture trust: An empirical examination. In P. W. Beamish & J. P. Killing (Eds.), *Cooperative strategies: Vol. 1. North American perspectives* (pp. 309–334). San Francisco: New Lexington Press.

Jones, G. R., & George, J. M. (1998). The experience and evolution of trust: implications for cooperation and teamwork. *Academy of Management Review, 23*(3), 531–546.

Jordan, A. (2006). *Tapping the power of social networks: Understanding the role of social networks in strengthening families and transforming communities.* Baltimore: Annie E. Casey Foundation.

Joseph, E. E., & Winston, B. E. (2005). A correlation of servant leadership, leader trust, and organizational trust. *Leadership and Organization Development Journal, 26*(1), 6–22.

Judge, T. A., & Piccolo, R. F. (2004). Transformational and transactional leadership: A meta-analytic test of their relative validity. *Journal of Applied Psychology, 89*(5), 755–768.

Jung, D. I., & Avolio, B. J. (2000). Opening the black box: An experimental investigation of the mediating effects of trust and value congruence on transformational and transactional leadership. *Journal of Organizational Behaviour, 21,* 949–964.

Kee, H. W., & Knox, R. E. (1970). Conceptual and methodological considerations in the study of trust and suspicion. *Journal of Conflict Resolution, 14,* 357–366.

Kenney, C. (2008). *The best practice: How the new quality movement is transforming medicine.* New York: Perseus.

Kerlinger, F. N. (1973). *Foundations of behavioral research* (2nd ed.). New York: Holt, Rinehart, & Winston.

Kimmel, M. J., Pruitt, D. G., Magenau, J. M., Konar-Goldband, E., & Carnevale, P. J. D. (1980). Effects of trust, aspiration, and gender on negotiation tactics. *Journal of Personality and Social Psychology, 38*(1), 9–22.

Kirby, M., & DiPaola, M. (2009). Academic optimism and achievement: A path model. In W. K. Hoy & M. DiPaola (Eds.), *Studies in school improvement* (pp. 77–94). Greenwich, CT: Information Age.

Kirsch, L. J. (1996). The management of complex tasks in organizations: Controlling the systems development process. *Organization Science, 7,* 1–21.

Knoop, H. H. (2007). Control and responsibility: A Danish perspective on leadership. In H. Gardner (Ed.), *Responsibility at work: How leading professionals act or don't act responsibly* (pp. 221–246). San Francisco: Jossey-Bass.

Kochanek, J. R. (2005). *Building trust for better schools: Research-based practices.* Thousand Oaks, CA: Corwin Press.

Koh, W. L., Steers, R. M., & Terborg, J. R. (1995). The effects of transformational leadership on teacher attitudes and student performance in Singapore. *Journal of Organizational Behavior, 16*(4), 319–333.

Konovsky, M. A., & Pugh, S. D. (1994). Citizenship behavior and social exchange. *Academy of Management Journal, 37*(3), 656–669.

Koontz, H., & O'Donnell, C. (1955). *Principles of management.* New York: McGraw-Hill.

Kramer, R. M., Brewer, M. B., & Hanna, B. A. (1996). Collective trust and collective action: The decision to trust as a social decision. In R. Kramer & T. Tyler (Eds.), *Trust in organizations: Frontiers of theory and research* (pp. 357–389). Thousand Oaks, CA: Sage.

Kramer, R. M., & Tyler, T. R. (1996). *Trust in organizations: Frontiers of theory and research.* Thousand Oaks, CA: Sage.

Larson, A. (1992). Network dyads in entrepreneurial settings: A study of the governance of exchange relationships. *Administrative Science Quarterly, 37,* 76–104.

Lee, S. M. (1971). An empirical analysis of organizational identification. *Academy of Management, 14*(2), 213–226.

Leifer, R., & Mills, P. K. (1996). An information processing approach for deciding upon control strategies and reducing control loss in emerging organizations. *Journal of Management, 22,* 113–137.

Leithwood, K., & Jantzi, D. (2000). The effects of transformational leadership on organizational conditions and student engagement with school. *Journal of Educational Administration, 38*(2), 112–129.

Leithwood, K., & Steinbach, R. (1993). Total quality leadership: Expert thinking plus transformational practice. *Journal of Personnel Evaluation in Education*, 7(4), 311–337.

LePine, J. A., Erez, A., & Johnson, D. E. (2002). The nature and dimensionality of organizational citizenship behavior: A critical review and meta-analysis. *Journal of Applied Psychology*, 87(1), 52–65.

Levin, B. (1998). An epidemic of education policy: (what) can we learn from each other? *Comparative Education*, 34, 131–141.

Lewicki, R. J., & Bunker, B. B. (1996). Developing and maintaining trust in work relationships. In R. Kramer, & T. Tyler (Eds.), *Trust in organizations*. Thousand Oaks, CA: Sage.

Lewis, D. J., & Weigert, A. (1985). Trust as a social reality. *Social Forces*, 63(4), 967–985.

Likert, R. (1967). *The human organization*. New York: McGraw Hill.

Lin, N. (1999). Social networks and status attainment. *Annual Review of Sociology*, 25, 467–487.

Lin, N. (2001). Building a network theory of social capital. *Connections*, 22(1), 28–51.

Lopez, G. R. (2001). The value of hard work: Lessons on parent involvement from an (im)migrant household. *Harvard Educational Review*, 71(3), 416–437.

Louis, K. S. (2007). Trust and improvement in schools. *Journal of Educational Change*, 8(1), 1–24.

Loury, G. C. (1977). A dynamic theory of racial income differences. In P. A. Wallace & A. M. LaMond (Eds.), *Women, minorities, and employment discrimination* (pp. 153–186). Lexington, MA: Heath.

Lowe, K. B., Kroeck, K. G., & Sivasubramaniam, N. (1996). Effectiveness correlates of transformational and transactional leadership: A meta-analytic review of the MLQ literature. *Leadership Quarterly*, 7(3), 385–425.

Luhmann, N. (1979). *Trust and power*. Chichester, UK: Wiley.

MacKenzie, S. B., Podsakoff, P. M., & Ahearne, M. (1996). [Unpublished data analysis]. Bloomington: Indiana University School of Business.

Maeroff, G. I. (1988). A blueprint for empowering teachers. *Phi Delta Kappan*, 69, 472–477.

Malen B., & Rice, J. K. (2009). School reconstitution and school improvement: Theory and evidence. In G. Sykes, B. Schneider, & D. N. Plank (Eds.), *Handbook of education policy research* (pp. 464–477). New York: Routledge.

Marks, H. M., & Printy, S. M. (2003). Principal leadership and school performance: An integration of transformational and instructional leadership. *Educational Administration Quarterly*, 39(3), 370–397.

Mayer, R. C., Davis, J. H., & Schoorman, F. D. (1995). An integrative model of organizational trust. *The Academy of Management Review*, 20(3), 709–737.

McEvily, B., Perrone, V., & Zaheer, A. (2003). Trust as an organizing principle. *Organization Science*, 14(1), 91–103.

McEvily, B., Weber, R. A., Bicchieri, C., & Ho, V. T. (2006). Can groups be trusted? An experimental study in collective entities. In R. Bachmann & A. Zaheer (Eds.), *Handbook of trust research* (pp. 52–84). Northampton, MA: Edward Elgar.

McGregor, D. (1960). *The human side of enterprise.* New York: McGraw-Hill.

McGuigan, L., & Hoy, W. K. (2006). Principal leadership: Creating a culture of academic optimism to improve achievement for all students. *Leadership and Policy in Schools, 5*(3), 203–229.

McLaughlin, M. W., & Talbert, J. T. (2006). *Building school-based teacher learning communities: Professional strategies to improve student achievement.* New York: Teachers College Press.

McLendon, M. K., & Cohen-Vogel L. (2008). Understanding education policy change in the American states: Lessons from political science. In B. S. Cooper, J. G. Cibulka, and L. D. Fusarelli (Eds.), *Handbook of education politics and policy* (pp. 30–51). New York: Routledge.

Merton, R. K. (1952). *Reader in bureaucracy.* Glencoe, IL: The Free Press.

Miller, G. J. (2004). Monitoring, rules, and the control paradox: Can the good soldier Svejk be trusted? In R. M. Kramer & K. S. Cook (Eds.), *Trust and distrust in organizations* (pp. 99–126). New York: Russell Sage Foundation.

Mills, T. M. (1967). *The sociology of small groups.* Englewood Cliffs, NJ: Prentice-Hall.

Mintrop, H. (2003). *Schools on probation: How accountability works (and doesn't work).* New York: Teachers College Press.

Mintrop, H., & Trujillo, T. (2005). *Corrective action in low-performing schools: Lessons for NCLB implementation from state and district strategies in first-generation accountability systems.* Los Angeles: National Center for Research on Evaluation, Standards, and Student Testing.

Mintzberg, H. (1989). *Mintzberg on management: Inside our strange world of organizations.* New York: The Free Press.

Mishra, A. K. (1996). Organizational responses to crisis: The centrality of trust. In R. Kramer & T. Tyler (Eds.), *Trust in organizations: Frontiers of theory and research* (pp. 261–287). Thousand Oaks, CA: Sage.

Miskel, C., Fevurly, R., and Stewart, J. (1979). Organizational structures and processes: Perceived school effectiveness, loyalty, and job satisfaction. *Educational Administration Quarterly, 15,* 97–118.

Miskel, C., McDonald, D., and Bloom, S. (1983). Structural expectancy linkages within schools and organizational effectiveness. *Educational Administration Quarterly, 19*(1), 49–89.

Mitchell, R. M., & Forsyth, P. B. (2004, November). *Trust, the principal, and student identification.* Paper presented at the annual meeting of the University Council for Educational Administration, Kansas City, MO.

Mitchell, R. M., & Forsyth, P. B. (2005, April). *Trust: The key to student identification with school.* Paper presented at the annual meeting of the American Educational Research Association, Montreal, Canada.

Möllering, G. (1998). The trust/control duality: An integrative perspective on positive expectations of others. *International Sociology, 20*(3), 283–305.

Moore Johnson, S. (2001). The aging of America's teachers. *Harvard University Gazzette.* Retrieved from http://www.news.harvard.edu/gazette/2001/10.04/13–njteachers.html

Mott, P. E. (1972). *The characteristics of effective organizations.* New York: Harper & Row.

Mulkay, M. J. (1971). *Functionalism, exchange and theoretical strategy.* New York: Schocken Books.

Napier, R. W., & Gershenfeld, M. K. (1999). *Groups: Theory and experience.* New York: Houghton Mifflin.

Nash, J. B. (1929). Leadership. *Phi Delta Kappan, 12,* 24–25.

Nooteboom, R. (2002). *Trust: Forms, foundations, functions, failures, and figures.* Cheltenham, UK: Edward Elgar.

Nooteboom, B., Berger, H., & Noorderhaven, N. (1997). Effects of trust and governance on relational risk. *Academy of Management Journal, 40,* 308–338.

Northcraft, G. B., Polzer, J. T., Neal, M. A., & Kramer, R. M. (1995). Diversity, social identity, and performance: Emergent social dynamics in cross-functional teams. In S. E. Jackson & M. N. Ruderman (Eds.), *Diversity in work teams* (pp. 17–46). Washington, DC: American Psychological Association.

Northouse, P. G. (2001). *Leadership: Theory and practice* (2nd ed.). London: Sage Publications.

O'Day. J. A. (2002). Complexity, accountability, and school improvement. *Harvard Educational Review, 72*(3), 293–329.

Ogawa, R. T. (2009). Improvement or reinvention: Two policy approaches to school reform. In G. Sykes, B. Schneider, & D. N. Plank (Eds.), *Handbook of Education Policy Research* (pp. 534–538). New York: Routledge.

Organ, D. W. (1988). *Organizational citizenship behavior: The good soldier syndrome.* Lexington, MA: Heath.

Organ, D. W. (1990). The subtle significance of job satisfaction. *Clinical Laboratory Management Review, 4,* 94–98.

Organ, D. W. (1997). Organizational citizenship behavior: It's construct clean-up time. *Human Performance, 10*(2), 85–97.

Organ, D. W., & Ryan, K. (1995). A meta-analytic review of attitudinal and dispositional predictors of organizational citizenship behavior. *Personnel Psychology, 48,* 775–800.

Ouchi, W. (1981). *Theory Z.* Reading, MA: Addison-Wesley.

Ouchi, W. G. (1979). A conceptual framework for the design of organizational control mechanisms. *Management Science, 25,* 833–848.

Parsons, T. (1960). *Structure and process in modern society.* Glencoe, IL: The Free Press.

Parsons, T. (1961). An outline of the social system. In T. Parsons, E. A. Shils, K. D. Naegle, & J. R. Pitts (Eds.), *Theories of society* (pp. 30–43). New York: The Free Press.

Parsons, T., Bales, R. F., & Shils, E. A. (1953). *Working papers in the theory of action.* New York: The Free Press.

Paul, M. F. (1982). Power, leadership, and trust: Implications for counselors in terms of organizational change. *Personnel and Guidance Journal, 60,* 538–541.

Pfeffer, J. (1982). *Organizations and organization theory.* Boston: Pitman.

Podgursky, M. J., & Springer, M. G. (2006). Teacher performance pay: A review. National Center on Performance Initiatives [Unpublished paper].

Podsakoff, P. M., Ahearne, M., & MacKenzie, S. B. (1997). Organizational citizenship behavior and the quantity and quality of work group performance. *Journal of Applied Psychology*, 82, 262–270.

Podsakoff, P. M., & MacKenzie, S. B. (1994). Organizational citizenship behaviors and sales unit effectiveness. *Journal of Marketing Reseach*, 3(1), 351–363.

Podsakoff, P. M., MacKenzie, S. B., & Bommer, W. H. (1996). Transformational leader behaviors and substitutes for leadership as determinants of employee satisfaction, commitment, trust, and organizational citizenship behaviors. *Journal of Management*, 22(2), 259–298.

Podsakoff, P. M., MacKenzie, S. B., Moorman, R. H., & Fetter, R. (1990). Transformational leader behaviors and their effects on followers' trust in leader, satisfaction, and organizational citizenship behaviors. *Leadership Quarterly*, 1(2), 107–142.

Podsakoff, P. M., MacKenzie, S. B., Paine, J. B., & Bachrach, D. G. (2000), Organizational citizenship behaviors: A critical review of the theoretical and empirical literature and suggestions for future research. *Journal of Management*, 26(3), 513–563.

Portes, A. (1998). Social capital: Its origins and applications in modern sociology. *Annual Review of Sociology*, 24, 1–24.

Prins, E., & Toso, B. W. (2008). Defining and measuring parenting for educational success: A critical discourse analysis of the parent education profile. *American Educational Research Journal*, 45(3), 555–596.

Putnam, R. (1995). Bowling alone: America's declining social capital. *Journal of Democracy*, 6, 65–78.

Putnam, R. (2000). *Bowling alone: The collapse and revival of American community*. New York: Simon & Schuster.

Putnam, R., & Feldstein, L. (2003). *Better together: Restoring the American community*. New York: Simon & Schuster.

Quinn, T. (2002). The impact of principal leadership behaviors on instructional practice and student engagement. *Journal of Educational Administration*, 40(5), 447–468.

Ravitch, D. (2010). *The death and life of the great American school system: How testing and choice are undermining education*. New York: Basic Books.

Riketta, M. (2005). Organizational identification: A meta-analysis. *Journal of Vocational Behavior*, 66(2), 358–384.

Ring, P. S., & Van de Ven, A. H. (1992). Structuring cooperative relationships between organizations. *Strategic Management Journal*, 13, 483–498.

Rogers, E. (2003). *Diffusion of innovations* (5th ed.). New York: The Free Press.

Romney, A. K., Boyd, J. P., Moore, C. C., Batchelder, W. H., & Brazill, T. J. (1996). Culture as shared cognitive representations. *Proceedings of the National Academy of Science*, 93, 4699–4705.

Rotter, J. B. (1967). A new scale for the measurement of interpersonal trust. *Journal of Personality*, 35, 651–665.

Rousseau, D., Sitkin, S. B., Burt, R., & Camerer, C. (1998). Not so different after all: A cross-discipline view of trust. *The Academy of Management Review*, 23(3), 393–404.

Rowan, B. P., Correnti, R. J., Miller, R. J., & Camburn, E. M. (2009). School improvement by design: Lessons from a study of comprehensive school reform programs. In G. Sykes, B. Schneider, & D. N. Plank (Eds.), *Handbook of Education Policy Research* (pp. 637–651). New York: Routledge.

Royeen, C. B. (1985). Adaptation of Likert scaling for use with children. *Occupational Therapy Journal of Research, 5*(1), 59–69.

Russell, R. F. (2001). The role of values in servant leadership. *Leadership and Organization Development Journal, 22*(2), 76–84.

Ryan, R. M., & Deci, E. L. (2000). Self-determination theory and the facilitation of intrinsic motivation, social development, and well-being. *American Psychologist, 55*(1), 68–78.

Schein, E. H. (2004). *Organizational culture and leadership* (3rd ed.). San Francisco: Jossey-Bass.

Schlechty, P. C. (1990). *Schools for the 21st century: Leadership imperatives for educational reform.* San Francisco: Jossey-Bass.

Schmidt, M. (2008). Risky policy processes: Accountability and school leadership. In E. A. Samier & A. G. Stanley (Eds.), *Political approaches to educational administration and leadership* (pp. 139–154). London: Taylor & Francis.

Schneider, B., & Reichers, A. (1983). On the etiology of climates. *Personnel Psychology, 36*(1), 19–40.

Seligman, M. E. P. (1998). Positive social science. *APA Monitor, 29,* 2–5.

Senge, P., Cambron-McCabe, N., Lucas, T., Smith, B., Dutton, J., & Kleiner, A. (2000). *Schools that learn: A fifth discipline fieldbook for educators, parents, and everyone who cares about education.* New York: Doubleday.

Serva, M. A., Fuller, M. A., & Mayer, R. C. (2005). The reciprocal nature of trust: A longitudinal study of interacting teams. *Journal of Organizational Behavior, 26,* 625–648.

Shapiro, S. P. (1987). The social control of impersonal trust. *American Journal of Sociology, 93*(3), 623–658.

Shaw, R. B. (1997). *Trust in the balance: Building successful organizations on results, integrity, and concern.* San Francisco: Jossey-Bass.

Sheldon, S. B. (2002). Parents' social networks and beliefs as predictors of parent involvement. *The Elementary School Journal, 102*(4), 301–316.

Shulman, L. (2007). Counting and recounting: Assessment and the quest for accountability. *Change, 39*(1), 20–25.

Silins, H., & Mulford, B. (2004). Schools as learning organizations: Effects on teacher leadership and student outcomes. *School Effectiveness and School Improvement, 15*(3), 443–466.

Sitkin, S. B. (1995). On the positive effect of legalization on trust. *Research on Negotiation in Organizations, 5,* 185–217.

Sitkin, S. B., & Roth, N. L. (1993). Explaining the limited effectiveness of legalistic "remedies" for trust/distrust. *Organization Science, 4,* 367–392.

Sitkin, S. B., & Stickel, D. (1996). The road to hell: The dynamics of distrust in an era of quality. In R. Kramer & T. Tyler (Eds.), *Trust in organizations* (pp. 196–215). Thousand Oaks, CA: Sage.

Smith, C. A., Organ, D. W., & Near, J. P. (1983). Organizational citizenship behavior: Its nature and antecedents. *Journal of Applied Psychology, 68*(4), 653–663.

Smith, P. A., & Birney, L. L. (2005). The organizational trust of elementary schools and dimensions of student bullying. *International Journal of Educational Management, 19*(6), 469–485.

Smith, P. A., & Hoy, W. K. (2007). Academic optimism and student achievement in urban elementary schools. *Journal of Educational Administration, 45*(5), 556–568.

Smith, P. A., Hoy, W. K., & Sweetland, S. R. (2001). Organizational health of high schools and dimensions of faculty trust. *Journal of School Leadership, 11*(2), 135–151.

Somech, A., & Ron, I. (2007). Promoting organizational citizenship behavior in schools: The impact of individual and organizational characteristics. *Educational Administration Quarterly, 43*(1), 38–66.

Spillane, J. P. (2000). Cognition and policy implementation: District policymakers and the reform of mathematics education. *Cognition and Instruction, 18,* 141–179.

Spillane, J. P. (2004). *Standards deviation: How schools misunderstand education policy.* Boston: Harvard University Press.

Spillane, J. P. (2006). *Distributed leadership.* San Francisco: Jossey-Bass.

Spillane, J. P., Gomez, L. M., & Mesler, L. (2009). Notes on reframing the role of organizations in policy implementation: Resources for practice, in practice. In G. Sykes, B. Schneider, & D. N. Plank (Eds.) *Handbook of education policy research* (pp. 409–425). New York: Routledge.

Stogdill, R. M. (1974). *Handbook of leadership.* New York: The Free Press.

Sykes, G. (1990). Fostering teacher professionalism in schools. In R. F. Elmore & Associates (Eds.), *Restructuring schools: The next generation of school reform* (pp. 59–96). San Francisco: Jossey-Bass.

Sykes, G., O'Day, J., & Ford, T. G. (2009). The district role in instructional improvement. In G. Sykes, B. Schneider, & D. N. Plank (Eds.), *Handbook of Education Policy Research* (pp. 767–784). New York: Routledge.

Tarter, C. J., Bliss, J. R., & Hoy, W. K. (1989a). Principal leadership and organizational commitment. *Planning and Changing, 20*(3), 131–140.

Tarter, C. J., Bliss, J. R., & Hoy, W. K. (1989b). School characteristics and faculty trust in secondary schools. *Educational Administration Quarterly, 25*(3), 294–308.

Tarter, C. J., & Hoy, W. K. (1988). The context of trust: Teachers and the principal. *High School Journal, 72,* 17–24.

Tarter, C. J., Sabo, D., & Hoy, W. K. (1995). Middle school climate, faculty trust, and effectiveness. *Journal of Research and Development in Education, 29,* 41–49.

Tead, O. (1935). *The art of leadership.* New York: McGraw-Hill.

Thompson, J. D. (1967). *Organizations in action.* New York: McGraw-Hill.

Tough, P. (2008). *Whatever it takes: Geoffrey Canada's quest to change Harlem.* New York: Houghton Mifflin.

Triandis, H. C., Hall, E. R., & Ewen, R. B. (1965). Member heterogeneity and dyadic creativity. *Human Relations, 18*(1), 33–35.

Tschannen-Moran, M. (2001). Collaboration and the need for trust. *Journal of Educational Administration, 39*(4), 308–331.

Tschannen-Moran, M. (2003). Fostering organizational citizenship in schools: Transformational leadership and trust. In W. K. Hoy & C. G. Miskel (Eds.), *Studies in leading and organizing schools* (pp. 157–179). Greenwich, CT: Information Age.

Tschannen-Moran, M. (2004). *Trust matters: Leadership for successful schools.* San Francisco: Jossey-Bass.

Tschannen-Moran, M. (2009). Fostering teacher professionalism in schools: The role of leadership orientation and trust. *Educational Administration Quarterly, 45*(2), 217–247.

Tschannen-Moran, M., & Goddard, R. (2001, April). *Collective efficacy and trust: A multilevel analysis.* Paper presented at the annual meeting of the American Educational Research Association, Seattle.

Tschannen-Moran, M., & Hoy, W. K. (1998). Trust in schools: A conceptual and empirical analysis. *Journal of Educational Administration, 36*(4), 334–352.

Tschannen-Moran, M., & Hoy, W. K. (2000). A multidisciplinary analysis of the nature, meaning, and measurement of trust. *Review of Educational Research, 70*(4), 547–593.

Tyack, D., & Cuban, L. (1995). *Tinkering toward utopia: A century of public school reform.* Boston: University of Harvard Press.

Tyler, T. R., & Degoey, P. (1996). Trust in organizational aurhtorities. In R. M. Kramer & T. R. Tyler (Eds.), *Trust in organizations: Frontiers of theory and research* (pp. 331–350). Thousand Oaks, CA: Sage.

Uekawa, K., Aladjem, D., & Zhang, Y. (2005, April). *The role of social capital in comprehensive school reform.* Paper presented at the annual meeting of the American Educational Research Association, Montreal.

U.S. Department of Education, Office of Planning, Evaluation and Policy Development. (2010). *A blueprint for reform: The reauthorization of the Elementary and Secondary Education Act.* Available at http://www2.ed.gov/policy/elsec/leg/blueprint/blueprint.pdf

Van Dyne, L., Cummings, L. L., & Parks, J. M. (1995). Extra role behaviors: In pursuit of construct and definitional clarity (a bridge over muddied waters). In L. L. Cummings & B. M. Staw (Eds.), *Research in organizational behavior* (Vol. 17, pp. 215–285). Greenwich, CT: JAI.

Vandenberghe, C., Bentein, K., & Stinglhamber, F. (2004). Affective commitment to the organization, supervisor, and work group: Antecedents and outcomes. *Journal of Vocational Behavior, 64*(1), 47–71.

Voelkl, K. E. (1997). Identification with schools. *American Journal of Education, 105*(3), 294–318.

Wagner, C., & DiPaola, M. (2009, April). *Academic optimism of high school teachers: Its relationship to student achievement and organizational citizenship behaviors.* Paper presented at the annual meeting of the American Educational Research Association, San Diego, CA.

Wagner, T. (1998). Change as collaborative inquiry: A constructivist methodology for reinventing schools. *Phi Delta Kappan, 79*(7), 512–518.

Wagner, T. (2001). Leadership for learning: An action theory of school change. *Phi Delta Kappan, 82*(5), 378–384.

Waldman, D. A. (1987, August). *Reducing the incongruence between formal organization and the development of individuals: A case for transformational leadership.* Paper presented at the 47th meeting of the Academy of Management, New Orleans.

Waldman, D. A., Bass, B. M., & Yammariono, F. J. (1990). Adding to contingent-reward behavior: The augmenting effects of charismatic leadership. *Group and Organization Studies, 15*(4), 381–394.

Walz, S. M., & Niehoff, B. P. (1996). Organizational citizenship behaviors and their effects on organizational effectiveness in limited-menu restaurants. In J. B. Keys & L. N. Dosier (Eds.), *Academy of Management Best Papers Proceedings* (pp. 307–311). Madison, WI: Omnipress.

Wang, H., Law, K. S., Hackett, R. D., Wang, D., & Chen, Z. X. (2005). Leader-member exchange as a mediator of the relationship between transformational leadership and followers' performance and organizational citizenship behavior. *Academy of Management Journal, 48*(3), 420–432.

Webb, T. W. (2005). The anatomy of accountability. *Journal of Education Policy, 20*(2), 189–208.

Webber, S. S. (2002). Leadership and trust facilitating cross-functional team success. *Journal of Management Development, 21*(3), 201–214.

Weber, M. (1947). *The theory of social and economic organizations.* New York: Oxford University Press.

Wech, B. A. (2002). Trust context: Effect on organizational citizenship behavior, supervisory fairness, and job satisfaction beyond the influence of leader-member exchange. *Business and Society, 41*(3), 353–360.

Whitener, E. M., Brodt, S. E., Korsgaard, M. A., & Werner, J. M. (1998). Managers as initiators of trust: An exchange relationship framework for understanding managerial trustworthy behavior. *Academy of Management Review, 23*(3), 513–530.

Williamson, O. E. (1993). Calculativeness, trust and economic organization. *The Journal of Law and Economics, 36*(1), 453–486.

Wong, K. K. (2008). Federalism, equity, and accountability in education. In B. S. Cooper, J. G. Cibulka, & L. D. Fusarelli (Eds.), *Handbook of Education Politics and Policy.* New York: Routledge.

Woolcock, M. (1998). Social capital and economic development: Toward a theoretical synthesis and policy framework. *Theory and Society, 27*(2), 151–208.

Young, S. A., & Parker, C. P. (1999). Predicting collective climates: Assessing the role of shared work values, needs, employee interaction, and work group membership. *Journal of Organizational Behavior, 20*(7), 1199–1218.

Zaheer, A., & Venkatraman, N. (1995). Relational governance as an interorganizational strategy: An empirical test of the role of trust in economic exchange. *Strategic Management Journal, 16*, 373–392.

Zand, D. E. (1972). Trust and managerial problem solving. *Administrative Science Quarterly, 17*, 229–239.

Zepeda, S. (2006). High stakes supervision: We must do more. *International Journal of Leadership in Education, 9*(1), 61–73.

Zielinski, A. E., & Hoy, W. K. (1983). Isolation and alienation in elementary schools. *Educational Administration Quarterly, 19*, 27–45.

Zimmerman, B. J. (1990). Self-regulated learning and academic achievement: An overview. *Educational Psychologist, 25*(1), 3–17.

Zimmerman, B. J., & Martinez-Pons, M. (1988). Construct validation of a strategy model of student self-regulated learning. *Journal of Educational Psychology, 80*(3), 284–290.

Zucker, L. G. (1986). Production of trust: Institutional sources of economic structure: 1840 to 1920. In L. L. Cummings & B. M. Staw (Eds.), *Research in organizational behavior* (pp. 53–111). Greenwich, CT: JAI Press.

Index

About the Authors

Patrick B. Forsyth is professor of education at the University of Oklahoma and has long been involved in the reform of educational leadership preparation, starting in 1984 when he became executive director of the University Council for Educational Administration (UCEA), a position he held for 15 years. He managed the National Commission on Excellence in Educational Administration, and together with Martha McCarthy (Indiana University), founded the UCEA convention. He secured Danforth funds to begin the National Policy Board for Educational Administration and, as its corporate secretary, was instrumental in obtaining Pugh support for the ISLLC project that put in place stricter standards for licensure of school leaders. Forsyth has worked with education leaders in China, Taiwan, Australia, Canada, and the United Arab Emirates. He has served the American Education Research Association in various capacities, including Division A vice president and Executive Council. Since returning to the professoriate in 2000, he has directed an extensive research project focused on parent trust. Forsyth has also explored work alienation, professionalization, and collective efficacy. He serves on several editorial boards, including those of AERA Books and *The Journal of Educational Administration*. He and his wife, Elena, have two sons, who are aspiring musicians.

Curt M. Adams is an assistant professor of educational leadership and policy studies at the University of Oklahoma and is a research scientist with the Oklahoma Center for Educational Policy, where he studies school reform initiatives. He is past founder and director of the San Miguel School of Tulsa, a nonprofit school based on the Lasallian philosophy of serving socially deprived students and families. Recent journal articles and book chapters include "The Formation of Parent-School Trust: A Multi-level Analysis" (*Educational Administrative Quarterly*), "The Nature and Function of Trust in Schools" (*Journal of School Leadership*), and "Social Determinants of Student Trust in High Poverty Elementary Schools" (a chapter in *Analyzing School Contexts: Influences of Principals and Teachers in Service of Students*).

Wayne K. Hoy, a public school mathematics teacher, received his D.Ed. from The Pennsylvania State University in 1965. He taught at Oklahoma State University before moving to Rutgers University in 1968, where he was a distinguished professor, department chair, and associate dean for academic affairs. In 1994, he was selected as the Fawcett Chair in Educational Administration, an endowed professorship at The Ohio State University. In 1973, he received the Lindback Foundation Award for Distinguished Teaching from Rutgers University; in 1987, he received the Alumni Award for Professional Research from the Rutgers University Graduate School of Education; in 1991, he received the Excellence in Education Award from The Pennsylvania State University; in 1992, he received the Meritorious Research Award from the Eastern Educational Research Association; and in 1996, he became an alumni fellow of The Pennsylvania State University. He is past secretary-treasurer of the National Conference of Professors of Educational Administration (NCPEA), past president of the University Council for Educational Administration (UCEA), a fellow of the American Educational Research Association (AERA), and recipient of the Roald Campbell Lifetime Achievement Award in Educational Administration. He has published more than 100 research articles and is the author or coauthor of 11 books in the fields of research and theory, educational administration, decision making, leadership, instructional supervision, and research methods. Three of his recent books include *Quantitative Research in Educational Administration: A Primer* (2010); *Educational Administration: Theory, Research, and Practice* (2008), with Cecil Miskel; and *Instructional Leadership: A Research-Based Guide to Learning in Schools* (2009), which he coauthored with his wife, Anita Woolfolk.